THE LIVING NOVEL

V. S. PRITCHETT

The
Living Novel

REYNAL & HITCHCOCK · NEW YORK

To My Wife

CONTENTS

The Ancestor   17
Clarissa   24
The Shocking Surgeon   32
The Crank   38
A Scottish Documentary   50
Scott   56
Our Half-Hogarth   70
Disraeli   77
Edwin Drood   83
George Eliot   89
An Irish Ghost   103
A Victorian Son   109
A Plymouth Brother   116
The Scientific Romances   122
The Five Towns   130
Sons and Lovers   136
A Pole in the Far East   143
The Irish R.M.   149
An East End Novelist   155
An Amateur   161
Two Writers and Modern War   167

7

CONTENTS

Cavalleria Rusticana   179

Poor Relations   186

The Bohemian   198

The English Frenchman   204

The Centenary of Anatole France   210

The Russian Day   216

The Hypocrite   222

The Great Absentee   228

The Minor Dostoevsky   235

A Russian Cinderella   241

A Russian Outsider   247

PREFACE

EXPERIENCE suggests that a writer is wise to avoid reading many novels when he is writing one himself; and Mr. Somerset Maugham, an efficient guide to the hygiene of authorship, has even laid it down that a novelist ought to have few books in his house at any time. I have never desired, indeed could never afford perfect health; and at the beginning of the war I was sitting half inside other people's novels and half inside a novel of my own. The war put a stop to that. Without leisure or freedom to write what I wanted, I could at least read what I wanted, and I turned to those most remarkable men and women: the great novelists of the past, those who are called the standard novelists. We were and are living through a revolution, and revolutions stir us to a total reconsideration of the past; a reconsideration of the novel might tell me where my own half-finished novel was wrong; it would certainly tell me, if I regarded each classic as it came along as a new just-published book, what a good novel ought to be. I set out therefore on a number of short journeys of rediscovery, too idle and specific in my inquiry to call myself a critic, but rather like the ordinary reader who has some private axe to grind. Some of the notes I made appeared from week to week in the columns of the *New Statesman and Nation* and now, occasionally lengthened, are collected in this volume. To the literary editor of that paper, Mr. Raymond Mortimer, I owe a great debt for encouraging and advising me in projects which, I must confess, often scared me.

For, except to the bookish, many of what are called the

Standard Novelists have the set air of an officially appointed committee. We had fallen into the error of believing that they were written for critics, for literary historians, for students or for leisured persons of academic tastes; and people who read only the best authors usually let one know it. We had easily forgotten that the masters, great and small, remembered or neglected, were the freshest, the most original, the most importunate and living novelists of their time; that they stood above their contemporaries and survived them, because they were more readable, more entertaining, more suggestive and incomparably more able than the common run of novelists. The forms of the novel are various, but it has enormously developed the field of its curiosity; new country has been subjugated in every generation; and the masters are those who have first invaded and liberated and added new territory. Let us admit that changes in style, method and belief often stand between us and the immediate enjoyment of many of the great novelists; but these barriers become unimportant when we perceive that the great are the great, not only because of their inherent qualities, but because they were the writers who were most sensitive to the situation of their time. They are, in the finer sense, contemporary. I do not mean necessarily that they explicitly responded to external events, though they often did; evidently even bad writers reflect the age in which they live; I mean that the great are sensitive to an intrinsic situation. We say today that we are living in an age of transition, "between two worlds"; the lesson of the master is that human life is always in transition; an essential part of his excellence is that he brings this clearly out in his work. We have only to glance at the second-rate novelists to see how they differ in this sense from the masters. The second-rate are rarely of their time. They are not on the tip of the wave. They are born out of date and out of touch and are rooted not in life but in literary convention. The Bohemian convention of the beloved vagabond who thrived just before 1914 when the Bohemians had ceased to exist—Verlaine was the last—is an example. More grotesque still are the modern historical novels which are so out of touch that they bind their pictures of, say, the American Civil War, with the thin *passe partout* of modern suburban morals and wishes. We have a glossy mixture of bad men and good housekeeping. The masters, on the contrary, have a direct apprehension of life. The secret of their eminence is not in style, form, experiment in narrative or manner alone, but also in their presentation of new material. This was the basis of the distinction of James Joyce when he put lower-middle-class Dublin on the page in *Dubliners* and *The Portrait of the Artist as a Young Man*; of Balzac who sought for the first time to import the catalogue of what he called "the material of civilization" in his novels and who set down the appetites of his gluttonous age; of Stendhal who detected that the conceit of risk, power and success, the calculation of adventure, were of the essence of his time.

But new material is always assimilated material. Arnold Bennett added nothing to the novel when he brought into it the enormous material relating to the hotel industry in *Imperial Palace;* and recent novels that have dealt in documentary fashion with mines and industries have added nothing either. New material is added only by new seeing not by new sights. *Moll Flanders* is a book of new material because it is old material— the conventional rogue's tale—seen in a new way. I do not pretend that the novelist is indebted only to life for his material or his inspiration. We analyze the ingredients of talent but we still do not know what it really is, why certain sociological or psychological types become novelists and others of the same breed become invalids, criminals, lunatics. A novelist owes a huge debt to other novelists, to his literary traditions. He begins by copying and imitation, as Balzac modeled his work and his life on Scott's, as Fielding began by satirizing Richardson, as Scott himself looked to the annalists of his country. Words beget words. But here we enter the world of the literary critic and historian, and when I set out to rediscover the masters I did so informally, not as a literary critic, but as an expectant novelist, and to the novelist the mass of literary criticism has very little to say. Here he has more in common with the ordinary and doubtfully instructed reader. It seemed to me that the ordinary reader, like myself, would not dismiss George Eliot as cold mutton or the Russian novelists because they were foreigners, if we could sometimes put our finger on the new point in life from which any given novel started. Ideally the critic should have read everything and know everything; the accretions of our culture, the vagaries of our taste, all the notes in the score of our achievement and standards should be familiar to him. If he has a theory it ought to be wide and just in its application. By comparison the novelist and the ordinary reader are persons of idle mind. Each of them goes for what interests him and what stimulates him. They would sooner skip to what they want, or ignore an issue, than miss the one or two things they are after. They put intensity of experience before everything else.

In this spirit I went almost haphazard from novel to novel. I was a raider, not a reader. I felt like someone who comes out of the darkness into some bright and crowded room, where things and people become ineffaceably vivid; and it was that dazzled moment of entry that I sought to set down when I wrote. Why is this room like no other room I ever saw before? That, I felt, must be the sensation of the novelist himself as he went from page to page, surprised by his own creations. If one could catch the novelist in the throb of writing. If one could see him taking his stance at some distance from his material, and if one could sometimes say how life itself had edged him into that position, and why that precise position had not been taken before. And then, from my own point of view, it was interesting to see difficulties mastered; to see how often a novelist is obliged to turn his deficiencies into virtues or new discoveries. A novelist like D. H. Lawrence was deficient in the sense of narrative and in the power of construction; he found himself in the middle of his subject striking out in all directions. It is precisely this temperamental disadvantage which Lawrence converted into a virtue. He makes us feel we are in the middle of life, in the confused core and center of a human being. Or again, Dickens had an almost fatal eye for eccentricity, the comic-sketch writer's habit of caricature; he transforms this tiring characteristic into something altogether more interesting: the sight of people talking, declaiming to themselves, in their inner world. Dickens, the histrionic egotist, is the poet of egotistical soliloquy, the poet of the ham-acting inner man, pleading his own fantasies.

The last thing this collection claims to be is a collection of epitaphs and last judgments. It is not a history of the novel. Many important names are missing; some have been discussed in an earlier volume; others like Jane Austen, Tolstoy, Trollope, Henry James and Proust, have moved me, but not to the labor of writing. A number of minor writers take their place, chiefly because they were forgotten and seemed worth reviving. It will seem strange that Hood and Whitman are included in a book on the novel; but Whitman has his place because of his reporting of the American Civil War; and Hood creeps in because of his grotesque poem, a novel in verse, called *Miss Kilmansegg and her Precious Leg*.

THE LIVING NOVEL

THE ANCESTOR

W HEN I was young and was reading too many novels
the works of Fielding were regarded as one of the
pleasant things in store for those about to reach the age of con-
sent. He was the last novelist, as Thackeray said, to be allowed
to describe a man, and there were book-soaked critics like Professor Saintsbury to expatiate over their wine upon Fielding's
use of the privilege. It is true that Dr. Johnson called Fielding
a blockhead and that Richardson—who had reason to spit and
squirm—dismissed him as an ostler; but on the whole the warm
impression of his genius and character prevailed, the impression
which was most frankly but tolerantly conveyed in one of the
letters of Lady Mary Wortley Montagu:

> I am sorry for H. Fielding's death, not only as I shall
> read no more of his writings, but I believe he lost more
> than others, and no man enjoyed life more than he did,
> though few had less reason to do so, the highest of his prefer-
> ment being raking in the lowest sinks of vice and misery. I
> should think it a nobler and less nauseous employment to be
> one of the staff-officers than conduct the nocturnal weddings.
> His happy constitution (even when he had, with great pains,
> half demolished it) made him forget everything when he was
> before a venison pastry, or over a flask of champagne, and I
> am persuaded he has known more happy moments than any
> prince upon the earth. His natural spirits gave him rapture
> with his cook-maid, and cheerfulness when he was fluxing in
> a garret. There was a great similitude between his character
> and that of Sir Richard Steele. He had the advantage both
> in learning and, in my opinion, genius; they both agreed in
> wanting money in spite of all their friends, and would have

17

wanted it, if their hereditary lands had been as extensive as their imaginations; yet each of them was so formed for happiness, it is a pity he was not immortal.

Alas, the vogue of Fielding had passed by the time I grew up. The secret reading of the mid-Victorians, and late, had lost its spell. The muscular Christians who were privately addicted to his muscular impropriety had given place to a generation with a feminine preoccupation with sex and the fortune-telling scene of psychology. If one was going to read the eighteenth-century novelists at all, Richardson was your man and the masculine tradition of Fielding was less congenial. It is typical of our taste that Proust was greatly influenced by Richardson; and that when we look back to the earliest realism, we prefer the ungarnished plate of Defoe to the stylish menu that is handed to us by the author of *Tom Jones* and *Joseph Andrews*. He is said to be altogether too hearty, towny and insensitive. He is said to be that most tiresome of bores, the man's man. He sets up as the shallowest of philosophers: the man of the world, whose world turns out to be a box of tricks. And what does the philosophy amount to beyond a number of small notions: that society is not what it seems, that self-love and self-interest are the beginning and end of human motive, and that the only real and virile view of human nature is the low one? His geniality labored the offense.

One has to admit the force of such a criticism of Fielding, but I am far from thinking it fatal to his rank as a novelist. In the first place the criticism is really aroused by his style rather than by his matter. Fielding is out to cut a figure. When he sets up as a satirist, he believes in the robust satire of the man who lives, not in the more cruel satire of the weak-livered man who abstains and snarls. In their rebellion against the poetic hyperbole of the early romances which had been imitated from the French, the Augustans parodied the heroic style; they were not thereby mocking the noble view of human nature; they were insinuating the sensible one.

Yet, even when we have acquiesced in the brilliant assumptiveness of Fielding's style and have seen beyond his sardonic preoccupation with men of honor and women of discretion, there remains the difficulty that Fielding is the ancestor. In Fielding we are haunted by almost the whole of the English novel. Pages of Dickens, Thackeray, Meredith, even, incongruously, of Kipling, Galsworthy and Wodehouse, become confused in the general panorama: Fielding has the disadvantage of being the "onlie begetter." Not only do we pick out the perennial characters of the main part of English fiction, but he has set many of its idiosyncrasies and limits. Sociable man, social problems, middle-class humor, the didactic habit, the club culture, the horseplay, the gregarious rather than the single eye, the habit of treating country life as an opportunity for the exercise of the body or of the fancy, as though Nature were a mixture of gymnasium and an open-air extension of the Established Church—these are some elements which have continued in the English novel and which date from Fielding. He expressed one kind of Englishness, so that many critics—Sir Hugh Walpole was one—seemed to think that conservative sociability or what is called "the creation of character" contains the whole English tradition; that people who speak of the novel as something inspired by ideas or concerned with a sense of the real situation of society at any given time, were importing tendentious and arid continental ideas. If these critics had considered Fielding's work they could never have made such a wild statement. Fielding was an old Etonian, but he was one of Eton's recalcitrants, sneered at and, in the end, pursued because he let the side down. The fact is that, from the beginning, the English novel set out to protest and to teach. Its philanthropic campaigns in the nineteenth century are paralleled in the eighteenth century by its avowed desire to reform the brutal manners of the age.

The explanation is not necessarily that there has been an extra allowance of public spiritedness in our novelists; it is

simply that the crucial problems of his own time provide a
novelist with his richest material, whether he deals with it directly or by inference. The reform of manners was as vital in
the eighteenth century as the reform of the Poor Law was in
the nineteenth. From Elizabethan times, the Dutch, the French
and the Spanish visitors had been appalled by the barbarity of
English life. When Fielding and Richardson filled their novels
with abducted heiresses, Tammany law, bribed judges, faked
weddings, duels in Hyde Park, with squalid fights between half-
naked women in Gin Alley or on the village commons; with
scoundrelly nincompoops, bailiffs and middle-men from the
Coffee House and the Court, they were not amusing themselves
with the concoctions of artificial comedy. They were attacking
the criminal violence and corruption that underlay the elegance of the time. There was a plea for the middle-class virtues
at a time when the aristocracy had left the country for the
Court and had abandoned its responsibilities in order to milk
the Exchequer. Public societies for the Reform of Manners had
existed in the early part of the century. Fielding spent his writing life fighting abuses and ended as an excellent Bow Street
magistrate, trying to clean up the London streets. "Great characters" there are in all his books, but they are inseparable from
his social purpose.

In an essay on his own work Fielding always said that he
drew from life. But like Cervantes, whom he hoped to copy,
and whom he so much admired, Fielding had been trained as a
writer in the theater. The English novel was not a development from the reporting of Defoe, a way of writing which, of
its nature, is prevented from imaginative development. In the
end the reporter can do no more than cover more and more
ground; his method gives him nothing to till the ground with.
Fielding took his slice of life, his chains of picaresque episode
which in *Joseph Andrews* had made a promising but inferior
version of *Gil Blas,* and let the artifice of the theater break
them up and rebuild them. The English novel started in *Tom*

Jones, because the stage taught Fielding to break the monotony of flat, continuous narrative. The methods of the theater are abstract and summary; there is an idea before there is a scene; and one of the fascinating things in *Tom Jones* is the use of the summary method to set the scene, explain the types of character, cover the preparatory ground quickly by a few oblique moralizings and antics so that all the realism is reserved for the main action. Is Tom Jones a loyal and honest man? Could he be the opposite if circumstances tempt him? No great paraphernalia of dialogue and literal detail has to be used in order to introduce such questions. Fielding puts them, then illustrates with action, and frames the whole in brief commentary. Scenes do not ramble on and melt into each other. They snap past, sharply divided, wittily contrasted, cunningly balanced. The pace of *Tom Jones* is as fast as farce, and indeed only a theater man's expertness in the dramatic, the surprising, the situation capped and recapped, could cover the packed intrigue of the narrative. The theater taught Fielding economy. It taught him to treat episodes as subjects and not as simple slices of life. Thackeray, who is the only English novelist to have learned from *Tom Jones*—Dickens learned from the inferior middlebrow *Amelia,* which has much more of the drudging realism of the later English novel—developed this method of Fielding's in *Vanity Fair,* going backwards and forwards in time, as well as to and fro in moral commentary. The difference is that Thackeray was born in the time of the sermon, and Fielding in the time of the chorus and the stage aside.

Fielding's own ancestor is Ben Jonson. Coleridge compared the formal excellence of *Tom Jones* with that of *The Alchemist.* The satire in both writers is meaty and brainy, very packed and prolific in ridiculous situations. To every character life is surprising and Fortune perverse. In the love-chase of Sophia Western and Tom Jones, there is the familiar stage situation that when one is willing the other is not available. Tom is a healthy young rake who does not intend to be one, and he reads a severe lecture to Nightingale, the professional Lovelace, who is merely satisfying sexual vanity. In the picaresque novels there is growth or decline in fortune, and rarely is there growth in character; but in *Tom Jones,* Partridge grows once he has got rid of his wife. Sophia, in London, learns to tell a lie to her rival—for which one admires her as much as when she comes headfirst off the horse—and Tom himself passes from the loyal to the careless and, after the shock of being caught out in his infidelities at Upton, into Tom the frantic who will commit any folly. He is a young man in a mess by the time he is mixed up with Lady Bellaston. This intrigue is the one in which first her ladyship and then the lady's maid are hidden behind the curtain in Tom's room, a piece of turn and turnabout which comes straight from the theater; it *does* strike one as artificial, but Fielding brings the whole intrigue to earth by the brilliant short chapter which introduces Mrs. Hunt. Many critics have objected to this chapter as a loose end; but the naïve proposal of marriage from someone to whom Tom has never spoken comes almost affectingly out of the blue. It is a *cri de cœur* among a lot of sharp practice, something beautifully silly in an ill-natured episode.

Joseph Andrews, Jonathan Wild and *Tom Jones* are the three important novels of Fielding, and *Jonathan Wild* is the diamond among them, the most dazzling piece of sustained satirical writing in our language. There remains *Amelia:* a hybrid that lies halfway between the Augustan and the Victorian novel. As a novelist Fielding was subject to two opposite influences which were to leave their mark on the English novel for a hundred years and to ensure that it had little resemblance to the French and Russian novels: he was trained in the rogue's tale which introduced untidiness and irresponsibility into the English novel; and, as I have said, he was trained in the theater, which gave our novel its long obsession with elaborate plot. *Amelia* is a compromise. By the time he came to write this novel, Fielding seems to have lost the heat of the theater's inspiration. The first chapter describing the prison is in the old manner, but presently the narrative digresses and dawdles. The didactic intention comes out frankly and, alas, unadorned. There is white-faced indignation where before there was irony, and indignation is the weaker strain, for it interrupts, where irony undermines. I do not suggest that his old comic gift is dead; far from it. There is Colonel Bath's remarkable duel. And there is the devastating Miss Mathews, the would-be murderess, who is a development from the drawing of that hard old rip, Lady Bellaston, out of *Tom Jones*. Miss Mathews is a superb tart. One is delighted that the Colonel refuses to drop her; delighted, too, though Fielding does not seem to be, that she grows fat. She will so obviously enjoy growing fat. It is she who makes the celebrated remark about the English taste for prudish women: do they attract, inquires the ever-curious Miss Mathews, because they appear to promise to cool the heat of love? In *Amelia,* there is more psychological complexity than there was in *Tom Jones;* it is the book of an older man who has grown tired. If we contrast Tom Jones with Mr. Booth of *Amelia,* we see that Tom commits his sins, repents in a moment and ingeniously forgets them. Mr. Booth is far more complicated. He is a married man to start with; he sins with caution, is transfixed by remorse and then settles down to brood with growing misanthropy. The wages of sin is not death, but worry —middle-class worry. His case never improves, for we see the subtle influence of his affair with Miss Mathews on his relations with other people. Fielding's rising interest in psychology marks a break with his interest in moral types. It is a signal of the coming age. And if *Amelia* indicates a decline from the brilliant fusing of gifts that went to make his earlier books, it points the way the English novel would go when a new genius, the genius of Dickens, seized it.

CLARISSA

THE modern reader of Richardson's *Clarissa* emerges from his experience exhausted, exalted and bewildered. The book is, I fancy, the longest novel in the English language; it is the one most crowded with circumstantial detail; it is written in the most dilatory of narrative methods, i.e. in the form of letters. It is a novel written through a microscope; it is a monstrosity, a minute and inordinate act of prolonged procrastination. And the author himself is a monster. That a man like Samuel Richardson should write one of the great European novels is one of those humiliating frolics in the incidence of genius. The smug, juicy, pedestrian little printer from Derbyshire, more or less unlettered, sits down at the age of fifty and instructs young girls in the art of managing their virtue to the best advantage. Yet, ridiculous as *Pamela* is, her creator disarms criticism by a totally new ingredient in the novel: he knows how to make the reader weep. And, stung by the taunts of the educated writers of his time, Richardson calmly rises far above *Pamela* when he comes to the story of Clarissa Harlowe; he sets the whole continent weeping. Rousseau and even Goethe bow to him and take out their handkerchiefs; the vogue of sensibility, the first shoots of the Romantic movement, spring from the pool of Richardson's pious tears like the grateful and delicate trees of an oasis. Yet there he is, plump, prosaic, the most middling of middling men, and so domestically fussy that even his gift of weeping hardly guarantees that he will be a major figure. Is there not some other strain in this dull and prodi-

giously painstaking little man? There is. Samuel Richardson
was mad.

I do not mean that Richardson was a lunatic. I do not
mean he was mad as Swift was mad. At first sight, an im-
measurable smugness, an endlessly pettifogging normality seem
to be the outer skin of Richardson's character. We know,
as I have already said, that from his youth he was an
industrious and timid young man who was, for some reason
or other, used by young women who wanted their love letters written. Profoundly sentimental, he sat like some pious
old cook in her kitchen, giving advice to the kitchen maids, and
when he came to write novels he was merely continuing this
practical office. He lived vicariously like some sedentary lawyer
who has to argue the disasters of other people's lives letter by
letter, but who himself never partakes. Genteel, he is, nevertheless, knowing; prim and cozy, he is, nevertheless, the victim
of that powerful cult of the will, duty and conscience by which
Puritanism turned life and its human relations into an inces-
sant war. There is no love in Puritanism; there is a struggle for
power. Who will win the daily battle of scruple and conscience
—Pamela or the young squire; Clarissa or Lovelace? And yet
what is urging Richardson to this battle of wills? What is it
that the Puritan cannot get out of his mind, so that it is a
mania and obsession? It is sex. Richardson is mad about sex.

His is the madness of Paul Pry and Peeping Tom. I said just
now that *Clarissa* is a novel written under the microscope;
really it is a novel written about the world as one sees it through
the keyhole. Prurient and obsessed by sex, the prim Richardson
creeps on tiptoe nearer and nearer, inch by inch, to that vantage
point; he beckons us on, pausing to make every kind of pious
protestation, and then nearer and nearer he creeps again, delaying, arguing with us in whispers, working us up until we
catch the obsession too. What are we going to see when we get
there? The abduction, the seduction, the lawful deflowering of
a virgin in marriage are not enough for him. Nothing short of

the rape of Clarissa Harlowe by a man determined on destroying her can satisfy Richardson's phenomenal day-dream with its
infinite delays.

The principle of procrastinated rape is said to be the ruling
one in all the great best-sellers. It was in Richardson's genius
that he was able to elevate the inner conflict of the passions and
the will to an abstract level, so that the struggle of Clarissa and
Lovelace becomes a universal battle-piece; and, in doing this,
Richardson was able to paint it with the highly finished realism
of the Dutch painters. At the beginning one might simply be
reading yet another novel of intrigue, which just goes on and
on; and but for the incredible suspense in the narrative I think
many readers must have given up *Clarissa* by the end of the
first volume. It is not until the third and fourth volumes
are reached, when Richardson transposes his intrigue into
the sustained and weeping music, the romantic tragedy of
Clarissa's rape and long preparation for death, that we get his
measure. She dies piously, yet like a Shakespearean conferring
greatness upon all around her by the starkness of her defeat.
At the beginning we are not prepared for this greatness in
Clarissa; even in that last volume we are often uncertain of her
real stature. It is not easy for virginity to become Virtue. Would
she be anything without Lovelace? And yet, we know, she is the
crown upon Lovelace's head. He too becomes tragic under her
judgment as she becomes tragic by his act. These two reflect
glory upon each other, like saint and devil. But in the first
volume there is no difficulty about deciding who is the greater
as a character or as an abstract conception. Lovelace has her
beaten hands down. A practical and languid correspondence
wakes up when he takes pen in hand. Anna Howe, the "pert"
friend, makes circles round her. Arabella, with her nose out of
joint, is livelier comedy. The scheming brother, the gouty father
with his paroxysms, the supplicating and fluttering mother, and
the endearing uncles with their unendearing family solidarity,
make a greater mark on our minds than the all-too-articulate

Clarissa does. Our one hope is that witty Miss Howe is right when she teases Clarissa with maidenly self-deception. "The frost piece," as Lovelace called her, looks exactly like one of those fascinating prudes whose minds are an alphabet that must be read backwards. But no; though she will enchant us when she is rattled, with cries like "Oh, my Nancy, what shall I do with this Lovelace?" her course and her motives are clear to her; and we begin the slow and painful discovery of a virtue which finds no exhilaration except in scruple. We face an inexhaustible determination, and this is exhausting to contemplate, for Clarissa is as interested in the organization of human motives as Richardson himself; and he insinuates himself in her character so thoroughly, niggling away with his "ifs" and his "buts," that he overwhelms her, as Flaubert overwhelmed Madame Bovary.

Still this does not take from the drama of Clarissa's situation, and does, in fact, increase the suspense of it. If we skip—and of course we do, looking up the letters in the obliging synopsis —we do not, as in other novels, find ourselves caught out by an overlooked sub-plot; we are back in the main situation. Will the family relent? Will Lovelace abduct, marry, rape or reform? There's hardly a sub-plot worth mentioning in this huge novel. It follows the labyrinth of a single theme. And though we turn to Anna Howe for glimpses of common sense, and for a wit to enliven the glum belligerents of what Lovelace—always a psychologist and nearly a Freudian—called "the Harlowe dunghill" with its wills and deeds of settlement, we see in Clarissa's stand something more than a virtuous daughter bullied by her parents. She is a lawyer in family morals, and in Lovelace's too; but she is the first heroine in English fiction to stand against the family. Richardson called them "the embattled phalanx," and in *Clarissa* he goes to the heart of the middle-class situation; money, accretion of estate, the rise in the world, the desire to found a family, in conflict with the individual soul. She and Lovelace complement each other here. She thinks her family ought not to do evil to her, yet takes their evil upon herself; she is not a rebel but is tricked and driven into becoming an outcast and at last a saint. Like Lovelace, she has asked too much, "for people who allow nothing will be granted nothing; in other words, those who aim at carrying too many points will not be able to carry any." Yes, and those who put up their price by the device of reluctance invite the violence of the robber. By setting such a price upon herself, Clarissa represents that extreme of puritanism which desires to be raped. Like Lovelace's, her sexuality is really violent, insatiable in its wish for destruction.

Lovelace is Richardson's extravagant triumph. How did such a burning and tormented human being come out of that tedious little printer's mind? In the English novel Lovelace is one of the few men of intellect who display an intellect which is their own and not patently an abstract of their author's intellectual interests. He is half-villain, half-god, a male drawn to the full, and he dominates English fiction. He is all the more male for the feminine strains in his character: his hatred of women, his love of intrigue, his personal vanity, his captiousness and lack of real humility. A very masculine novelist like Fielding is too much a moralist, and too confidently a man, to catch a strain like that. And how Lovelace can write! When Clarissa's letters drag, like sighing Sunday hymns, or nag at us in their blameless prose, like the Collect for the day, the letters of Lovelace crackle and blaze with both the fire and the inconsequence of life. His words fly back and forth, throwing out anecdotes and the characters of his friends, with wonderful transitions of mood. In one paragraph he is writing a set apostrophe to Clarissa, full of longing and half-way to repentance. He shakes the mood off like a man who is drunk with grief and throws off this description of his gouty old kinsman:

> And here (pox of his fondness for me; it happens at a very bad time) he makes me sit hours together entertaining him with my rogueries (a pretty amusement for a sick man!) and

yet, whenever he has the gout, he prays night and morning with his chaplain. But what must *his* notions of religion be, who, after he has nosed and mumbled over his responses, can give a sigh or groan of satisfaction, as if he thought he had made up with Heaven; and return with a new appetite to my stories?—encouraging them, by shaking his sides with laughing at them, and calling me a sad fellow, in such an accent as shows he takes no small delight in his kinsman.

The old peer has been a sinner in his day, and suffers for it now; a sneaking sinner, *sliding,* rather than *rushing* into vices, for fear of his reputation; or rather, for fear of detection, and positive proof; for this sort of fellow, Jack, has no real regard for reputation. Paying for what he never had, and never daring to rise to the joy of an enterprise at first hand, which bring him within view of a tilting or the honor of being considered as the principal man in a court of justice.

To see such a Trojan as this just dropping into the grave which I hoped ere this would have been dug, and filled up with him; crying out with pain and grunting with weakness; yet in the same moment crack his leathern face into a horrible laugh, and call a young sinner charming varlet, encoring him as formerly he used to do the Italian eunuchs; what a preposterous, what an unnatural adherence to old habits.

Or there is the awful description of that old procuress, Mrs. Sinclair, a horror out of Rowlandson, who advances upon Clarissa on the night of the rape, when all Richardson's fascination with carnal horror breaks out. There is a double terror in it, because Lovelace himself is writing as if trying to drive evil out of his mind by a picture of evils still greater:

The old dragon straddled up to her, with her arms kemboed again, her eyebrows erect like the bristles upon a hog's back, and, scowling over her shortened nose, more than half hid her ferret eyes. Her mouth was distorted. She pouted out her blubber-lips, as if to bellow up wind and sputter into her horse-nostrils, and her chin was curdled, and more than usually prominent with passion.

The temperate, lawyer-like mind of Richardson does not prepare one for passages like this. When there is matter-of-factness

in the eighteenth century, one expects it to be as regular as
Pope's couplets were. But Richardson is not consistent. In the
sheer variety of their styles the letters in this novel are astonishing. The bovine uncles, the teasing parenthetical Miss Howe, the
admonitory Belford, the curt Colonel Morden, heading for his
duel, the climbing neurotic brother whose descendants were no
doubt in the British Union of Fascists, all have their styles, and
they are as distinctive as Lovelace's or Clarissa's. Richardson is
the least flat, the most stereoscopic novelist of an age which ran
the plain or formal statement to death in the end. Another
point: he is a writer of indirect narrative. We are shown scenes
at second hand, for the epistolatory method requires it so; and
we become used to a sort of memoranda of talk and action
which will tire our inward eye because our judgment is called
upon at the same time. So there are many reported scenes which
are relative failures, for example, the early and rather confusing ones between Clarissa and her mother. One has a muddled
impression of two hens flying up in the air at each other and scat-
tering their feathers. Yet even in this kind of scene Richardson
can, at times, write talk which is direct and put action wonderfully under our eye. The scene of the rape is tremendous in
this respect; and so is the awful picture of the brothel when
Mrs. Sinclair breaks her leg and the harridans come out in their
night attire; and there is the comic, savage picture of Lovelace
defeating the attempt of his family to try him. But where Richardson shook off the slavery of his own method is shown at its
best, I think, in Belford's letter describing the prison scene
where the two prostitutes offer to bail Clarissa out:

"We are surprised at your indifference, Miss Harlowe.
Will you not write to any of your friends?"
"No."
"Why, you don't think of tarrying *here* always."
"I shall not live always."

Even in those few lines one sees Richardson advancing his inner
narrative and, if one continues this conversation, one also sees

him patiently and unerringly preserving character. One might almost say that prolix as it was, his method was economical, given his chosen end. The slowness comes from an excess of examination, not an excess of words. No prose has fewer redundancies.

We come to the death scene. The torment of Lovelace pacing his horse past the gate of the house he dare not enter, though Clarissa lies dying within, is not rhetorical. It is defiant as fits a being so saturnine, it is in the mind as becomes a man of intellect, it is the changeable, imploring, raging madness of a clever mind that has met its conqueror. Lovelace is a villain no man hates, because he is a man. He is candid, if he is vain. He can argue like Iago or debate like Hamlet, and in between send a purse of a few guineas to a rogue who has helped him to his present catastrophe. It is strange to think of him—the only Don Juan in English fiction and done to the last Freudian detail. Clarissa dies like a swan amid the formal melody of a prose into which Richardson fell without affectation.

> Her breath being very short, she desired another pillow. Having two before, this made her, in a manner, sit up in her bed; and she spoke then with more distinctness; and seeing us greatly concerned, forgot her own stutterings to comfort us; and a charming lecture she gave us, though a brief one, upon the happiness of a timely preparation, and upon the hazards of a late repentance, when the mind, as she observed, was so much weakened, as well as the body, as to render a poor soul hardly able to contend with its natural infirmities.

It is a strong test of the illusion that Richardson has cast upon us, that we think of Lovelace like a shadow cast upon Clarissa as she dies; and of Clarissa rather than of Lovelace when *he* appears. These lives are known by their absences; they are inextricable, tangled in the thousands of words they have spoken about each other, and are swept away at last into other people's words.

THE SHOCKING SURGEON

THE disappearance of illustrations from the English novel, and indeed the decline of the art of illustrating, is a loss to literary criticism. For one of the obligations of the critic is to possess himself of the eyes with which a novelist's contemporaries read him, and this the good illustrator helped him to do. Of course we never achieve this sight, but we can approach it. And how far off the mark we can be is shown by the shock that a good illustrator gives. Cruikshank, for example: he upsets all the weary pieties of realism that lie between us and a comprehension of Dickens; half the silly criticisms of Dickens need never have been written if Cruikshank had been studied as closely as the text. And Rowlandson: pick up an edition of Smollett that has Rowlandson's illustrations and see Smollett come into focus once more, so that his page is almost as fresh to us as it must have appeared to the eighteenth-century reader. It is true that outside this school of illustration the argument weakens; the wooden severity of late-Victorian realism was a lugubrious travesty of the text and one is glad that illustration has been dropped. The fact is that illustration was at its best when the English novel also was in its brash, vital, fantastic youth; when, though wigged in a judicious style, it had only a simple and crude concern with caricature, anecdote and the bad manners of society. Once the novel abandoned travel and developed plot and form, the English novel ceased to need the illustrator, or at any rate ceased to get the right one.

There are two pointers in the engravings which Rowlandson did for *Humphrey Clinker,* pointers the reader of Smollett

ought to follow. Look at the scrawny figure of that malign
virgin, Tabitha Bramble, as she comes accusing into the room
where her philanthropical brother has been caught with a
lady; look at Humphrey in the jail, moaning out his grotesque
Methodism to the felons; look at her ladyship, gluttonous, dis-
eased and warty, tearing out her friend's hair. They are not
human beings. They are lumps of animal horror or stupidity.
To Rowlandson the human race are cattle or swine, a reeking
fat-stock done up in ribbons or breeches, which has got into
coffee-houses, beds and drawing-rooms. He was nauseated by
the domesticity and the grossness of the eighteenth century's
new rich. In fact, every eighteenth-century artist and writer
jibbed at the filth of domestic life, at some time or other. These
pictures of Rowlandson's (of Hogarth's too) show how urgent
was the task of the reform of manners which the writers of the
eighteenth century had set themselves, from Addison onwards.
(The movement had been revived by William III, who, when
he came from Holland, was horrified by the brutality of English
life. He encouraged Defoe, especially, to write in the cause of
reform.) The second point is that Rowlandson's people are portraits of Swift's Yahoos. In these pictures we see the nightmare
lying behind the Augustan manner. The nightmare of the pox,
the scurvy, delirium tremens, of obesity and gout, the nightmare of the insanitary streets, of the stairway which was a dunghill, of the sedate Georgian window which was a place for the
emptying of chamber-pots; the nightmare of the suppurations
that flowed into the waters at Bath, of the stenches that rose
from the "elegant" crowds at Assemblies; the nightmare of the
lives of children flogged into stupidity—see the boyhood of
Peregrine Pickle—so that, in Rowlandson and Hogarth, all the
virtuous people look like lumps of suet; and, haunting this
scene, the nightmare religion of Wesley. Smollett and Rowlandson run so closely together in the drawing of these things
that one borrows from the other's brutality. Yet are they brutal?
I do not know enough about Rowlandson to say, but I am

pretty sure that Smollett, for all his obsession with the bladder and the backside, was not a brutal nor a filthy man. He enjoyed being the shocking surgeon who brings out horrors at the dinner-table; but because he was shocked himself. Smollett's sensibility is close to Swift's. There is enough proof of Smollett's intention in the reforms which followed his descriptions of the brutalities of naval life at his time in *Roderick Random*. And though there is a good deal of horseplay, battery and assault in his books, from the comic scene where Hawser Trunnion picks up a turkey from the table to beat an unwelcome visitor, to the one in *Roderick Random* where the hero and a friend tie up the schoolmaster and flog his naked backside with a rope, Smollett has strong views on the stupefying effects of flogging. These are clearly stated in *Peregrine Pickle*. It is true that Perry, after a period of beating, himself becomes the bully of the school, to Hawser Trunnion's great delight, but Trunnion's views are always presented as further fantastic examples of a fantastic and maimed character. We see more of what Smollett was like in the portrait of Dr. Bramble in *Humphrey Clinker*. Generosity and goodness of heart go together with an impetuous temper and a good touch of hypochondria. He has a morbid nose which smells out every stench that Bath, Edinburgh and Harrogate can provide; and Smollett's own nose, in his book of travels in France and Italy, was as fastidious. Smollett may have enjoyed the brutality he described, but his protests and his hypochondria suggest that he felt the pleasure and the agony of the man who has a skin too few. His coarseness, like that of Joyce, is the coarseness of one whose senses were unprotected and whose nerves were exposed. Something is arrested in the growth of his robust mind; as a novelist he remains the portrayer of the outside, rarely able to get away from physical externals or to develop from that starting-point into anything but physical caricature.

A course of Smollett is hard for the modern reader to digest. The theater advised and animated Fielding and gave him form

and discipline. Smollett might have remained a ship's surgeon
—and would probably have been a happier man. (Smollett figures in the elder Disraeli's gallery of literary calamities.) The
difficulty of digestion is that he is raw and piquant meat; course
follows course without abating, and one has a surfeit. One
begins *Peregrine Pickle, Roderick Random, Humphrey Clinker*
or *Count Fathom,* exclaiming with pleasure at the physical zest
and the racing speed of the narrative, but after a hundred and
fifty pages one has had enough of the practical jokes, the heiresses and duelists, the cheats and the bawds. Our trouble is that
the English novel changed direction after its early lessons with
the French and Spanish picaresque writers. The novel of travel
gave place to plot and developed character. The kind of thing
that Smollett did in *Humphrey Clinker*—which all the critics,
except the unerring Hazlitt, over-praise—was turned into
Young's *Tours* or Cobbett's *Rural Rides.*

One book of Smollett's can be recommended to the modern
reader without reservations: the very original *Travels Through
France and Italy,* the first ill-tempered, captious, disillusioned
and vigorously personal travel book in modern literature. It is a
tale of bad inns, illness, cheating customs officials, a thoroughly
British book of grousings and manias—the aim of every Frenchman is to seduce your wife, or if not your wife, your sister, and if
not your sister, your daughter, as a token of his esteem for you!—
but packed with the irritable author and moments of fresh,
unperturbed judgment. It annoyed Sterne and was meant to
annoy him. Against Sterne's fancies stand Smollett's manias,
and how well they stand. Elsewhere, in the novels, one thinks
less of whole books than of scenes. *Peregrine Pickle* is not as
vigorous in its strokes and movements as *Roderick Random,*
but my favorite scenes come from the former book. Hawser
Trunnion and his "Garrison" are wonderful fantasies, which
tumble upon the reader uproariously as if a party were going
on upstairs and the ceiling had given way in the middle of it.
Trunnion lying about his naval engagements, fooled by publi-

cans, entrapped by women, and tacking across country to his wedding, is, as they say, "a beauty and no mistake." And his death—that is one of the great scenes of English literature, to be compared with that great death scene at the end of Dostoevsky's *The Possessed*. You can see, as you read, how Fielding's wittier and better-formed imagination would have improved this novel; though Smollett surpasses Fielding, I think, in female portraiture; his leading ladies have more spirit than Fielding's and can amuse themselves quite well without the help of the hero. *Roderick Random* is altogether more sardonic and violent; *Count Fathom* is more polished, an essay after the manner of *Jonathan Wild*. It contains two scenes which stand out—a robber scene, suggested, I suppose, by an early episode in *Gil Blas,* and an appalling chapter describing the Count's mother, who was a camp follower in Marlborough's wars and made a good living by cutting the throats of the wounded and robbing them. This is the kind of scene that reveals the exposed nerve in Smollett.

The physical realism of Smollett and his chamber-pot humor are one other link with Joyce and shows how his mind may have had not dissimilar obsessions. Perhaps that is going rather far; but there is some hint of *Anna Livia* in the Welsh maid's letters in *Humphrey Clinker*. Smollett extended the farce of punning and misspelling into new regions for his times:

> Last Sunday in the parish crutch, if my own ars may be trusted, the clerk called the banes of marridge betwist Opaniah Lashmeheygo and Tapitha Bramble, spinster; he mought as well have called her inkle weaver, for she never spun a hank of yarn in her life. Young Squire Dollison and Miss Liddy make the second kipple and there might have been a turd, but times are changed for Mr. Clinker:

Or:

> Who would have thought that mistriss, after all the pains taken for the good of her prusias sole, would go for to throw away her poor body? that she would cast the heys of infec-

tion upon such a carrying crow as Lashmyhago, as old as Mathewsullin, as dry as a red herring, and as poor as a starved veezel. . . . He's a profane scuffle, and as Mr. Clinker says, no better than an imp-fiddle, continually playing upon the pyebill and the new burth.

That's going farther than any Malaprop could go. It is more than the rollicking *double entendre* of Rowlandson's letter-press. It is a Scotsman making a Welsh woman play ducks and drakes with the English language. It is imaginative, festive and, like all Smollett's comedy, broad, bizarre and bold.

THE CRANK

IF WE are to define the spirit of the eighteenth century by
its favorite word, I think the word "man" or "mankind"
even more than words like "order" or "reason," is the one we
ought to choose. Man dominates the minds and ultimately the
hearts of the eighteenth-century writers, where God had dominated the mind of the seventeenth century. After the battles,
the factions, the treasons, the private and partisan faiths of the
religious wars, the men of the eighteenth century were concerned to impose an order on that chaos, to seek the common
denominator, to reassemble the judgment of divided human nature. The warring consciences were to be fused once more into
an amenable moral animal with all his greatness and all his
folly. The lines of Pope proclaim him:

> Know then thyself, presume not God to scan,
> The proper study of Mankind is Man.
> Plac'd on this isthmus of a middle state,
> A Being darkly wise, and rudely great:
> With too much knowledge for the Sceptic side,
> With too much weakness for the Stoic's pride,
> He hangs between; in doubt to act or rest;
> In doubt to deem himself a God, or Beast;
> In doubt his Mind or Body to prefer;
> Born but to die, and reas'ning but to err;
> Alike in ignorance, his reason such,
> Whether he thinks too little or too much:
> Chaos of Thought and Passion, all confus'd;
> Still by himself abus'd or disabus'd;
> Created half to rise, and half to fall;
> Great lord of all things, yet a prey to all;

THE CRANK

Sole judge of Truth, in endless Error hurl'd:
The glory, jest, and riddle of the world!

And Man is not yet trapped in our later prefixes and qualifications. He is not yet industrial man, economic man, evolutionary man, civilized man, mass man or man in transition. He is simply himself, a wonder ordained, like a tree watched in a garden. Inconstancy, levity, cruelty may be his habits; but so are generosity, the noble and the useful virtues. Even Swift declares that he loves plain John, Peter and Thomas. The name of Candide is itself a commendation. However ferocious the satire of the eighteenth century it is always balanced by a pleasure, sometimes trite and complacent, but always ingenuous and warm, in the habits of the new-discovered species; and we ourselves respond to such a fundamentally sanguine and well-found conception of human nature, even as we smile at the neat eighteenth-century labels. The Age of Reason was a revised, replanted and well-tended Eden; the serpent himself did obeisance to the great landscape gardener; and when we look back upon that world we cannot but suspect that half our present miseries date from the dissipation of the common feeling and philosophy that ensured the sanity of the age.

The notion of the sufficiency of man in himself encouraged the growth of peculiar character. The century enjoyed its fantastics. It allowed people to grow as they willed. One delighted in inventing more and more deformities and vices for one's enemies, more and more foibles and scandals for one's friends. The eccentrics of the age grew like cultivated blooms for all to admire; and its cranks could rely on the affection if not on the support of their circle. Misanthropy was especially respected, for among people who live well the meloncholy man is slipped in by nature as a kind of sport and to restore the balance; and when the misanthropic man was a crank into the bargain, he was observed with that delighted eagerness which a naturalist feels for the smallest hint of a new mutation.

39

In this period, there is no more suggestive example than the author of *Sandford and Merton*. Mr. Day is the modest and entrancing crank of the century. He is a crank who is the guide to all cranks, the pattern of the tribe. In their lives few earnest men have been more ridiculous. After his death, the growth of his influence indicated the cranks' embarrassing usefulness: if he was ridiculous, we were dreadful; if he was to be laughed at, we were to be wept over. For the case of Mr. Day perfectly illustrates the point that the crank is one of the growing points of society. He shows us not indeed what we shall become, but the direction we are likely to take. The special madness of Mr. Day was the belief that the errors of life were not due to original sin, but to stupidity and the formation of bad habits. If we could be caught young enough, in the age of natural innocence, we could be trained to be wiser and better than our stupid fathers. It was the madness of education. We shall see that when we come to *Sandford and Merton,* but before we do so, a glance at Mr. Day himself, as he is drawn full-length in the *Memoirs* of his friend Richard Edgeworth, is indispensable.

Nature is malicious. She is likely to arrange that those who have revolutionary ideas about the education of children shall have no children of their own; and here we come upon the first flaw in Mr. Day's private life. He did not succeed in getting any children of his own; he was without the recklessness of the philoprogenitive. An abnormal caution governed the revolutionary life of Mr. Day. He was unable for many years to master the initial difficulty of getting a wife. Women surrounded him, but none came up to his severe requirements. He believed, like any rationalist, in the sufficiency of man; his cross was the insufficiency of woman. The heart of the problem was that Mr. Day was a perfectionist; he not only believed in the perfectibility of man which is arguable, but he also believed in the perfectibility of women, and women take unkindly to the notion that they can be improved. The susceptible Mr. Day—and he was very susceptible—had either to take what he could get

and like what he got, as the common run of men have to do, or
—the logic is unanswerable—construct his own wife from blue
prints in advance. Admirable mind of the eighteenth century:
Mr. Day chose the second course.

What were the requirements of Mr. Day? Like a planner, he
wanted to begin from the beginning, to make a fresh start. The
whole invention called woman was in error. First of all one had
to persuade women of this fundamental error in creation. Then
one isolated them, cured them of silliness, frivolity, caprice,
love of clothes, love of flirtation, love of chatter, flattery and
society, the tendency to disobedience, lying and deception. One
cured them of their slavery to fashion. Into the resulting
vacuum, one poured modesty, decorum and the higher mental
interests; the sex would learn, not indeed to converse themselves, but to follow a man's conversation and to assimilate his
opinions. And they would be the most advanced opinions. Mr.
Day was sick of the silly women of the eighteenth century, the
creatures who were seduced, abducted and swindled, who gig-
gled and fainted, danced and gambled and talked of nothing
but clothes. The story is well-known. Cautiously he obtained
the two famous orphans—two because he realized there might
be a failure. Lucretia and Sabrina were immured in the country, and Day waited for them to grow to the point where he
could attend to their minds. Alas, the reformer who did not
believe in original sin, had not reckoned with invincible dullness! Lucretia turned out to be quarrelsome and trivial. She
was married off quickly to a draper. For a time Sabrina seemed
more hopeful. But it could not be concealed that she disliked
reading. She could not bear science. She could not keep a secret.
And she had no control over her emotions. Day established all
these points by experiment. For example, to test her self-control
he fired pistols close to her ears and her petticoats. She
screamed. More serious—she was found secretly to be buying
hats and putting lace on her dresses.

The experiment of Mr. Day's is notorious. It caused the

greatest astonishment in France where he took the two girls on
an educational tour; but incredulous Frenchmen were at last
convinced that Mr. Day was genuinely engaged in an educational exercise, and retired from his party in terror. Mr. Day
was prepared to fight a duel with anyone who imperilled the
curriculum. But the experiment is a mere episode in Mr. Day's
search for the right partner. He was only twenty-one when he
undertook it.

At this point it is important to reveal the existence of another character who had been experimenting also, and who was
the close witness and associate in some of Day's adventures. I
refer to Richard Edgeworth. Here comedy fills out. Day is the
initiator, but Richard Edgeworth is the foil. One man is the
making of the other; and it is through the delightful memoirs
of Maria Edgeworth's father that we see Mr. Day drawn full-
length with all the century's love of strange human beings and
with its special regard for friendship. The two men are examples of the dyspeptic and the eupeptic schools of experiment.
They were both rich. They were both country gentlemen.

On the one hand there is the ingenious Mr. Day, the exem-
plary Mr. Day, the Mr. Day who talked like a book, who neglected his appearance, who refused to dress like a man of
fashion, who despised the polite conventions, who began his
addresses to women by denouncing the sex. A clumsy man,
greasy-haired in the days of wigs, pock-marked and brilliant,
Mr. Day scowled cautiously all day over his scruples. At a time
when a good masculine leg was admired he was painfully knock-
kneed. On the other hand there was Richard Edgeworth, Irish,
headstrong, handsome, generous, hot-tempered and gallant, the
best dancer in Europe. Like Day he was a man with theories of
education—he was bringing up his son on the lines laid down
by Rousseau, to the astonishment of his neighbors and the
despair of his lamenting wife—like Day he was a man of scruples. But his passions were always growing stronger and his
scruples growing less.

And then Day was the theorist and Edgeworth was the man of practice. Day would a thousand times sooner read a book on housing than address a carpenter. His theories about women could be seen as a protective device. Edgeworth's character was the opposite. In the matter of education he got a son and tried his educational theories on him. In the matter of women—Edgeworth married four times, three times very happily. He was an incurable inventor of contraptions—one-wheeled coaches, patent turnip cutters, railway lines, interlocking carriages, telegraphs, patent tips and loading devices, a notable forerunner of the next century's engineers. One can see that a love of mischief was part of his ingenuous temperament, and that it must have directed his affection for the prosaic Mr. Day.

There is one remarkable episode in their friendship. It happened when Day had reached the point of desperation in his search for a wife. A delightful young woman called Elizabeth Sneyd who was Edgeworth's sister-in-law (years later she was to become Edgeworth's wife) agreed to consider Mr. Day if he would improve his appearance and polish his manners. Not a simple decision for a man like Day; for him, polish was the Arch-Enemy, fashion the Pollution of life. To his drastic and puritan mind, the wearing of a wig meant the renunciation of his republican principles. But he was a desperate man. He agreed. He went off to France with Edgeworth, and, in his own mind, sold himself to the devil. Edgeworth describes how they got to Lyons where he had an enormous social success, while Day went through the pitiless school of a French dancing master. They cropped Day's lank Cromwellian locks. They piled a huge horsehair wig on his head. They dressed his ungainly body in the latest Parisian clothes. They taught him to bow and to dance. It was difficult for him to do this gracefully because of his knees and so soon they had him between boards which were screwed tight so that he could not move. Edgeworth had engineering projects of his own on the Saône, but he took a special and wicked interest in Mr. Day's knee-straightening machine. It was no good. The knees still knocked. "I could not help pitying my philosophic friend," says Richard Edgeworth, "pent up in durance vile for hours together, with his feet in the stocks, a book in his hand and contempt in his heart." Day returned at last to England, but when Elizabeth Sneyd saw the puritan Malvolio come bowing into the room, she collapsed with laughter, and that was the end of that.

Let us leave Mr. Day standing with unbendable rectitude amid the debris of his personal comedy. He did find a wife in the end, exactly the wife he desired, who was delighted to abandon all her personal tastes, including her love of music—an art which distressed him—and to devote her ear to his endless conversation. It was usually about education, and education killed him in the end. Kindness to animals was one of his principles, and Day was killed trying out a new "natural" method of educating an unbroken horse. The Age of Reason conceived wild nature and the noble savage to be tamer than they were.

When we read *Sandford and Merton* we feel that Day had this delusion about children. He had none of his own. Would they have broken him? Or would he have broken them? The father-prig, endlessly eloquent, mellifluously disposed to draw the ever-recurring moral, always pat with the tendentious anecdote, is a strain on his children. They relieve it at last by laughter. Perhaps Day would have become the ridiculous father as *Sandford and Merton* is the father's ridiculous book.

But not basically ridiculous. I have already suggested that *Sandford and Merton* is the fruit of the eighteenth century's humane belief in the sufficiency of man and the light of reason. The book is not merely a child's book with a purpose; it is a child's book with a coherent philosophy, and that humane philosophy seems to me to have made *Sandford and Merton* far superior to the religious literature prescribed for children up to and, indeed, after that time. In how many biographies do we read of children who were terrified by *Foxe's Book of Mar-*

tyrs? How many have been made to snivel in misery over *Sandford and Merton's* pious rival of the nineteenth century, *The Fairchild Family*? Some undoubtedly enjoyed the terrors, and I am not sure that it is wise to prevent a child from transposing his inheritance of the guilt and crimes of human nature into the pages of imaginative literature. Throughout the nineteenth century Day's book was disliked because it was said to ignore religion. In fact it did not, for it contains a simple account of Christ's morality; but Day certainly was no friend to the idea of original sin, and he did not set out to take the growing mind from a consideration of its responsibilities to the world outside itself, by nagging it continually with morbid images of the world within. If he was going to talk about hell, it was the hell of poverty, the several hells which men make for their fellows, not the hell invented by sadistic servants. One of the important aims of Day—and also of Edgeworth, who had some claim to be called the father of modern education—was to free the children of the well-to-do from the corrupting influence of nurses, chambermaids and butlers. But Day's philosophy must be judged by the kind of interests it encouraged. No doubt, as Edgeworth at last came to see, we are not certain to choose virtue just because our reason tells us that vice leads to misery and unhappiness; no doubt authority and discipline are required. But what new fields the freedom of philosophy opened to the curious mind! While the fearful and pious child was sobbing over the catastrophes of sin and was enclosed in the dank cloisters of self-pity, the prim little rationalists of *Sandford and Merton* were seeing the world. They were exploring South America, studying elephants and tigers, conducting experiments with the sun and the moon, and learning about the society they lived in.

It is strange that such an uninspiring man as Day, a man so full of crotchets and so devoid of instinct, so poor in response to everything except a generality, should have written a book as limpid and alive as *Sandford and Merton*. He hits one or two tastes of children with nicety: the complacency of children, their priggish and fierce delight in codes of conduct and honor; their love of a crude argument in black and white; their cocky moments of discovery; their passion for being heroes. Day understands the elementary principle that children are human beings who are growing taller and more powerful every day. "We are but little children strong"—not weak. It is true that the tears and the piety of the awful little Harry Sandford mark a stage in the "too noble by half" tradition; but I imagine that the child reader identifies himself with the willful Tommy Merton, and attends only to Harry Sandford's remarkable practical capabilities—he knows how to deal with snakes, for example, and can take a thrashing without turning a hair—without being much perturbed by his virtues. Even the sentimentality about the honest poor, with its underhand appeal to childish pity, catches the child's love of showing off and making himself important. Old Mr. Barlow, to do him justice, has an inkling of this.

But the important charm of *Sandford and Merton* is extraneous to these matters. Day succeeds because he has created a kind of traveling zoo, an elegant and orderly zoo whose head keeper maintains a lively and picaresque running commentary. Now he is telling the visitor about the elephant, about elephants he has seen, elephants in the wild, elephants he has tamed, how you ought to handle them, and what happened to a tailor who made the mistake of playing a trick on one. The jungle, the native village, the regal procession are thrown in; and the whole stream of pictures flows smoothly by. They flick away before boredom starts. We have the pleasure of listening to someone talking to himself. This musical and vivid manner comes straight out of Day's own character. He was a man who never stopped talking. The ladies found this suffocating. But a child would listen forever, for Day was so delightfully unreal. "Is not that the country, Sir, where the cruel animal, the crocodile, is found?" asks Harry Sandford, when Mr. Barlow shows the human weakness of stopping for breath. The invitation is not to be resisted. "It is an animal," says the invincible Mr. Barlow, off again for another couple of pages, "that lives sometimes upon the land, sometimes in the water. It comes originally from an egg. . . ." Little Harry Sandford, so liable to be infected by every germ of virtue blowing casually on the air, catches this manner in his talks with Tom Merton. Harry has just been thrashed by the wicked Squire for refusing to tell him which way the hare went, and Tom is sympathizing:

H. Oh! it's nothing to what the young Spartans used to suffer.
T. Who were they?
H. Why, you must know they were a brave set of people that lived a great while ago; and as they were but few in numbers and were surrounded by enemies . . .

And so, by yet another happy dislocation of the narrative, the babbling stream of information resumes its cheerful flow.

Sandford and Merton is one of those books which are rich because they have taken a long time to mature and have outgrown their original plan. Day's first notion was to rewrite a number of well-known stories and fables for children; but he gradually saw that the stories could lead to Socratic dialogues and the arguments to still more stories.

Mr. B. But when a person is not good to him, or endeavors to hurt him, it is natural for an animal to run away from him, is it not?
T. Yes.
Mr. B. And then you say he is wild, do you not?
T. Yes, Sir.
Mr. B. Why, then, it is probable that animals are only wild because they are afraid of being hurt, and that they only run away from the fear of danger. I believe you would do the same from a lion or a tiger.
T. Indeed I would, Sir.
Mr. B. And yet you do not call yourself a wild animal?
Tommy laughed heartily at this and said No. Therefore,

said Mr. Barlow, if you want to tame animals, you must be good to them, and treat them kindly, and then they will no longer fear you, but come to you and love you. Indeed, said Harry, that is very true; for I knew a little boy that took a great fancy to a snake that lived in his father's garden; and, when he had milk for breakfast, he used to sit under a nut tree and whistle, and the snake would come to him, and eat out of his bowl.

T. And did it not bite him?

H. No; he sometimes used to give it a pat with his spoon if it ate too fast; but it never hurt him.

The aim of Day was to give a tendentious education. He loathed all that was meant by a man of fashion. He loathed everything that Lord Chesterfield stood for, almost as much as Lord Chesterfield's son came to do. He loathed idleness, profligacy, the self-indulgence of the rich. He loathed the man of fashion's attitude to children. He was a plain Republican who believed that no one should eat who did not work. He was one of the earliest Abolitionists. All these views are directed at Tommy Merton, whose father is a rich slave-owner:

And what right have the people who sold the poor negroes to your father to sell them, or what right has your father to buy them? Here Tommy seemed a good deal puzzled, but at length he said: They are brought from a country that is a great way off, in ships, and so become slaves. Then, said Mr. Barlow, if I take you to another country in a ship I shall have a right to sell you? —T. No, but you won't, sir, because I was born a gentleman. —Mr. B. What do you mean by that, Tommy? —Why (said Tommy, a little confounded) to have a fine house and fine clothes, and a coach, and a great deal of money, as my papa has. —Mr. B. Then if you were no longer to have a fine house, nor fine clothes, nor a great deal of money, somebody that had all these things might make you a slave, and use you ill, and beat you, and insult you, and do whatever he liked with you? —T. No, Sir, that would not be right, neither, that anybody should use me ill. —Mr. B. Then one person should not use another ill? —T. No, Sir. —Mr. B. To make a slave of anybody is to use him

48

ill, is it not? —T. I think so. —Mr. B. Then no one ought to make a slave of you? —T. No, indeed, Sir. —Mr. B. But if no one should use another ill, and making a slave is using him ill, neither ought you to make a slave of anyone else. —T. Indeed, Sir, I think not.

If Day's instruction was tendentious and was written on the revolutionary impulse of the eighteenth century, his methods were also new. Lord Chesterfield's son was intended to be a miniature Lord Chesterfield, an awed and suitably diminished reflection of his father. Day's notion was that a child is a new and independent life. His education in fact and morality was to be gained in the course of living; he was not to inherit a convention. If father's gluttony leads to gout, if father's wealth leads to restlessness, cruelty and guilt, if mother's spoiling leads to ill-health, the child's rational faculty must be strengthened until he sees that other courses are better. Education is a guidance in the choice of good habits and the cultivation of a humane disposition.

This was revolutionary. So revolutionary that old Edgeworth was obliged to disinherit his own son who had taken the bit of freedom between his teeth. Reason, alas, could not control him; neither a parent's reason nor his own. Edgeworth hastened to warn parents that he and his friends had been laboring under an appalling error. This was years later; and there is no doubt that Tommy Merton was drawn from Edgeworth's dashing and willful eldest son. And then there was another aspect to the revolution. The coddled manikin of the eighteenth-century portraits was given a healthier life. He was given lither, freer clothes and was sent to harden himself to sun and cold. The Spartan ideal was established. But, excellent as a revolution and adventure, the Spartan ideal itself became a kind of grim, vested interest, a terrifying convention in the English public schools of the nineteenth century. The cult of nature became the cult of neglect. The gentleman of fashion was succeeded by the gentleman tough.

A SCOTTISH DOCUMENTARY

WHILE Byron and Hobhouse were at Malta refusing to leave the ship until the Governor ordered the guns of the harbor to salute their arrival, there was another writer in the background. He was getting quiet pleasure out of the fact that the Governor had evidently no intention of wasting his honors on literature. This third person was John Galt, hitherto only a dull Scottish poet and young businessman, but later to become one of the most delightful humorous novelists of the Scottish hearth. Of his work, *The Annals of the Parish* is still entertaining, even for those who, like myself, never take kindly to the Scottish dialect and whose taste for glens, kirks, lochs and kailyards has suffered from an early excess of Scott, George Macdonald and Stevenson. With less pleasure one can also read Galt's *Ayrshire Legatees* and skip through his long novel *The Entail*. There is some well-tipped satire in both these books. Byron said that the Leddy Grippy of *The Entail* was the finest portrait of a woman in English literature since Shakespeare, but he was thinking, I am afraid, not of literature, but of the women who had annoyed him.

Of the three men who waited on board at Malta and who met several times later during Byron's Mediterranean travels, Galt was easily the most versatile, one almost had said the most original. At that time he was traveling with a scheme for capturing the Turkish trade and with an eye for any deal that came by the way. (He just missed buying the Elgin marbles as a speculation and was actually their nominal owner for a week or two while they were on the sea.) Galt showed the same sort of efficiency and enterprise in business which Peacock had, a capacity for large and problematical undertakings; and when one looks at the long list of plays, poems, hack biographies, pamphlets and novels which he wrote, it is a surprise to discover that the main business of his life was buying and selling, pushing plans for colonization, or for damming great rivers like the Clyde and the St. Lawrence, getting canal bills through Parliament and founding towns in Canada. The now thriving town of Guelph, in Ontario, was founded by him; he chose its site and planned its institutions; one other town in the same province bears his name.

Versatility, especially if this includes practical gifts, is a great danger to writers. To Galt, literature was always a side-line, a means of making a little extra, which he needed very badly. His work suffers accordingly. But there is always something sympathetic about the businessman novelist, the man who gets a little private amusement out of the Byrons, and himself never quite surrenders to the aberrations of the profession. Into the posing, frantic life of Grub Street, with its suggestion of the intellectual nudist colony, a man like Galt brings the mystery, indeed it amounts to the richness and romance of the conventional; he has the self-possession of one who does not carn his living by exposing his shame. *Tout se paie,* of course; Galt knew that he was a part-timer if not an amateur by temperament. But those writers whose main occupation keeps them on the outside of literary circles preserve a kind of innocence, a modest but all the more determined sense of their merits, and are less tempted to imitate and follow a school. Galt had such an individuality. He was brilliantly inventive by nature. He made a virtue of his inability to concoct plots and fables by writing documentary works, which in his *Autobiography* he calls "theoretical histories." And it is interesting to know that *The Annals of the Parish* was written long before *Waverley*— and was for twenty years without a publisher until Scott's work started the interest in Scottish subjects. Galt was indeed an innovator, and innovators do not generally reap fully where they have sown. Not many writers can say that they have founded a town, invented a new kind of book, and have given an important new word to the language: the word Utilitarian was taken by John Stuart Mill from the lips of the Rev. Mr. Balwhidder of *The Annals of the Parish*.

Galt's inspiration for this book came from *The Vicar of Wakefield*. He set out to create a Scottish Dr. Primrose. In fact, the Rev. Mr. Balwhidder, timid, twittering, pious, cautious, decorous, yet possessed of a salty tolerance of nature, is very different. One is never quite certain whether the minister knows how comical he really is. And when I say that *The Annals* is an amusing book I am not addressing myself to the literary critic who can take his amusement spread very, very thin as long as he is sure he is dealing with a standard work. *The Annals* is brisk and diverting, and as succulent, within the bounds of clerical decorum, as local scandal itself. We see the life of the parish of Dailmailing year after year, growing, waning, growing again.

Smuggling seizes Dailmailing's fancy for a time, and along come the illegitimate babies; soldiering seizes it; revolutionary ideas get into its heads; the old laird gives place to a new order; a mill absorbs the free weavers. And on top of these main episodes there is the froth of gossip. Old ladies fly into tantrums, young girls elope, justices roar, and wicked old women conceal smuggled tea in their mattresses and go to bed on them, feigning illness when the Excise officer and his informer come round. If one is in any doubt about the character of this book the first page settles it at once. The Minister of Dailmailing, whose prudence drove him to marry three wives in the course of his lifetime, belongs to the best dry vintage of Scottish humor, with its strange conflicting tangs of primness and animal spirits. He was put in by a patron over the heads of the angry villagers, and over their heads he had to go the Sunday he was "placed" at the church. Pelted with mud and guarded by soldiers, he had to climb in at a window because the church door was locked, only to be greeted inside by one of the zealots with the appropriate Scripture about those who enter "not by the door of the sheepfold but by some other way." And as the dismayed but long-suffering Mr. Balwhidder kneeled at the induction ceremony a loud laugh went up from the congregation when the neighboring minister gave him a tap on the head with a staff, and said, "Timber to timber." Having come in at the window, the minister was obliged to leave by it as well.

The inhabitants of Dailmailing, as can be seen, were people of spirit and with a turn for fantasy, but the quiet Minister was soon their equal. A gamekeeper had seduced the Rev. Mr. Balwhidder's parlormaid, and the Minister obliged the couple to stand in church. This happened after the death of the first Mrs. Balwhidder and was a warning to the prudent Minister that he had better get a second wife. Very different she was from the first, a managing woman with an "overearnestness to gather gear." She turned the meditative manse into a raucous farm, and worked day and night in the dairy, so that the Minister was left in his study most evenings as lonely as a bachelor. He might have married a factory. But he outlived her, too, and the third one, married in his old age, was nearer his own nature. She was a professor's widow, and the Minister's courtship of her is one of the most remarkable I ever remember in English comic literature. It is like something from Sterne, without the leer. One catches in this scene the frosty sparkle of Galt's comedy at its best:

> On the Thursday the company was invited, came, and nothing extraordinary was seen; but in cutting up and helping a hen, Dr. Dinwiddie put one wing on Mrs. Nugent's plate, and the other wing on my plate, and said there have been greater miracles than these two wings flying together, which was a sharp joke, that caused no little merriment at the expense of Mrs. Nugent and me. I, however, to show that I was none daunted, laid a leg also on her plate, and took

53

another on my own, saying, in the words of the reverend doctor, there have been greater miracles than that these two legs should lie in the same nest, which was thought a very clever come off; and at the same time I gave Mrs. Nugent a kindly nip in her sonsy arm, which was breaking the ice in as pleasant a way as could be.

The American war drains the Minister's parish, and then the French revolution divides the village into Government men and Jacobins and the new cults of philosophy, philanthropy and utility grow among the weavers. One angry Tory J.P., on being asked by an arrested weaver whether Christ was not a reformer, replied in a rage: "And what the devil did He make of it? Was He not crucified?" Which, I should say, is a very accurate report of what Christians who are sitting pretty really think of Christ, without realizing it.

The Annals is, besides its comedy, a fascinating social history; and Galt succeeds, where so many artists fail, in showing how his place, his people and their interests grow and change. At the end the Rev. Mr. Balwhidder is far from being the pious clown he was at the beginning. The zest of the narrative springs from its use of everyday speech. Here the dialect words are used sparsely but with vivid effect. Words like "yellyhoo" and "oustrapulous," full of sound and picture, are the hi-jinks of a vastly living vernacular. When we turn to the homely farce of *The Ayrshire Legatees* or the more complicated satire of Glasgow manners in *The Entail,* it is by these phrases and especially by the realism of Galt's dialogue that the eye is taken. A natural, stoical charm, a racy, nutty equanimity, unperturbed and unembittered by the shocks of the world, are in all Galt's books, and in his life too, which was filled with the disappointments that fall to a man who is more inventive than his fellows, as the reader of his *Autobiography* may see. The disappointments of affairs may indeed prepare a writer to take the dramas of the imagination less extremely and certainly rid him of the artist's temptation to pose. Galt, the part-timer, who

54

reverenced the poet in Byron and wrote his life, was not in the least overawed by him nor deceived. So easily might Galt have sneered or, worse still, have become the prosaic toady; it is the mark of Galt's independence and talent that he kept his moderate Tory head. And in those times it was something to have a level head. When Godwin's works were banned for their Jacobinism in the Ayrshire library, Galt, who detested Godwin's opinions, fought to get the ban removed, and was successful.

SCOTT

"NO ONE reads Scott now": how often one has heard these words! I have no doubt they are true, at any rate true of English readers. At some time in the last thirty years feeling against dialect and especially the Scottish dialect has hardened into a final dislike. It is troublesome to the eye, it is a language which nags and clatters; one would as soon read phonetics. And then dialect suggests the overweening conceit of local virtue, and if anything has died in the last thirty years, it is regionalism. Our society—why pretend—has made war on regionalism and has destroyed it. We may question whether, under any disguise, it can be reborn in the modern world. That is the first difficulty when we look at the long brown row of the Waverley Novels that have stood high out of reach on our shelves, unopened since our childhood. And here the second difficulty arises. We read Scott in our childhood and he is not suitable reading for children; few of the great novelists are. Why should a man, writing in his maturity, scarred by life, marked by the evils of the world, its passions and its experience in his blood, be consigned to the young who know nothing of themselves or the world? The fault is partly Scott's: this great man, the single Shakespearean talent of the English novel, drew far too often the heroes and heroines which have always appealed to the adolescent and gently reared reader—wooden idealizations, projections of our more refined, sixteen-year-old wishes. At sixteen we are in love with those sexless heroines with their awful school-mistressy speeches. We are in love with those stick-in-the-mud heroes whose disinterestedness and honor pervert the minds of boys with a tedious and delusive idealism. One grows up in the day-dream that Scott has generated to discover it is a swindle; and one never forgives him.

Yet, if we except this serious criticism for the moment, and measure Scott in the light of the full noon of life, we see that he belongs to that very small group of our novelists—Fielding and Jane Austen are the chief of them—who face life squarely. They are grown-up. They do not cry for the moon. I do not mean that to be grown-up is the first requirement of genius. To be grown-up may be fatal to it. But short of the great illuminating madness, there is a power to sustain, assure and enlarge us in those novelists who are not driven back by life, who are not shattered by the discovery that it is a thing bounded by unsought limits, by interests as well as by hopes, and that it ripens under restriction. Such writers accept. They think that acceptance is the duty of a man.

An error of our boyhood reading of Scott is, I fancy, the easy assumption that Scott is primarily an historical novelist. There is more reason to think of him as a comic writer. We would make a similar kind of error about Defoe, Fielding or Richardson if we took them at their word and believed that their only aim was to reform morals. The historical passion of Scott or the moral passion of these other novelists was the engine of their impulse. Where that engine took them is another matter. Hazlitt saw this when, in his too drastic way, he said that Scott was interested in half of life only: in the past of man and not in what he might become; and Hazlitt went to the length of thinking Godwin's *Falkland* fit to be compared with *Waverley*. But Scott's history meant simply his preoccupation with what is settled—and, after all, a great deal *is* settled for better or worse, in human life and character. One might even see in Scott's history the lame man's determination to impose and ennoble normality. The feuds of the clans are done with, the bloody wars of the Border are over, Jacobitism is a mere sentiment notable for its ironical inconsistencies as well as its heroic gestures. A period has ended and, for a novelist, there is no more favorable moment. Now he can survey. Scott gazes upon it all like a citizen who has dressed up. Now, vicariously, he can be physically heroic; but the real result of the historical impulse is not history but an immense collection of small *genre* pieces, a huge gallery of town and country faces in their inns, their kitchens, their hovels, their farms and their rambling houses. And the painting of them is as circumstantial, as middle-class—in the anti-romantic sense—and as non-aristocratic as anything of Hogarth's. Scott does not revive the past or escape into it; he assimilates it for his own time and for his own prejudices. He writes like a citizen. He asserts the normal man, the man who has learned to live with his evil; what his evil might have done with him if he had not learned to live with it can be guessed from the grotesque declamations of *The Black Dwarf,* the creature who cuts himself off from mankind.

The Black Dwarf is not a good novel. There are awkward lumps of unreality in it. The bad thing is the central drama, and this points to Scott's obvious fault as a novelist. He has an immense memory and the necessary taste for improving on memory. He has the power to present the outside of a character and to work from the outside to the inside. But once inside, he discovers only what is generic. That is the fault. He has, I would say, no power to work from the inside to the outer man. There is nothing feminine in him. So the black dwarf is excellent when he is seen as local recollection, a piece of Border hearsay, and no one could surpass Scott in portraying that tortured head, with its deep-sunken pin-point eyes, the almost legless and hairy little body with its huge feet, and the enormous voice that issues from the abortion. But when we come to the mind of this tortured creature, when he speaks, what we get is not horror but a dreary, savage Calvinist lecture. The black dwarf's misanthropy is a mere exercise, a sermon turned inside out. There is a complete breakdown of the imagination: compare this story with Turgenev's *Lear of the Steppes.* I suspect that as we continue our rediscovery of Scott we shall often find that the chief drama of the novels breaks down in this way, for the great protagonists of fiction begin from the inside of a writer. One is inclined to divide the Scott characters into two classes: the secondary and minor ones who are real and are truly recollected, the children of his wonderful memory; and the major ones who are the awkward, stage figures of an imagination that is cut off from the sap of life. To go back to Hazlitt: Scott lacked a vital sense, the sense of what people may become. His history was not real history. It was the settled, the collectable, the antique.

I turn to *The Chronicles of the Cannongate,* the tales of the second series, to see whether my last sentence is too sweeping. There is *The Highland Widow.* Here is real history—but you notice at once—history without costume. History in the rags of the people. The widow's husband has been a bandit, the Robin Hood of a clan that has almost died out. Her son perceives that times have changed; he enlists in the army which was once his father's enemy. The mother is appalled by the disgrace and plots to restore her son to a life of crime. The tragedy which is enacted springs from the clash of two orders of virtue, and the virtue of one age has become the vice of the age that succeeds it. There is no dialect in this story. It is heroic and not Hogarthian. It is the kind of thing that Mérimée and Pushkin took from Scott. And here, better than in his more elaborate compositions, we see the mark of Scott's genius as a story-teller. I say nothing of the suspense of which he is always a master; I am thinking of his power of suggesting the ominous, the footsteps of fate coming to meet one on the road. Frequently Scott used the supernatural and the hints of second sight to get this effect, and they are all the more effective for being explained as the domestic beliefs of his characters which the author himself hesitates to accept. But in *The Highland Widow* we come upon one of those real omens, one of those chance remarks made by a stranger which have another meaning to the one who hears. It is a device much used by Hardy. In Scott's story the young soldier has been drugged by his fanatical mother so that he shall not return to his regiment. The boy wakes up and rushes out to find what day of the week it is, for he fears more than anything else the degradation of his honor. The first person he meets is a minister, who replies: "Had you been where you should have been yesterday, young man, you would have known that it was God's Sabbath." The two meanings of those words mark the crisis of the tale, and after looking back upon it one realizes how ingenious and masterly has been the construction of a simple story. The end we could foresee; the means we could not, and it is in the means that Scott always shows the power of a master.

It is less the business of the novelist to tell us what happened than to show how it happened. The best things in Scott arise out of the characters. He especially understands, as I said before, the generic differences between people. He understands the difference between the fisherman and the farmer, the shepherd and the drover, and so on. He understands, in other words, what all ordinary, simple, observant men know about one another: the marks of their trade, their town, their family. (His view of women is that of the simple man: he knows them by their habits in the house. In love he does not know them at all.) The tale called *The Two Drovers* is a fine example of Scott's watchfulness of male character. The honor of Robin, the Highland drover, seems to be quaint silliness to Wakefield, the stolid Yorkshireman; the sense and fair play of Wakefield, who cannot believe that enmity will survive a little amateur boxing, are meaningless to the Highlander. Each is reasonable—but in a different way. The clash when it comes is tragic; again two kinds of virtue are irreconcilable. The scene in the inn is wonderfully true to the men there, and the talk slips naturally off their clumsy tongues. Wakefield has challenged Robin to fight with his fists. Robin can't see how this will mend a quarrel.

Harry Wakefield dropped the hand of his friend or rather threw it from him.

"I did not think I had been keeping company for three years with a coward."

"Coward pelongs to none of my name," said Robin, whose eyes began to kindle, but keeping the command of his temper. "It was no coward's legs or hands, Harry Waakfelt, that drew you out of the fords of Frew, when you was drifting ower the plack rock, and every eel in the river expected his share of you."

"And that is true enough, too," said the Englishman, struck by the appeal.

"Adzooks!" exclaimed the bailiff—"sure Harry Wakefield, the nattiest lad at Whitson Tryste, Wooler Fair, Carlisle Sands, or Stagshaw Bank, is not going to show the white feather? Ah, this comes of living so long with kilts and bonnets—men forget the use of their daddles."

"I may teach you, Master Fleecebumpkin, that I have not lost the use of mine," said Wakefield, and then went on. "This will never do, Robin. We must have a turnup or we shall be the talk of the countryside. I'll be d——d if I hurt thee—I'll put on the gloves gin thou like. Come, stand forward like a man!"

"To be peaten like a dog," said Robin, "is there any reason in that? If you think I have done you wrong, I'll go before your shudge, though I neither know his law nor his language."

A general cry of "No, no—no law, no lawyer, a bellyful and be friends" was echoed by the bystanders.

"But," continued Robin, "if I am to fight, I have no skill to fight like a jackanapes, with hands and nails."

And here once more the agent of tragedy is moving slowly down the road towards the two friends—the drover who is carrying Robin's dirk for him, to keep him out of trouble and to circumvent the fate that was foretold at the beginning of the story.

Except in the outbursts of *The Black Dwarf*, Scott appears to see evil as a fatality that ensues from the nature of the times. The civil wars have made men narrow and ruthless, and he writes at the end of an era, surveying the broken scene and pleading for tolerance. The crimes in *The Chronicles of the Canongate* are "errors of the understanding," not examples of absolute wickedness. When we turn to *The Antiquary* we meet another side of his talent; his humor. I wonder how many of those who, like myself, have not read Scott since their school-days will recall that Scott is one of the great comic writers? It is not purely Scottish humor, depending on the canniness of the speaker or on a continuous sly, nervous snigger, or on the grotesque and pawky asides of dialect. Scott's humor, like his best prose, is cross-bred with the English eighteenth century. Sterne and Fielding have put red blood into it. A character like Jonathan Oldbuck does not make thin jokes down his nose, but stands solidly and aglow beside all the well-found comics of our literature. The secret is that Scott's animal spirits are high, as Fielding's were. I have always enjoyed that strange scene in the early pages of *The Antiquary* in which Oldbuck supervises the rescue of the foolish, snobbish, bankrupt, treas-ure-hunting Sir Arthur, and his stick of a daughter, from the rising tide. Jonathan Oldbuck who has only an hour before been snubbed by the angry baronet, now watches the men heave the scarcely conscious gentleman up the rock:

> "Right, right, that's right, too—I should like to see the son of Sir Gamelyn de Guardover on dry land myself—I have a notion he would sign the abjuration oath, and the Ragman-roll to boot, and acknowledge Queen Mary to be nothing better than she should be, to get alongside my bottle of old port that he ran away from, and left scarce begun. But he's safe now, and here a' comes—(for the chair was again low-ered, and Sir Arthur made fast in it, without much con-sciousness on his own part)—— Here a' comes—bowse away, my boys!—canny wi' a tenpenny tow—the whole barony of Knockwinnock depends on three plies of hemp—respice finem, respice funem—look to your end—look to the rope's end."

I can read about half of *The Antiquary* and enjoy the flavors of what I read. After that I skip through the preposterous plot and willingly leave the wooden Lovel and the disdainful Miss Wardour to the pleasure of talking like public statues to each other. In one respect it must be admitted they do surpass modern lovers. Severely regulated by their families and by circumstance, these antique couples are obliged to know their subject. The obstacles to love ensure that the lovers shall concentrate.

The criticism that Scott cannot draw a heroine has to be modified after we have read *The Heart of Midlothian*. To judge by this book Scott could not draw a hero. For neither the pious, pettifogging Butler nor the wicked George Staunton can be called human beings of anything but conventional interest. Effie and Jeanie Deans are quite another matter. They are peasants and Scott condescends to them with the gentlemanliness of his time, but they are alive as his peasants always are. Scott's inability to draw women life-size seems to be due to the fact that he can think of them only as creatures high above him, or safely below him; and the ones below are drawn better than the ones above. The maid is more interesting than the mistress. We owe this romantic and pedestalled conception of women partly to the lame man's feeling of inferiority. He idealized what he could not approach. But these idealizations also arise from that curious split in the puritan middle-class mind which had begun to unsex itself so that it might devote all its will to the adventure of getting on in the world of money or honor, leaving the warmer passions to the lower orders. But unlike the early Victorian novelists, Scott is not a prude. Miss Bellendon's maid, in *Old Mortality*, nudges, winks and uses all her enticements on the soldiery; speech is very free in the farms and the inns; only Miss Bellendon in her castle stands like a statue and talks like an epitaph. Once Scott is free of these inhibitions —and in the main they are fixed by considerations of class— Scott describes women as well as they can be described from the point of view of a man in the house; that is as scolding, fussing, gossiping, pestering, weeping, willful and mercenary adjuncts of domestic life. They can always answer back. They never forgive a slight, they can always be persuaded to condone a crime. Expressed without satire but with sense and geniality this view has inspired many robust minor portraits of womanhood in Scott. The loveliness and attraction of Di Vernon in *Rob Roy* is due, I fancy, to the fact that she has a good deal of male in her. What is missing from all these portraits is the vitalizing element: the sense a woman has of herself, the sense of what she may become—that sense of our fate which alone gives meaning to our character. And as I have said before, Scott's direct intuitive sense of that fate seems to have been weak; he grasps the importance of it only through the labors of the historian and the documentary artist. His researches, not his instinct, gave us his remarkable portrait of the passionate mother in *The Highland Widow,* and his researches also revealed to him, in the same way, the larger meaning of Jeanie Deans' character in *The Heart of Midlothian.*

A modern novelist who rewrote *The Heart of Midlothian* would certainly stress the unconscious jealousy which Jeanie must have felt towards her younger sister by her father's second marriage. We would say that Jeanie's refusal to tell the lie that would save Effie from the scaffold was not a stern moral act, but an animal retaliation; for psychology has altered for us the nature of many ethical dilemmas. Scott ignores the evident jealousy. And though Effie, in a remarkable prison scene, flies out at her sister, we are left with the impression that Jeanie is either too stupid or too conceited in her conscience to be endured. But Scott's strength in the handling of the situation between the two women comes from his knowledge of the effect of history upon them. They are children of history. And the one part of history Scott knew inside out was its effect upon the conscience. Jeanie's refusal to tell a lie had generations of Calvinistic quarreling behind it, the vituperations of the secretaries who had changed the sword of the clan wars and the civil wars for the logic-chopping of theology. Instead of splitting skulls, they had taken to splitting hairs. The comedies, the tragedies, the fantastic eloquence and tedious reiteration of these scruples of conscience are always brilliantly described by Scott, who has them in his blood. And so Jeanie's refusal to lie and her journey to London on foot to seek her sister's pardon are not the result of conceit, heartlessness or even literalness of mind: they are the fruit of history.

And a history which produces not only plump, dumb, resolute figures like hers, but men of roystering violence like the bloody Porteous, tortured believers in predestination like Staunton, fanatics like old Deans, cranks like Saddlebright, lunatic harlots like Madge Wildfire, adventuresses like Effie, wonderful sea-lawyers of the criminal world of old Edinburgh like Ratcliffe, the thief, and wonderful fools like the gaping old laird of Dumbiedikes. There is none of the sentimentality which Dickens spread like a bad fog over the suffocated bastards, baby-farmers, harlots and criminals of his novels; none of the melodrama. Scott's realism belongs to the time when gentlemen knew the mob because they were not yet afraid of the mob. There is only one false episode in *The Heart of Midlothian;* and that is the wildly improbable meeting between Jeanie and George Staunton at his father's vicarage in England, and we owe that to the influence of the theater on the English novel. For that matter, none of the English scenes is really good and the final third of the novel is a failure. Here Jeanie is diminished as a character by the condescension of the author. But when she is in Scotland, we feel the force of her country and her fate in her, and these make her into a woman. One sees her even more clearly and fully late in the book when it is she, the rescuer, who has to pay tribute to Effie, the adventuress, who has, after all, got away with it. Scott was too much the man of the world to prevent Effie getting away with a good deal more than Dickens or even Thackeray were later on to allow their giddy-pated or wicked women. Scott recorded willfullness in women with an appreciative eye; and an ear cocked for the back answer.

It has often been said that the decay of our interest in problems of conscience is a major cause of the feebleness of the modern novel; but there have been many poor novels stuffed tight with conscience. Might we not say more justly that the problems of conscience have changed? Our habit is to weigh man against society, civilization against man or nature, individuals against groups. The greatness of *The Heart of Midlothian* arises, first of all, in the scope that the problem of conscience gave to Scott's imagination. He was not arguing in a void. His argument was creating real people and attracting real people to it. He made the story of Effie's murdered baby a national story. And then how wide his range is! The scenes in the Tolbooth are remarkable, and especially those that are built about the figure of Ratcliffe when the governor is working to turn him into an informer. Scott had the eighteenth-century taste for rogues, and their talk is straight from nature.

"Why, I suppose you know you are under sentence of death, Mr. Ratcliffe?" replied Mr. Sharpitlaw.

"Ay, so are a', as that worthy minister said in the Tolbooth Kirk the day Robertson wan off; but naebody kens when it will be executed. Gude faith, he had better reason to say than he dreamed of, before the play was played out that morning!"

"This Robertson," said Sharpitlaw, in a lower and something like a confidential tone, "d'ye ken, Rat—that is, can ye gie us ony onkling where he is to be heard tell o'?"

"Troth, Mr. Sharpitlaw, I'll be frank wi' ye: Robertson is rather a cut abune me—a wild deevil he was, and mony a daft prank he played; but except the Collector's job that Wilson led him into, and some tuilzies about run goods wi' the gaugers and the waiters, he never did ony thing that came near our line o' business."

"Umph! that's singular, considering the company he kept."

"Fact, upon my honour and credit," said Ratcliffe, gravely. "He keepit out o' our little bits of affairs, and that's mair

66

than Wilson did; I hae dune business wi' Wilson afore now. But the lad will come on in time; there's nae fear o' him; naebody will live the life he has led, but what he'll come to sooner or later."

"Who or what is he, Ratcliffe? You know, I suppose?" said Sharpitlaw.

"He's better born, I judge, than he cares to let on; he's been a soldier, and he has been a playactor, and I watna what he has been or hasna been, for as young as he is, sae that it had daffing and nonsense about it."

"Pretty pranks he has played in his time, I suppose?"

"Ye may say that," said Ratcliffe, with a sardonic smile, "and" (touching his nose) "a deevil amang the lasses."

"Like enough," said Sharpitlaw. "Weel, Ratcliffe, I'll no stand niffering wi' ye; ye ken the way that favour's gotten in my office; ye maun be usefu'."

"Certainly, sir, to the best of my power—naething for naething—I ken the rule of the office," said the ex-depredator.

Then there is Scott's power of describing a crowded scene. I am thinking of the long narrative about the crowd's storming of the Tolbooth and the killing of Porteous. Scott has looked it all up, but his own version is so alive, so effortless, so fast-moving. Every detail tells; the very pedantry of it is pedantry washed down by the rough wine of life. Everything is carried off with the authority of a robust and educated style, the style of a man fit to understand, master and govern, a man endlessly fair and excitingly patient in his taste for human nature. He understands popular clamor. He understands the mysteries of loyalty—all the diverse loyalties of a man's life and trade.

And after that Scott has the story-teller's ability to build a great scene and to make a natural use of it. I'm thinking of the search in the dark on Salisbury Crag when the police have persuaded Ratcliffe to help them catch Robertson, and Ratcliffe has brought Madge Wildfire with him to show them all the way. Madge is semi-lunatic, and Ratcliffe has to use all his guile to keep her to the job. He knows her mind is stuffed full of old wives' tales, and he reminds her of a notorious murder that was done on the Crag years before—a story the reader has already been prepared for: Scott's antiquarian asides ought never to be skipped—but Ratcliffe's cunning is turned against him at the moment of success by the madness of the woman. She accuses him of being as bad as the murderer.

"I never shed blood," he protested.
"But ye hae sauld it, Ratton—ye hae sauld blood mony a time."

That chance shaft hits Ratcliffe's conscience and wrecks the expedition. In a short chapter Scott has ingeniously extracted every kind of surprise and apprehension; and without any frivolity or artifice. The adventure could have happened; indeed, we say, if we had had eyes at the back of our heads, we would have known that it *must* have happened so, fabulous as it is. Scott's knowledge gives a sense of necessity to his picture of life, and his freedom in mixing the comic with the serious, even at the most dramatic moments, adds to this pleasant sense. He is not overdriven by his imagination, whereas a writer like Dickens was. Scott, like Fielding, has both feet firmly on the ground.

Rob Roy is admired—but for one or two scenes only when we examine the matter, and it is really a poor novel. At first sight the claims of *Old Mortality* are less emphatic upon the reader's attention, and since Scott repeated himself so often one is tempted to neglect this novel. It should not be neglected. Into this book Scott put all his tolerance and civilization, his hatred of fanaticism, and illuminated the subject of the religious wars in Scotland with all his irony, humor, all his wiriness of intellect and all his human sympathy. In Burley he drew the rise and the corruption of the fanatical character, and I do not know any other in Scott whose character grows and changes so convincingly. There is real movement here; elsewhere the sense of movement in his character is more the result of Scott's habit of dissertation than a real enacting of change. The portrait of Claverhouse is debonair, and the battle scene when the insurgents rout him is almost Tolstoyan. How much Scott owes to a sincere pleasure, even a joy, in the accoutrement of life. One can see how the Russians, like Tolstoy, Gogol and Pushkin first of all, must have been caught by Scott's wonderful pictures of the eccentric lairds. The miser in *Old Mortality,* or the ridiculous, gaping laird in *The Heart of Midlothian* must have fathered many a landlord in *Dead Souls* and other Russian stories. Where the Russians were to succeed and where Scott failed was in conveying the sense of an abiding destiny going on beyond the characters described. For Scott life is a book that one closes; to the Russians it is a book that one opens. And although one feels his animal zest for life, one feels it as a delightful recollection of hours that are ended, not as the perturbation or languor of the hour which has still to go by on the clock as we read.

One looks up the critics. What did Scott add to the English novel? Is he just another Fielding, but planted in Scottish history? Has he simply added a change of scene and material? It looks like that at first glance; he is a writer from the outside looking in. But I think there is something else. I would like to argue that Scott is a complement to Richardson—an analytical and psychological novelist who describes to us the part of our motives formed by public events. He is certainly the first novelist to describe the political influence of religion and the peculiar significance of superstitions and legend in the mind; and he uses them to illustrate the prompting of unconscious guilt and fear. One sees this in the character of Ratcliffe in *The Heart of Midlothian* and in innumerable instances elsewhere; Scott does not use his apparitions and legends merely for the purpose of putting a shiver or a laugh in his story. They are there to convey hidden processes of mind. No English novelist has added to that sense of a general or public mind, and certainly no great novelist—Hardy is the atheistical exception—has used religion as Scott used it.

OUR HALF-HOGARTH

THE English humorists! Through a fog compounded of tobacco smoke, the stink of spirits and the breath of bail-iffs, we see their melancholy faces. Look at Thomas Hood, his eyes swollen with the cardiac's solemnity, his mouth pouting after tears. There is a terrible account of his last days in Canon Ainger's *Memoir,* where we see the poet famous, forty-six, bank-rupt and dying of heart disease, writing farewells to his friends and unable to stop making puns. They beset him like a St. Vitus' dance. They come off his lips in an obsessional patter as if his tongue had become a cuckoo-clock and his mind a lunatic asylum of double meanings. And around him his doting family and his friends are weeping, "Poor Tom Hood." This is, alas, one of the too many crying-scenes of Victorian biography. It brims with that home-made beverage of laughter and tears which is handed round like a negus from the chiffonier of the lighter Victorian literature. The savage and vital indignation of the eighteenth century, its moral dogmatism, its body full of laughter and its roars of pain, have gone; melodrama replaces morality, a sprite-like pathos, all grace and weeping, and inked by fear of life, steps in where Caliban groaned and blubbered. I believe it was Charles Lamb who called Thomas Hood "our half-Hogarth," and that is the measure of the difference between the two periods.

Hood marks the difference well. Only in Goldsmith do we find a tenderness comparable to his. We look at the eighteenth century and, when all is said, we can hardly deny that it had a coherent and integrated mind, a mind not deeply divided

70

against itself. The proper study of mankind is man, who is very corrupt, but presently Divine Reason will teach him to cast off his chains and he will become a free child of nature. By the end of the century the chains are removed. And what is the result? Hood's early nineteenth century shows us. Man has not become free; he has vanished. Or rather, that humane abstraction called Man has been succeeded by two warring groups. Man has degenerated and has become the middle classes and the poor. No longer, like Swift, do the Victorians feel horror of mankind; on the contrary, looking at the little circle of mankind in which they live, they find the species has very much improved. At Clapham, at Wanstead Flats, even in Russell Square and Fleet Street, he is kindly, charitable and good. Their horror moves from man as a whole to a section of men. They are horrified, they are frightened—philanthropical and well policed though they are—by the poor. For generations now they will not stop talking about the poor. Did they pull down the Venetian blinds and turn to conceits and fancies because this fear is outside the window after dark? The feeling is that outside the sitting room is an undefined world of wickedness, hunger, catastrophe and crime. Pickpockets are nabbed, poachers are imprisoned, desperate laborers threaten arson, and children go to the mills and up the chimneys; the press gang and transportation are living memories, and sailors drown—oh, how many sailors drown!—in calamitous storms. These terrible things happen—to the poor. There we have Hood's background. There is his material. But writers are urged and taught to write not by society only but by other writers whose background and intention make them utterly different from their pupils. It is a strange fact that the England of Hood is not delineated by revolutionary realists, but has come down to us in the fantastic dress of German Gothic. The Cruikshank who frightens us; Mr. Punch, with his pot-belly, his fairy legs and the arching nose like some cathedral fragment, who squats on Dicky Doyle's cover, are part of the Gothic colony that settle like a migration of gargoyles among the English chimneys and their myth-creating smoke.

Hood, who was a Cockney of Scottish parentage, writes very early in his career of "doing something in the German manner." In his serious verses he is a Romantic, with his eye on Shakespeare, Scott and Keats. But this is the less readable part of Hood. His serious verses, if one excepts pieces of singular purity like "I remember, I remember," hardly amount to more than poetic dilutions for the family album, though contemporaries like Lamb, Southey and Byron had a higher opinion of them. Hood's best work is inflected, I suggest, by the basic early-Victorian fear and the fancies to which it led. He is on the side of the poor, of course, and wrote for the early, unsuccessful Radical *Punch*: but the Hood of *The Song of the Shirt*—which trebled the circulation of *Punch*—*The Lay of the Labourer* and *The Bridge of Sighs* is the dying Hood who is touched by the indignation of the hungry Forties. The earlier Hood thinks the poor are quaint and that their crimes can be sardonically disinfected. The result is a vein of fanciful horror which fathered a whole school of ballad writing:

> The body-snatchers they have come,
> And made a snatch at me;
> It's very hard them kind of men
> Won't let a body be!

> You thought that I was buried deep
> Quite decent-like and chary,
> But from her grave in Mary-bone
> They've come and boned your Mary.

That is from *Mary's Ghost*. I could have quoted from *The Volunteer* or *Death's Ramble*. There is *The Careless Nurse Mayd*:

> I saw a Mayd sitte on a Bank
> Beguilded by Wooer fayne and fond;

And whiles his flatteryinge Vowes she drank,
Her Nurselynge slipt within a Pond!

All Even Tide they Talkde and Kist
For She was Fayre and He was Kinde;
The Sunne went down before she wist
Another Sonne had sett behinde!

Or from *Sally Simpkin's Lament*:

Oh! What is that comes gliding in
And quite in middling haste?
It is the picture of my Jones,
And painted to the waist.

Oh Sally dear, it is too true—
The half that you remark
Is come to say my other half
Is bit off by a shark.

Gilbert, Lear, Carroll, Thackeray, the authors of *Struwelpeter*
and the cautionary tales continue this comic macabre tradition,
which today appears to be exhausted. There is Mr. Belloc,
who digressed intellectually; and there are the sardonic ballads
of Mr. William Plomer. He has added brilliantly the horrors of
vulgarity to the horrors of crime and accident.

Hood's special idiosyncrasy is to turn the screw of verbal conceit upon his subject. In *Eugene Aram* alone he cut out these
tricks, even forbearing in the last verse when his temptation
was always strongest. (How was it Hood failed to ruin what
are, surely, the most frightening dramatic lines in English
narrative verse?) But if Hood's puns are often disastrous, they
do frequently show, as Walter Jerrold (his biographer) has said,
a kind of second sight. They are like the cackle out of the grave
in *Hamlet*. They add malice to the knife and give the macabre
its own morbid whimsicalities. Take that terrible poem, *The
Last Man*. The earth has been desolated by plague and only
two men are left alive. They meet at a gallows and one, out of

jealousy, decides to hang the other. He does so and is left, wracked by conscience, to lament that he cannot now hang himself:

> For there is not another man alive,
> In the world to pull my legs.

The wit in *Death's Ramble* shocks one first of all and then freezes the blood one degree colder. Death sees two duellists:

> He saw two duellists going to fight,
> In fear they could not smother;
> And he shot one through at once—for he knew
> They never would shoot each other.

And the comic funk of *The Volunteer* gets a grotesque double meaning. He fears the alarm:

> My jaws with utter dread, enclos'd
> The morsel I was munching,
> And terror lock'd them up too tight,
> My very teeth went crunching
> All through my bread and tongue at once
> Like sandwich made at lunching.

To the poor, Hood draws our attention by shuddering and laughing with them at the same time. His detachment, when he is writing about crime and catastrophe, is dropped when he is putting the case of the poor. Then he writes with something like the garrulous, flat statement of the broadsheets. These odes and poems lumber along. There is the washer-woman's attack on the new steam laundry which has taken her living. There is the chimney-boy's lament that the law against street cries forbids him to cry "Sweep" in the streets. Drapers' assistants plead politely with people to shop early. These are pieces of topical journalism which time has blunted, and Hood's pen dipped deeply into that sentimentality which the philanthropical outlook of the period demanded. He was a pro-lific writer, and knew how to turn out his stuff. Like Dickens he was a sentimental Radical who hoped, as Dickens also hoped, that the problem of the poor could be solved by kindness; but the abiding note is that unpleasant one of Uriah Heep's: "Me and mother is very humble."

Hood prefers to let the poor or oppressed describe their lives uncouthly, rather than to attack the rich. The grotesque poem called *Miss Kilmansegg and her Precious Leg* is an exception. This poem startles because it is the first documented account of the upbringing of the perfect middle-class young lady whose parents are rising in the world. She is brought up to be a proud heiress, and the wonderful picture of arrogant surfeit recalls the awful overfed daughter of the mine-owner in Zola's *Germinal*. Money is the only subject of conversation. Then one day Miss Kilmansegg has an accident, her leg is amputated and is replaced by a golden one. A wooden one would not be good enough. Far from spoiling her chances, the golden leg doubles the number of her suitors. Her parents select the most plausible and least trustworthy one who is an alleged aristocrat. He turns out to be a bankrupt gambler who, very soon after the wedding night, gives a knowing look at the leg and

> The Countess heard in language low
> That her Precious leg was precious slow,
> A good 'un to look at, but bad to go
> And kept quite a sum lying idle.

She refuses to sell it. But unhappily she is in the habit of taking it off at night, and the Count sees his chance. Using the leg as a cudgel he bashes her brains out and absconds.

This long poem is like a grotesque novel, something of de la Mare's, perhaps, packed with realistic descriptions, and if its plot groans the lines scamper along as fast as Browning's dramatic narratives and are delighted with their own wit. And here the puns give the poem a kind of jeering muttered undertone. Hood had a great gift for domestic realism and the conversational phrase. In *Miss Kilmansegg* he is not half a Hogarth, but Hogarth whole. Or ought one to say, half a Hogarth and the other half that fanciful melodramatic sermonizer—as Dickens was in *The Christmas Carol*—which the nineteenth century loved? The poem is labored but it is alive.

Hood's wit quietened and compassion melted him in his last years. *The Song of the Shirt* and *The Lay of the Labourer* last very well in their *genre*, because of their metrical brilliance and because they are taken directly from life. One would want to remove only two or three lines of self-parody from *The Bridge of Sighs*. Hood is as well-documented as the realistic novelists were to become. *The Lay of the Labourer* is based on a true incident. An agricultural laborer was convicted for threatening arson because he could not get work or food, and Hood kept the newspaper cutting about the event on his mantelpiece until he wrote the poem. The sentiment is bearable, the rant is bearable, because the facts cry out and are so tellingly reported. One must regret that his feeling for narrative, his instinct for the right tune to put it in and his kind of conscience too, died out of verse with the Victorians. In the higher regions where Hardy lived, as in the lower regions of the music hall, the art of writing dramatic stories in verse seems to have gone for good.

DISRAELI

"The leaders of the People are those whom the People trust," said Sybil rather haughtily.

"And who may betray them," said Egremont.

"Betray them!" said Sybil. "And you can believe that my father . . ."

"No, no, you can feel, Sybil, though I cannot express, how much I honour your father. But he stands alone in the singleness and purity of his heart. Who surround him?"

"Those whom the People have chosen; and from a like confidence in their virtues and abilities. They are a senate supported by the sympathy of millions with only one object in view—the emancipation of their race. It is a sublime spectacle these delegates of labor advocating the sacred cause in a manner which might shame your haughty factions. What can resist a demonstration so truly national! What can withstand the supremacy of its moral power!"

SO WRITES Disraeli of the rise of the Chartists in *Sybil or The Two Nations*. His people are speaking the language of opera; yet, after a hundred years, how exactly Disraeli has defined the English political situation. He is our only political novelist; I mean, the only one *saturated* in politics; the only one whose intellect feasts on polity. Strikes, riots, questions of social justice, elections and backstairs politics enliven the other Victorian novelists of the period frequently; but of Mrs. Gaskell, George Eliot, Meredith, Trollope it cannot be said that politics are their blood. These writers do not convert us to this view or that; they are cautious; they do not inflame us; on the whole they leave us with the impression that political action is a disagreeable duty, distracting us from the major interests of human nature. Children of a competitive society, heirs of the Utilitarians, they see politics as the indispensable but tedious regulator. Politics are a method, a humane technique of adjustment; and, in general, it must be said that this has been the English view throughout the nineteenth century and after. To Disraeli, the Jew and alien, such a theory was pragmatic and despicable.

In his early years, at least, and especially in the trilogy of novels of which *Sybil* is the second volume, Disraeli brought to political thought the electric heat of the Jewish imagination and the order of its religious traditions. He demanded the glory of a dogma, the sensation of a re-birth, the emotion of a "new era"—a phrase used for the first time at the accession of Queen Victoria. And when we pick up *Sybil* or *Coningsby*, with their captivating pictures of aristocratic life and their startling, documented pictures of the squalor of the industrial poor, we feel that here at last is a novelist who is impatient of immediate social issues and who has gone back dramatically to the historic core of the English situation. The tedium has gone. We may now be carried away by a faith, snared by a passion. How precise is the diagnosis of the failure of his own party; they are not Conservatives but concessionaries, a party without beliefs. As we read *Sybil* and *Coningsby* we are swept along by a swift exultant mind. It takes us, by a kind of cinematic magic, from the gold plate and languid peers of the Derby dinner to the delectable mansions and heavenly countenances of the exalted, and from them to the sunken faces of the starved and enslaved. We may find ourselves converted to a new medievalism, to those heady "Young England" politics which read like a mixture of Marx, William Morris, Hall Caine and romantic Fascism. Disraeli was wrong; wrong, that is to say, as things turned out. Young England came to nothing, and the English workers followed the solemn prophecies of Sybil and not the aristocratic theory of Egremont; but whether he was right or wrong is not the point. The secret of Disraeli's superiority as a political novelist is that he introduces imagination into politics; he introduces questions of law, faith and vision. He looked upon the English scene with the clear intellect of the alien who, as a Jew, identified himself with both the two English nations; with the race that was to be emancipated and with the aristocracy that ruled them. The romantic, Byronic pride of Disraeli—if we are to take the figure of Sidonia in *Coningsby* as a projection of himself, several times larger than life—is measureless. Under the ancient gaze of the hollow eye of Asia, the Norman family is as crude as a band of tourists standing before the ruin of Ozymandias, king of kings.

Disraeli's gift is for the superb and the operatic. And if there is more than a touch of the *de luxe* and meretricious in his understanding of the superb, that fits in with the political picture; politics is the world of façade and promises. Disraeli knew God and Mammon. So many political novels have known God, the party line, alone; and without Mammon the people fainteth. He was the romantic poet and yet the *rusé*, satiate, flattering and subtle man of the world. When we are exhausted by visions he can soothe us with scandal. No one, said Queen Victoria with delight when she read his letters,—no one had ever told her *everything* before. The novels of Disraeli tell us everything. He not only plants the main spectacle, the house party of history; but he tells us the club gossip and the boudoir gossip—especially that—and speculates with malice on the dubious political career, on the unelevating comedies of political muddle and panic. He knows ambitious human nature. His eye is bright, his wit is continuous. His general surveys, notably those of the shams and disasters which overtook the regime of the Duke of Wellington, are wonderful destructive criticisms. No one describes a ball, or a house party, or a dinner as well as Disraeli, for no one so quickly and neatly gives one the foibles and background of the guests. His family histories are master-pieces of irony; he knows the private cankers of grandeur, the long machinations that have produced a Lord Monmouth or a Lord Marney. (In our own time we can imagine the late Lord Curzon modeling himself on Disraeli's personages.) All his ladies are ravishing; nevertheless, though never losing his sympathy for the female character and never ceasing to flatter, he sets it out with the coolest impartiality. "Although the best of wives and mothers she had some charity for her neighbours"—does that not "get" the good woman precisely? Or take the portraits of Lucretia Colonna and her mother in *Coningsby*. They are social generalizations like all his characters, and yet how definite they are! I find it difficult to get the hard, grasping, silent and daring daughter out of my mind. Eighteen and a monster of imperiousness already; silent because ill-educated; how she will exploit the old peer who all his life has been exploiting others! Disraeli knows exactly how society has created the character of Lucretia; like Sidonia, he has flattered and observed her. The Lucretia episode in *Coningsby* is rich comedy; for it entangles the egregious Mr. Rigby, Lord Monmouth's awful agent. There is nothing more amusing in this novel than the sight of Mr. Rigby being sent off to subdue the emotions of the mother who has been jilted in favor of her secretive daughter. The vulgar Rigby is a master of tactics:

> He talked wildly of equipages, diamonds, shawls, opera boxes; and while her mind was bewildered with these dazzling objects he, with intrepid gravity, consulted as to the exact amount she would like apportioned independent of her general revenue for the purpose of charity.

Having flown at him like a tigress and poured out epithets—"some of them true"—like a fishwife, the Princess calms down, fanned by his promises, and ends with the faint, pouting complaint that Lord Monmouth "might have broken the news himself." The aristocrat is admired for doing what we would all like to do. Who would not pay a Mr. Rigby to go down and break the brunt of the scenes that are being prepared for one? Still, we cannot call Rigby a great comic character. He is too rapidly generalized in his appearances. He is an essay on a comic character. Libelously drawn from the notorious Croker, he is a portrait, not a person. He is a rich and perennial political type, the yes-man. We add him to our collection of cads and buffoons. The summary of his character is exact:

> The world took him at his word because he was bold, acute and voluble; with no thought but a good deal of desultory information; and though destitute of all imagination and noble sentiment, he was blessed with a vigorous and mendacious fancy, fruitful in small expedients and never happier than when devising great men's scrapes.

Coningsby is a novel of static scenes. There is one that is rightly famous. This is where Coningsby, as a youth, goes to call on Lord Monmouth, his grandfather, for the first time and proceeds from stairway to stairway, apartment to apartment in the great house, until at last he comes into the presence. The emotion is too much for the sensibility of the shy youth, who bursts into tears; and the disgusted old peer, who cannot bear displays of feeling, dismisses him at once. This is one of the human scenes which stands out so movingly against the excess of artificial ones. Where *Coningsby* is still, *Sybil* moves. We pass from the sight of society to the pictures of working-class starvation and slavery. Disraeli investigated the conditions of the poor for himself, and his remarkable eye and ear collected a number of unforgettable notes and dialogues. There is nothing as terrifying in Dickens, for example, as Disraeli's picture of the slum town of locksmiths run by the toughest working men alone, a kind of frontier town without institutions. We see the knocker-up on his rounds, the starving weaver at his loom, the fever and the gloom of the rain-sodden houses, the new pubs and entertainment halls, the good factories and the bad ones.

The conversation of the people is not falsified, but is indeed indigenous and racy. Disraeli drew miners, for example, very well and understood their lives. He could also draw the working-class girl. We have entered into a world already made familiar to us by the prophetic books of Blake. Blake-like cries come out of this darkness: "I wish there was no such thing as coal in the land," says the weaver's dying wife. "And then the engines would not be able to work and we should have our rights again." It is a cry from *The Daughters of Albion*.

Sybil is melodramatic—it would make an excellent opera or film—it lacks the closely finished texture of *Coningsby* but is looser, bolder in argument, wildly romantic in scene. The satire at the expense of the Whig families, who are driving the cottagers off their land and selling out to the railway companies, is scathing: "Sympathy is the solace of the Poor: but for the Rich there is compensation."

The rioting and the attack on Mowbray Castle at the end is tremendous theatrical stuff, though—it must be remembered—Disraeli claimed that all his material about the Chartists was carefully documented. The unreality of certain characters, especially Sybil herself, is, of course, comical; but such characters are not unreal in their context. They are ideals walking and so romantic in their carriage that, in the end, one accepts them and their theatrical lamentations over their stolen heritage.

The *roman à thèse* is not commended as a rule by English critics; we read, as a rule, to be contented, and Disraeli's novels have caused a good deal of polite laughter. Such a world of superlatives invited ridicule. One can never be absolutely sure that Disraeli's imagination would distinguish between a great palace and a great Corner House; just as we can never be quite sure, as Lytton Strachey pointed out, that Disraeli was not himself carried away by the luxurious flatteries he poured into the ears of Queen Victoria.

EDWIN DROOD

WHEN lately I was reading *The Mystery of Edwin Drood* I felt extremely the want of some sort of guidance on the Victorian fascination with violent crime. What explains the exorbitant preoccupation with murder, above all? In earlier periods, when life was cheaper, rape, seduction, incest were the crimes favored by literature. If we look to literature rather than to life, it is certain the Victorian writers took over murder from the popular taste of the eighteenth century, and succeeded—against the outcry of the older critics—in making it respectable. But in the nineteenth century one detects, also, the rise of a feeling (so curiously expressed by a popular writer on the melodrama a few years ago; I have forgotten his name) that "murder is cleaner than sex." There is a clue there, I think. There is a clue, too, in the fact that organized police forces and systems of detection were not established until the Napoleonic wars—we are bound to become fascinated by the thing we punish—and another more sinister clue lies in the relative freedom from war after 1815. A peaceful age was horrified and fascinated, for example, by the ritual murders of the Indian thugs. Where else can we look? To the megalomania that was a natural field for the Romantic movement? To the guilt that is deposited in the mind after a ruthless exertion of the will, such as the Victorians made at the time of the Industrial Revolution? To the social chaos before the 'fifties, when tens of thousands were uprooted, and if they did not rise with the rising tide were left to sink into the slums or to stand out alone in violent rebellion? The more one reads of the unrest and catastrophes of the nineteenth century, in social or in private life, the more one is appalled by the pressure which is revolution applied to human beings. And when we read again the rant of the melodramas, when we listen to the theater organ of Bulwer-Lytton in *Eugene Aram,* and read the theatrical pages of Dickens, we feel, after the first shock of distaste, that these people are responding to a pressure which is not exerted upon us in the same degree. The violence of the scene suggests a hidden violence in the mind, and we begin to understand how assuaging it must have been, in novels like *Oliver Twist* or *The Mystery of Edwin Drood,* to see the murderer's conscience displayed in terms of nightmare and hysteria.

Assuaging to the Victorians, but not to us. We are not driven by the same dynamo. *Edwin Drood* stands at the parting of the ways between the early Victorian and the modern attitude to murder in literature, and also, I suspect, at the beginnings of a change in Dickens himself. The earlier murders of Dickens belong to the more turbulent decades of the nineteenth century. By the late 'fifties a calm had been reached; the lid had been levered back on to the pot of society and its seething had become a prosperous simmer. When Wilkie Collins wrote *The Moonstone* and Dickens, not to be outdone, followed it with *Edwin Drood,* we begin the long career of murder for murder's sake, murder which illustrates nothing and is there only to stimulate our skill in detection and to distract us with mystery. The sense of guilt is so transformed that we do not seek to expiate it vicariously on the stage; we turn upon the murderer and hunt him down. Presently, in our time, the hunt degenerates into the conundrums of the detective novel which, by a supreme irony, distracts us from our part in the mass murders of two wars. One or two critics have suggested that the struggle with the unfamiliar technique of the hunt was too much for Dickens and that it killed him and his novel. We cannot know whether this is so; but both those who dismiss the book as the last leaden effort of a worn-out man, and those who observe that it is the most careful and private of Dickens's novels, are agreed that it is pitched in a key he has never struck before.

What is that key? Before I add my answer to the dozens that have been made, it seems important to define one's own attitude to Dickens. I am totally out of sympathy with the hostile criticism of Dickens which has been made during the last twenty years, which has ignored his huge vitality and imaginative range and has done no more than to say he lacked taste and that he sacrificed a profound view of human nature to the sentimentalities and falsities of self-dramatization. To me it is a perversion of criticism to suggest that you can have the virtues of a writer without his vices, and the discovery of Dickens's failures does not make his achievement less. I swallow Dickens whole and put up with the indigestion. I confess I am not greatly interested in the literary criticism which tells me where he is good and where he is bad. I am glad to be instructed; but for us, at the present time, I think there is far more value in trying to appreciate the nature of his creative vitality and the experience that fed it—a vitality notably lacking in our own fiction. Now when we turn to *Edwin Drood* we do find some of the old Dickens. There is Mr. Sapsea, for example, with his own account of his courtship, that beautiful shot plum in the middle of romantic love and Victorian marriage:

"Miss Brobity's Being, young man, was deeply imbued with homage to Mind. She revered Mind, when launched or, as I say, precipitated, on an extensive knowledge of the world. When I made my proposal, she did me the honor of being so over-shadowed with a species of Awe, as to be able to articulate only the two words 'Oh Thou!' meaning myself. Her limpid blue eyes were fixed upon me, her semi-transparent hands were clasped together, pallor overspread her aquiline features, and, though encouraged to proceed, she never did proceed a word further. . . . She never did and never could find a phrase satisfactory to her perhaps—too—favorable estimate of my intellect. To the very last (feeble action of the liver) she addressed me in the same unfinished terms."

That is the old Dickens, but a shadow is upon Mr. Sapsea. The tomb of Mrs. Sapsea is, we are told, to be used by Jasper, the murderer, for his own purpose. Durdles, the drunken verger, tapping the walls of the Cathedral for evidence of the "old uns," is to be roped in. The muscular Christian, Mr. Crisparkle, sparring before his mirror in the morning, is marked down by the plot; and that terrifying small boy, the Imp or Deputy, who is employed by Durdles to stone him homewards when he is drunk, will evidently be frog-marched into the witness box. Dickens is submitting to discipline, and how fantastically severe it was may be seen in Edmund Wilson's *The Wound and the Bow*. The background loses some of its fantasy, but the best things in *Edwin Drood* are the descriptions of the cathedral, the town and countryside of Rochester which are recorded with the attentive love one feels for things that are gracious and real. Chesterton thought that something of the mad, original Dickens was lost in this realism; other critics explain it as the influence of mid-Victorian settling down. Mr. Edmund Wilson seems to suggest that in *Edwin Drood* one finds the mellowness and the bitterness of the man who sets out with some confidence equipped to master his devil and to dominate his wound. I do not find a loss in this picture of Cloisterham:

Cloisterham is so bright and sunny in these summer days, that the cathedral and the monastery-ruin show as if their strong walls were transparent. A soft glow seems to shine from within them, rather than upon them from without, such is their mellowness as they look forth on the hot cornfields and the smoking roads that distantly wind among them. The Cloisterham gardens blush with ripening fruit. Time was when travel-stained pilgrims rode in clattering parties through the city's welcome shades; time is when wayfarers, leading a gypsy life between haymaking time and harvest, and looking as if they were just made of the dust of the earth, so very dusty are they, lounge about on cool doorsteps, trying to mend their unmendable shoes, or giving them to the city kennels as a hopeless job, and seeking others in the bundles that they carry, along with their yet unused sickles swathed in bands of straw. At all the more public pumps there is much cooling of the bare feet, together with much bubbling and gurgling of drinking with hand to spout on the part of these Bedouins; the Cloisterham police meanwhile looking askant from their beats with suspicion, and manifest impatience that the intruders should depart from within the civic bounds, and once more fry themselves on the simmering high roads.

The shocks in *Edwin Drood* come not from the sudden leveling of his fantasy and the appearance of realism. They occur when Dickens acts his realism—see the showdown between Jasper and Rosa—and we realize that it is really alien to Dickens's gift that his people should be made to talk to each other. When he attempts this he merely succeeds in making them talk *at* each other, like actors. His natural genius is for human soliloquy not human intercourse.

In criticism of the English novel and in appeals to what is called "the English tradition," there has been a misunderstanding, I think, about this intrinsic quality of Dickens. One hears the word Dickensian on all sides. One hears of Dickens's influence on the English novel on the one hand, and of the failure of the English novel to produce a comparable genius. While the word Dickensian lasts, the English novel will be suffocated. For the convivial and gregarious extravagance and the picaresque disorder which are supposedly Dickensian are not Dickens's especial contribution to the English novel. They are his inheritance from Sterne, Smollett and, on the sentimental side, from Richardson, an inheritance which may be traced back to the comedy of Jonson. What Dickens really contributed may be seen by a glance at the only novelists who have seriously developed his contribution—in Dostoevsky above all and, to a lesser degree, in Gogol. (There is more of Dickens, to my mind, in James Joyce's *Ulysses* than in books like *Kipps* or *Tono*

Bungay.) For the distinguishing quality of Dickens's people is that they are solitaries. They are people caught living in a world of their own. They soliloquize in it. They do not talk to one another; they talk to themselves. The pressure of society has created fits of twitching in mind and speech, and fantasies in the soul. It has been said that Dickens creates merely external caricatures, but Mr. Sapsea's musings on his "somewhat extensive knowledge" and Mr. Crisparkle's sparrings in front of his mirror are fragments of inner life. In how many of that famous congress of "characters"—Micawber, Barkis, Moddles, Jingle, Mrs. Gamp or Miss Twitteron: take them at random—and in how many of the straight personages, like Jasper and Neville Landless in *Edwin Drood,* are we chiefly made aware of the individual's obliviousness of any existence but his own? The whole of Dickens's emotional radicalism, his hatred of the utilitarians and philanthropists and all his attacks on institutions, are based on his strongest and fiercest sense: isolation. In every kind of way Dickens was isolated. Isolation was the foundation not only of his fantasy and his hysteria, but also—I am sure Mr. Edmund Wilson is correct here—of the twin strains of rebel and criminal in his nature. The solitariness of people is parallel by the solitariness of things. Fog operates as a separate presence, houses quietly rot or boisterously prosper on their own. The veneer of the Veneerings becomes almost tangible, whipped up by the repetitions. Cloisterham believes itself more important than the world at large, the Law sports like some stale and dilapidated circus across human lives. Philanthropy attacks people like a humor or an observable germ. The people and the things of Dickens are all out of touch and out of hearing of each other, each conducting its own inner monologue, grandiloquent or dismaying. By this dissociation Dickens brings to us something of the fright of childhood, and the kind of realism employed in *Edwin Drood* reads like an attempt to reconstruct and co-ordinate his world, like a preparation for a final confession of guilt.

GEORGE ELIOT

*She looked unusually charming today from the very fact
that she was not vividly conscious of anything but of having a mind near her that asked her to be something better
than she actually was.*

IT IS easy to guess which of the mid-Victorian novelists wrote
these lines. The use of the word "mind" for young man,
the yearning for self-improvement in the heroine, and, lastly,
the painful, reiterating English, all betray George Eliot. This
description of Esther Lyon in *Felix Holt* might have been
chipped out in stone for George Eliot's epitaph and, as we take
down a novel of hers from the shelf, we feel we are about to
lever off the heavy lid of some solid family tomb. Yet the epitaph
is not hers alone. The unremitting ethic of self-improvement
has been the sepulcher of all mid-Victorian fiction except *Wuthering Heights*. Today that ethic no longer claims the Esther
Lyons of the English novel. The whole influence of psychology
has turned our interest to what George Eliot would have called
the downward path, to the failures of the will, the fulfillment
of the heart, the vacillations of the sensibility, the perception
of self-interest. We do not wish to be better than we are, but
more fully what we are; and the wish is crossed by the vivid
conflicts set up in our lives by the revolution that is going on
in our society. The bottom has fallen out of our world and our
Esthers are looking for a basis not for a ceiling to their lives.

But this does not mean that Esther Lyon is falsely drawn or
that she is not a human being. Using our own jargon, all we

have a right to say is, that the objects of the super-ego have changed; and, in saying this, we should recall a minor point of importance. It is this. Not only English tradition from Fielding onwards, but no less a person than the author of the *Liaisons Dangereuses* delight in the delectable evasions of the prig and the reserve of the prude; and it would indeed be absurd to cut the aspirations to virtue out of characters and to leave only the virtue that is attained or is already there. The critic needs only to be clear about the kind of aspiration that is presented to him; and here we perceive that what separates us from Esther Lyon and her creator is a matter of history. She is impelled by the competitive reforming ethic of an expanding society. One might generalize without great danger and say that in all the mid-Victorian novels the characters are either going up in the world, in which case they are good; or they are going down in the world, in which case they are bad. Whereas Goldsmith and Fielding revelled in the misadventures of the virtuous and in the vagaries of Fortune—that tutelary goddess of a society dominated by merchant-speculators—a novelist like George Eliot writes at a time when Fortune has been torn down, when the earned increment of industry (and not the accidental coup of the gambler) has taken Fortune's place; and when character is tested not by hazard but, like the funds, by a measurable tendency to rise and fall.

Once her ethic is seen as the driving force of George Eliot we cease to be intimidated by it, and she emerges, for all her lectures, as the most formidable of the Victorian novelists. We dismiss the late-Victorian reaction from her work; our fathers were bored by her because they were importuned by her mind; she was an idol with feet of clay and, what was worse, appeared to write with them. But it is precisely because she was a mind and because she was a good deal of the schoolmistress that she interests us now. Where the other Victorian novelists seem shapeless, confused and without direction, because of their melodramatic plots and subplots and the careless and rich diversity of their characters, George Eliot marks out an ordered world, and enunciates a constructed judgment. If we read a novel in order to clarify our minds about human character, in order to pass judgment on the effect of character on the world outside itself, and to estimate the ideas people have lived by, then George Eliot is one of the first to give such an intellectual direction to the English novel. She is the first of the simplifiers, one of the first to cut moral paths through the picturesque maze of human motive. It is the intimidating role of the schoolmistress. And yet when we read a few pages of any of her books now, we notice less the oppression of her lectures and more the spaciousness of her method, the undeterred illumination which her habit of mind brings to human nature. We pass from the romantic shadows into an explicit, a prosaic but a relieving light.

Two of George Eliot's novels, it seems to me, will have a permanent place in English literature. As time goes by *Adam Bede* looks like our supreme novel of pastoral life; and I cannot see any novel of the nineteenth century that surpasses *Middlemarch* in range or construction. With *Adam Bede*, it is true, the modern reader experiences certain unconquerable irritations. We are faced by a sexual theme, and the Victorians were constitutionally unable to write about sexual love. In saying this we must agree that no English writer since the eighteenth century has been happy in this theme, for since that time we have lost our regard for the natural man and the equanimity required for writing about him. The most we have a right to say about the Victorians is that, like the ingenious people who bricked up the windows of their houses and painted false ones on the wall, in order to escape the window tax, the Victorian novelists always chose to brick up the bedroom first.

Now in *Adam Bede* we are shocked by two things: the treatment of Hetty Sorel and the marriage of Dinah and Adam at the end. It is clear that George Eliot's attitude to Hetty is a false one. The drawing of Hetty is neither observation from life nor a true recasting of experience by the imagination; it is a personal fantasy of George Eliot's. George Eliot was punishing herself and Hetty has to suffer for the "sins" George Eliot had committed, and for which, to her perhaps unconscious dismay, she herself was never punished. We rebel against the black and white view of life and when we compare *Adam Bede* with Scott's *Heart of Midlothian,* to which the former confessedly owes something of its plot, we are depressed by the decline of humanity that has set in since the eighteenth century. Humanity has become humanitarianism, uplift and, in the end, downright cruelty. The second quarrel we have with this book arises, as I have said, from the marriage of Adam and Dinah. There is no reason why a man who has suffered at the hands of a bad woman should not be rewarded and win the consolations of a good woman. If Adam Bede likes sermons, we say, better than infidelity let him have them: we all choose our own form of suffering. But George Eliot told lies about this marriage; or rather, she omitted a vital element from it. She left out the element of sexual jealousy or if she did not leave it out, she did not recognize it, because she cannot admit natural passions in a virtuous character. In that scene where Hetty pushes Dinah away from her in her bedroom, where Hetty is dressing up and dreaming her Bovary-like dreams, the reader sees something that George Eliot appears not to see. He is supposed to see that Hetty is self-willed; and this may be true, but he sees as well that Hetty's instincts have warned her of her ultimate rival. The failure to record jealousy and the attempt to transmute it so that it becomes the ambiguous if lofty repugnance to sin, springs from the deeper failure to face the nature of sexual passion.

This failure not only mars George Eliot's moral judgment but also represses her power as a story-teller. When Adam comes to Arthur Donnithorne's room at the Hermitage, Arthur stuffs Hetty's neckerchief into the wastepaper basket out of Adam's sight. The piece of silk is a powerful symbol. The reader's eye does not leave it. He waits for it to be found. But no, it simply lies there; its function is, as it were, to preach the risks of sin to the reader. Whereas in fact it ought to be made to disclose the inflammatory fact that the physical seduction took place in this very room. George Eliot refuses to make such a blatant disclosure not for æsthetic reasons, but for reasons of Victorian convention; and the result is that we have no real reason for believing Hetty *has* been seduced. Her baby appears inexplicably. The account of Hetty's flight is remarkable—it is far, far better than the corresponding episode in *The Heart of Midlothian*—but the whole business of the seduction and crime, from Adam's fight with Arthur Donnithorne in the woods to Hetty's journey to the scaffold, seems scarcely more than hearsay to the reader. And the reprieve of Hetty at the gallows adds a final unreality to the plot. It must also be said—a final cruelty.

Yet, such is George Eliot's quality as a novelist, none of these criticisms has any great importance. Like the tragedies of Hardy, *Adam Bede* is animated by the majestic sense of destiny which is fitting to novels of work and the soil. Majestic is perhaps the wrong word. George Eliot's sense of destiny was prosaic, not majestic; prosaic in the sense of unpoetical. One must judge a novel on its own terms; and from the beginning, in the lovely account of Dinah's preaching on the village green, George Eliot sets out the pieties which will enclose the drama that is to follow. Her handling of the Methodists and their faith is one of the memorable religious performances of English literature, for she neither adjures us not satirizes them, but leaves a faithful and limpid picture of commonplace religion as a part of life. When she wrote of the peasants, the craftsmen, the yeomen, the clergy and squires of Warwickshire, George Eliot was writing out of childhood, from that part of her life which never betrayed her or any of the Victorians. The untutored sermons of Dinah have the same pastoral quality as the poutings of Hetty at the butter churn, the harangues of Mrs. Poyser at her cooking, or the remonstrances of Adam Bede at

his carpenter's bench. In the mid-Victorian England of the railway and the drift to the towns, George Eliot was harking back
to the last of the yeomen, among whom she was born and who
brought out the warmth, the humor, the strength of her nature.
We seem to be looking at one of Morland's pictures, at any of
those domestic or rustic paintings of the Dutch school, where
every leaf on the elm trees or the limes is painted, every gnarl
of the bark inscribed, every rut followed with fidelity. We follow the people out of the hedgerows and the lanes into the
kitchen. We see the endless meals, the eternal cup of tea; and
the dog rests his head on our boot or flies barking to the yard,
while young children toddle in and out of the drama at the
least convenient moments. Some critics have gibed at the dialect,
and dialect is an obstacle; but when the great moments come,
when Mrs. Poyser has her "say out" to the Squire who is going
to evict her; or, better still, when Mrs. Bede laments the drown-
ing of her drunken husband, these people speak out of life:

"Let a-be, let a-be. There's no comfort for 'e no more,"
she went on, the tears coming when she began to speak,
"now they poor feyther's gone, as I'n washed for and mended,
an' got's victual for him for thirty 'ear, an' him allays so
pleased wi' iverything I done for him, an' used to be so
handy an' do the jobs for me when I war ill an' cambered wi'
th' babby, an' made me the posset an' brought it upstairs as
proud as could be, an' carried the lad as war as heavy as two
children for five mile an' ne'er grumbled, all the way to War-
son Wake, 'cause I wanted to go an' see my sister, as war
dead an' gone the very next Christmas as e'er come. An' him
to be drowned in the brook as we passed o'er the day we war
married an' come home together, an' he'd made them lots o'
shelves for me to put my plates an' things on, an' showed 'em
me as proud as could be, 'case he know'd I should be pleased.
An' he war to die an' me not to know, but to be a-sleepin' i'
my bed, as if I caredna nought about it. Eh! an' me to live to
see that! An' us as war young folks once, an' thought we
should do rarely when we war married. Let a-be, lad, let
a-be! I wonna ha' no tay; I carena if I ne'er ate nor drink no

more. When one end o' th' bridge tumbles down, where's th' use o' th' other stannin'? I may's well die, an' foller my old man. There's no knowin' but he'll want me."

Among these people Dinah's religion and their quarrels with her about it are perfectly at home; and George Eliot's rendering is faultless. English piety places a stress on conduct and the guidance of conscience; and George Eliot, with her peasant sense of the laws and repetitions of nature, easily converted this working theology into a universal statement about the life of man. Where others see the consequences of sin visited upon the soul, she, the Protestant, saw them appear in the events of a man's or woman's life and the lives of others. Sin is primarily a weakness of character leading to the act. To Arthur Donnithorne she would say, "Your sin is that your will is weak. You are unstable. You depend on what others say. You are swayed by the latest opinion. You are greedy for approbation. Not lust, but a weak character is your malady. You even think that once you have confessed, your evil will turn out good. But it cannot, unless your character changes." And to Hetty she says, "Your real sin was vanity." It is a bleak and unanswerable doctrine, if one is certain that some kinds of character are desirable and others undesirable; psychologically useful to the novelist because it cuts one kind of path deeply into human nature, and George Eliot knows each moral character like a map. If her moral judgment is narrow, it enlarges character by showing us not merely the idiosyncrasy of people but propounds their type. Hetty is all pretty kittenish girls; Arthur is all careless young men. And here George Eliot makes a large advance on the novelists who preceded her. People do not appear haphazard in her books. They are not eccentrics. They are all planned and placed. She is orderly in her ethics; she is orderly in her social observation. She knows the country hierarchy and how a squire is this kind of man, a yeoman another, a teacher, a publican, a doctor, a clergyman another. They are more than themselves;

they are their group as well. In this they recall the characters of Balzac. You fit Dinah among the Methodists, you fit Methodism into the scheme of things, you fit Adam among the peasants. Behind the Poysers are all the yeomen. George Eliot's sense of law is a sense of kind. It's a sense of life which has been learned from the English village where every man and woman has his definition and place.

I doubt if any Victorian novelist has as much to teach the modern novelists as George Eliot; for although the English novel was established and became a constructed judgment on situations and people after she had written, it did not emulate her peasant sense of law. Hardy alone is her nearest parallel, but he differed from her in conceiving a fate outside the will of man and indifferent to him. And her picture of country life is really closer to the country we know than Hardy's is, because he leaves us little notion of what the components of country society are. The English peasant lived and still lives in a milder, flatter world than Hardy's; a world where conscience and self-interest keep down the passions, like a pair of gamekeepers. It is true that George Eliot is cut off from the Rabelaisian malice and merriment of the country; she hears the men talk as they talk in their homes, not as they talk in the public-houses and the barns. But behind the salty paganism of country life stands the daily haggle of what people "ought" and "didn't ought" to do; the ancient nagging of church and chapel. All this is a minor matter beside her main lesson. What the great schoolmistress teaches is the interest of massive writing, of placing people, of showing how even the minds of characters must be placed among other minds.

When we turn from *Adam Bede* to *Middlemarch* we find a novel in which her virtues as a novelist are established and assured; and where there is no sexual question to bedevil her judgment. No Victorian novel approaches *Middlemarch* in its width of reference, its intellectual power, or the imperturbable spaciousness of its narrative. It is sometimes argued by critics of contemporary literature that a return to Christianity is indispensable if we are to produce novels of the Victorian scale and authority, or indeed novels of any quality at all; but there are the novels of unbelievers like George Eliot and Hardy to discountenance them. The fact is that a wide and single purpose in the mind is the chief requirement outside of talent; a strong belief, a strong unbelief, even a strong egoism will produce works of the first order. If she had any religious leanings, George Eliot moved toward Judaism because of its stress on law; and if we think this preference purely intellectual and regard worry, that profoundly English habit of mind, as her philosophy, the point is that it was strong, serious, comprehensive worry. A forerunner of the psychologists, she promises no heaven and threatens no hell; the best and the worst we shall get is Warwickshire. Her world is the world of will, the smithy of character, a place of knowledge and judgments. So, in the sense of worldly wisdom, is Miss Austen's. But what a difference there is. To repeat our earlier definition, if Miss Austen is the novelist of the ego and its platitudes, George Eliot is the novelist of the idolatries of the super-ego. We find in a book like *Middlemarch*, not character modified by circumstance only, but character first impelled and then modified by the beliefs, the ambitions, the spiritual objects which it assimilates. Lydgate's schemes for medical reform and his place in medical science are as much part of his character as his way with the ladies. And George Eliot read up her medical history in order to get his position exactly right. Dorothea's yearning for a higher life of greater usefulness to mankind will stay with her all her days and will make her a remarkable but exasperating woman; a fool for all her cleverness. George Eliot gives equal weight to these important qualifications. Many Victorian novelists have lectured us on the careers and aspirations of their people; none, before George Eliot, showed us the unity of intellect, aspiration and nature in action. Her judgment on Lydgate as a doctor is a judgment on his fate as a man:

He carried to his studies in London, Edinburgh and Paris the conviction that the medical profession as it might be was the finest in the world; presenting the most perfect interchange between science and art; offering the most direct alliance between intellectual conquest and the social good. Lydgate's nature demanded this combination: he was an emotional creature, with a flesh and blood sense of fellowship, which withstood all the abstractions of special study. He cared not only for "Cases," but for John and Elizabeth, especially Elizabeth.

The Elizabeth, who was not indeed to wreck Lydgate's life, but (with far more probability) to corrupt his ideals and turn him into the smart practitioner, was Rosamund, his wife. Yet, in its own way, Rosamund's super-ego had the most distinguished ideals. A provincial manfacturer's daughter, she too longed idealistically to rise; the desire was not vulgar until she supposed that freedom from crude middle-class notions of taste and bearing could only be obtained by marriage to the cousin of a baronet; and was not immoral until she made her husband's conscience pay for her ambitions. The fountain, George Eliot is always telling us, cannot rise higher than its source.

Such analyses of character have become commonplace to us. When one compares the respectable Rosamund Lydgate with, say, Becky Sharp, one sees that Rosamund is not unique. Where *Middlemarch* is unique in its time is in George Eliot's power of generalization. The last thing one accuses her of is unthinking acceptance of convention. She seeks, in her morality, the positive foundation of natural law, a kind of Fate whose measures are as fundamental as the changes of the seasons in nature. Her intellect is sculptural. The clumsiness of style does not denote muddle, but an attempt to carve decisively. We feel the clarifying force of a powerful mind. Perhaps it is not naturally powerful. The power may have been acquired. There are two George Eliots: the mature, experienced, quiet-humored Midlander who wrote the childhood pages of *The Mill on the*

Floss; and the naïve, earnest and masterly intellectual with her half-dozen languages and her scholarship. But unlike the irony of our time, hers is at the expense not of belief, but of people. Behind them, awful but inescapable to the eye of conscience, loom the statues of what they ought to have been. Hers is a mind that has grown by making judgments—as Mr. Gladstone's head was said to have grown by making speeches.

Middlemarch resumes the observation and experience of a lifetime. Until this book George Eliot often strains after things beyond her capacity, as Dorothea Casaubon strained after a spiritual power beyond her nature. But now in *Middlemarch* the novelist is reconciled to her experience. In Dr. Casaubon George Eliot sees that tragedy may paralyze the very intellect which was to be Dorothea's emancipation. Much of herself (George Eliot said, when she was accused of portraying Mark Pattison) went into Casaubon, and I can think of no other English novel before or since which has so truthfully, so sympathetically and so intimately described the befogged and grandiose humiliations of the scholar, as he turns at bay before the vengeance of life. Casaubon's jealousy is unforgettable, because, poisonous though it is, it is not the screech of an elderly cuckold, but the voice of strangled nature calling for justice. And notice, here, something very characteristic; George Eliot's pity flows from her moral sense, from the very seat of justice, and not from a sentimental heart.

Middlemarch is the first of many novels about groups of people in provincial towns. They are differentiated from each other not by class or fortune only, but by their moral history, and this moral differentiation is not casual, it is planned and has its own inner hierarchy. Look at the groups. Dorothea, Casaubon and Ladislaw seek to enter the highest spiritual fields —not perhaps the highest, for us, because, as we have seen, the world of George Eliot's imagination was prosaic and not poetic —still, they desire, in their several ways, to influence the standards of mankind. There is Lydgate, who is devoted to science and expects to be rewarded by a career. He and his wife are practical people, who seek power. The pharisaical Bulstrode, the banker, expects to rise both spiritually and financially at once, until he sits on the right hand of God, the Father; a businessman with a bad conscience, he is the father of the Buchmanites and of all success-religions. The Garths, being country people and outside all this urban world, believe simply in the virtue of work as a natural law and they are brought up against Fred Vincy, Rosamund's brother. He, as a horsey young man educated beyond his means, has a cheerful belief in irresponsible Style and in himself as a thing of pure male beauty with a riding crop. We may not accept George Eliot's standards, but we can see that they are not conventional, and that they do not make her one-sided. She is most intimately sympathetic to human beings and is never sloppy about them. When Vincy quarrels with Bulstrode about Fred's debts, when Casaubon's jealousy of Ladislaw secretes its first venom, when Lydgate tries vainly to talk about money to his wife or Fred goes to his mad old grandfather for a loan, vital human issues are raised. The great scenes of *Middlemarch* are exquisite, living transpositions of real moral dilemmas. Questions of principle are questions of battle; they point the weapons of the human comedy, and battle is not dull. In consequence, George Eliot's beliefs are rarely boring, because they are a dynamism. They correspond to psychological and social realities, though more especially (on the large scale) to the functions of the will; they are boring only when, in the Victorian habit, she harangues the reader and pads out the book with brainy essays.

I see I have been writing about *Middlemarch* as though it was a piece of engineering. What about the life, the humor, the pleasure? There are failures: Dorothea and Ladislaw do not escape the fate of so many Victorian heroes and heroines who are frozen by their creator's high-mindedness. Has George Eliot forgotten how much these two difficult, sensitive and proud people will annoy each other by the stupidity which so frequently afflicts the intellectual? Such scruples, such playing-act-ing! But Lydgate and Rosamund quarreling about money; Rosamund quietly thwarting her husband's decisions, passing without conscience to love affairs with his friends and ending as a case-hardened widow who efficiently finds a second father for her family—these things are perfect. Mary Garth defying the old miser is admirable. But the most moving thing in the book—and I always think this is the real test of a novelist—is given to the least likeable people. Bulstrode's moral ruin, and his inability to confess to his dull wife, is protrayed in a pic-ture of dumb human despondency which recalls a painting by Sickert. One hears the clock tick in the silence that attends the wearing down of two lives that can cling together but dare not speak.

The humor of George Eliot gains rather than loses by its mingling with her intellect. Here we feel the sound influence of her girlish reading of the eighteenth-century novelists who were above all men of education. This humor is seen at its best in scenes like the one where the relations of the miser come to his house, waiting to hear news of his will; and again in the sar-donic description of the spreading of the scandal about Bul-strode and Lydgate. George Eliot followed causes down to their most scurrilous effects. She is good in scandal and public rumor. Her slow tempo is an advantage, and it becomes exciting to know that she will make her point in the minor scenes as surely as she will make it in the great ones. Mrs. Dollop of The Tankard has her short paragraph of immorality:

> (She had) "often to resist the shallow pragmatism of cus-tomers disposed to think their reports from the outer world were of equal force with what had 'come up' in her mind."

Mr. Trumbull, the auctioneer, is another portrait, a longer one, smelling of the bar and the saleroom. Dickens would have caricatured this gift from heaven. George Eliot observes and savors. Characteristically she catches his intellectual preten-

sions and his offensive superiority. We see him scent the coming
sale and walk over to Mary Garth's desk to read her copy of
Scott's *Anne of Geierstein,* just to show that he knows a book
when he sees one:

> "The course of four centuries," he reads out unexpectedly,
> "has well enough elapsed since the series of events which are
> related in the following chapters took place on the conti-
> nent."

That moment is one of the funniest in the English novel, one
of those mad touches like the insertion of a dog stealing a bone,
which Hogarth put into his pictures.

There is no real madness in George Eliot. Both heavy feet
are on the ground. Outside of *Wuthering Heights* there is no
madness in Victorian fiction. The Victorians were a histrionic
people who measured themselves by the Elizabethans; and
George Eliot, like Browning and Tennyson, was compared to
Shakespeare by her contemporaries. The comparison failed, if
only because madness is lacking. Hysteria, the effect of the
exorbitant straining of their wills, the Victorians did, alas, too
often achieve. George Eliot somehow escapes it. She is too level-
headed. One pictures her, in life, moralizing instead of making
a scene. There is no hysteria in *Middlemarch*; perhaps there are
no depths because there is so much determination. But there
is a humane breadth and resolution in this novel which offers
neither hope nor despair to mankind but simply the necessity
of fashioning a moral life. George Eliot's last words on her
deathbed might, one irreverently feels, be placed on the title-
page of her collected works: "Tell them," she is reported to
have said, "the pain is on the left side." Informative to the last
and knowing better than the doctor, the self-made positivist
dies.

AN IRISH GHOST

THE leaves fly down, the rain spits and the clouds flow like a dirty thaw before the wind, which whines and mews in the window cracks and swings the wireless aerial with a dull tap against the sill; the House of Usher is falling, and between now and Hogmanay, as the drafts lift the carpets, as slates shift on the roof and mice patter behind the wainscot, the ghosts, the wronged suitors of our lives, gather in the anterooms of the mind. It is their moment. It is also the moment to read those ghosts of all ghosts, the minor novelists who write about the supernatural. Pushed into limbo by the great novelists with their grandiose and blatant passion for normality, these minor talents flicker about plaintively on the edges of fame, often excelling the masters in a phrase or a character, but never large enough to take the center of the stage. Such a writer is J. Sheridan Le Fanu. In mid-Victorian literature Le Fanu is crowded out by Dickens and Thackeray, talked off the floor by Lever, that supreme raconteur, surpassed or (should one say?) by-passed on his own ground by Wilkie Collins: yet he has, within his limits, an individual accent and a flawless virtuosity. At least one of his books, a collection of tales republished sixteen years ago with Ardizzone's illustrations and entitled *In a Glass Darkly* is worth reading; it contains the well-known *Green Tea*. His other books show that, like so many talented Irishmen, he had gifts, but too many voices that raise too many echoes.

Le Fanu brought a limpid tributary to the Teutonic stream which had fed mysterious literature for so long. I do not mean

that he married the Celtic banshee to the Teutonic poltergeist
or the monster, in some Irish graveyard; what he did was to
bring an Irish lucidity and imagination to the turgid German
flow. Le Fanu's ghosts are what I take to be the most disquieting of all: the ghosts that can be justified, blobs of the unconscious that have floated up to the surface of the mind, and
which are not irresponsible and preambulatory figments of
family history, mooning and clanking about in fancy dress. The
evil of the justified ghosts is not sportive, willful, involuntary
or extravagant. In Le Fanu the fright is that effect follows
cause. Guilt patters two-legged behind its victims in the street,
retribution sits adding up its account night after night, the
secret doubt scratches away with malignant patience in the
guarded mind. We laugh at the headless coachman or the leg-
endary heiress grizzling her way through the centuries in her
nightgown; but we pause, when we recognize that those other
hands on the wardrobe, those other eyes at the window, those
other steps on the landing and those small shadows that slip
into the room as we open the door, are our own. It is we who are
the ghosts. Those are *our* own steps which follow us, it is *our*
"heavy body" which we hear falling in the attic above. We
haunt ourselves. Let illness or strain weaken the catch which
we keep fixed so tightly upon the unconscious, and out spring
all the hags and animals of moral or Freudian symbolism, just
as the "Elemental" burns sharp as a diamond before our eyes
when we lie relaxed and on the point of sleep.

Some such idea is behind most of Le Fanu's tales. They are
presented as the cases of a psychiatrist called Dr. Helvetius,
whose precise theory appears to be that these fatal visitations
come when the psyche is worn to rags and the interior spirit
world can then make contact with the external through the
holes. A touch of science, even bogus science, gives an edge to
the superstitious tale. The coarse hanging judge is tracked
down by the man whom he has unjustly hanged and is hanged
in turn. The eupeptic sea captain on the point of marrying an

Irish fortune is quietly terrorized into the grave by the sailor whom, years before, he had had flogged to death in Malta. The fashionable and handsome clergyman is driven to suicide by the persecutions of a phantom monkey who jumps into his Bible as he preaches, and waits for him at street corners, in carriages, in his very room. A very Freudian animal this. Dark and hairy with original sin and symbolism, he skips straight out of the unchaste jungle of a pious bachelor's unconscious. The vampire girl who preys on the daughter of an Austrain count appears to be displaying the now languid, now insatiate, sterility of Lesbos. I am not, however, advancing Le Fanu as an instance of the lucky moralist who finds a sermon in every spook, but as an artist in the dramatic use of the evil, the secret, and the fatal, an artist, indeed, in the domestic insinuation of the supernatural. With him it does not break the law, but extends the mysterious jurisdiction of nature.

Le Fanu might be described as the Simenon of the peculiar. There is the same limpid narrative. He is expert in screwing up tension little by little without strain, and an artist in surprise. The literature of the uncanny scores crudely by outraging our senses and our experience, but the masters stick to the simple, the *almost* natural, and let fall their more unnerving revelations as if they were all in the day's work. And they are. The clergyman in *Green Tea* is describing the course of his persecution, how it abates only to be renewed with a closer menace.

"I traveled in a chaise. I was in good spirits. I was more— I was happy and grateful. I was returning, as I thought, delivered from a dreadful hallucination, to the scene of duties which I longed to enter upon. It was a beautiful sunny evening, everything looked serene and cheerful and I was delighted. I remember looking out of the window to see the spire of my Church at Kenlis among the trees, at the point where one has the earliest view of it. It is exactly where the little stream that bounds the parish passes under the road by a culvert; and where it emerges at the roadside a stone with an old inscription is placed. As we passed this point I drew my head in and sat down, and in the corner of the chaise was the monkey."

Again:

"It used to spring on a table, on the back of a chair, on the chimney piece, and slowly to swing itself from side to side, looking at me all the time. There is in its motion an indefinable power to dissipate thought, and to contract one's attention to that monotony, till the ideas shrink, as it were, to a point, and at last to nothing—and unless I had started up, and shook off the catalepsy, I have felt as if my mind were on the point of losing itself. There are other ways," he sighed heavily, "thus, for instance, while I pray with my eyes closed, it comes closer and closer, and I see it. I know it is not to be accounted for physically but I do actually see it, though my lids are closed, and so it rocks my mind, as it were, and over-powers me, and I am obliged to rise from my knees. If you had ever yourself known this, you would be acquainted with desperation."

And then, after this crisis, the tortured clergyman confides once more to his doctor and makes his most startling revelation in the mere course of conversation. The doctor has suggested that candles shall be brought. The clergyman wearily replies:

"All lights are the same to me. Except when I read or write, I care not if night were perpetual. I am going to tell you what happened about a year ago. The thing began to speak to me."

There is Henry James's *second* turn of the screw.

We progress indeed not into vagueness and atmosphere, but into greater and greater particularity; with every line the net grows tighter. Another sign of the master is Le Fanu's equable eye for the normal. There is a sociability about his stories, a love of pleasure, a delight in human happiness, a tolerance of folly and a real psychological perception. Only in terms of the vampire legend would the Victorians have permitted a por-trayal of Lesbian love, but how lightly, skillfully and justly it is told. Vigilance is a word Le Fanu often uses. We feel a vigilance of observation in all his character drawing, we are aware of a fluid and quick sensibility which responds only to the essential things in people and in the story. He is as detached as a *dompteur;* he caresses, he bribes, he laughs, he cracks the whip. It is a sinister but gracious performance.

One doesn't want to claim too much for Le Fanu. For most of his life he was a Dublin journalist and versatility got the better of him. He is known for two of his many novels: *Uncle Silas* and *The House by the Churchyard. Uncle Silas* has ingenious elements. Le Fanu saw the possibility of the mysterious in the beliefs and practices of the Swedenborgians, but the book goes downhill half-way through and becomes a crime puzzle. A good man dies and puts his daughter in his brother's care, knowing his brother is reputed to be a murderer. By this reckless act the good man hopes to clear his brother's name. On the contrary, it puts an idea into his head. This brother, Uncle Silas, had married beneath him, and the picture of his illiterate family has a painful rawness which is real enough; but such a sinister theme requires quiet treatment, and Le Fanu is too obviously sweating along in the footsteps of Dickens or Wilkie Collins. Lever is another echo. It is his voice, the voice of the stage Irishman which romps rather too nuttily about *The House by the Churchyard,* into which Le Fanu seems to have thrown every possible side of his talent without discrimination. There are ghosts you shrink from, ghosts you laugh at, cold murder is set beside comic duels, wicked characters become ridiculous, ridiculous ones become solemn and we are supposed to respect them. It is all a very strange mixture, and Sterne and Thackeray, as well as Lever, seem to be adding their hand. A good deal is farcical satire of the military society in eighteenth-century Dublin, and Le Fanu is dashing and gaudy with a broad brush:

> Of late Mrs. Macnamara had lost all her pluck and half her colour, and some even of her fat. She was like one of those

portly dowagers in Nubernip's select society of metamorphosed turnips, who suddenly exhibited sympathetic symptoms of failure, grew yellow, flabby and wrinkled, as the parent bulb withered and went out of season.

His comic subalterns, scheming land agents and quarreling doctors, his snoring generals and shrill army wives, are drawn close up, so close up that it is rather bewildering until you are used to the jumpy and awkward angles of his camera. One gets a confused, life-size impression, something like the impression made by a crowded picture of Rowlandson's, where so much is obviously happening that one can't be sure exactly what it is and where to begin. Le Fanu was spreading himself as Lever had done, but was too soaked in the journalist's restless habits to know how to define his narrative. He became garrulous where Lever was the raconteur. He rambles on like some rumbustious reporter who will drop into a graceful sketch of trout fishing on the Liffey or into fragments of rustic idyll and legend, and then return to his duels, his hell-fire oaths and his claret. I can see that this book has a flavor, but I could never get through it. The truth is that Le Fanu, the journalist, could not be trusted to *accumulate* a novel. You can see in *Uncle Silas* how the process bored him, and how that book is really a good short story that has unhappily got itself into the family way. His was a talent for brevity, the poetic sharpness and discipline of the short tale, for the subtleties and symbolism of the uncanny. In this form Le Fanu is a good deal more than a ghost among the ghosts.

A VICTORIAN SON

THE WAY OF ALL FLESH is one of the time-bombs of
literature. One thinks of it lying in Butler's desk at Clif-
ford's Inn for thirty years, waiting to blow up the Victorian
family and with it the whole great pillared and balustraded
edifice of the Victorian novel. The book Thackeray failed to
write in *Pendennis* had at last been written. After Butler we
look back upon a scene of devastation. A spiritual slum has
been cleared, yet one is not entirely heartened. Was that the
drawing-room where mamma day-dreamed about marrying off
her daughters to the school-friends of her sons? Was that the
fireplace where papa warmed the seat of his trousers and
worked up the power politics of divine inertia? Did guilty sons
go up those stairs? Did catty sisters hiss from those landings and
aunts conduct their warfare of headaches and slammed drawers
in those upper rooms? Yes, says Samuel Butler, this was Heart-
break House. Yet not all of his very few admirers agreed with
him. Butler writes to Miss Savage in 1883 when the book was
circulating in manuscript:

> "Mr. Heatherley said I had taken all the tenderest feelings
> of our nature and, having spread them carefully on the floor,
> stamped upon them till I had reduced them to an indistin-
> guishable mass of filth, and then handed them round for in-
> spection."

I think it must be agreed that at least Butler spread them on
the floor. Now that the floor has collapsed twice in a generation we begin to wonder whether it is still the best place for

them; whether Norman Douglas was not right when he said, in *South Wind,* that Butler lacked the male attributes of humility, reverence and sense of proportion?

As Irish life runs to secret societies, so English life seems to run naturally to parricide movements. We are a nation of father-haters. *The Way of All Flesh* assuaged a thirst which, one supposes, began with the law of primogeniture and the disinheritance of younger sons. In the working class which gets little material start in life from its parents and which has to support them and house them in their old age, the obsession is noticeably rare. The normal human desire seems to be to bite the hand that feeds us, and not the hand we feed. But one has only to compare the quarrels of fathers and sons in, say, the eighteenth-century theater, with Butler's development of the theme, to see a private struggle turning into a national disease. The thunder of the eighteenth-century father as he is helped out of the coach toward the trembling figure of a young scapegrace who has rejected one heiress in order to abduct another and prettier one, comes from a Jupiter engorged (by the generosity of nature) with biological authority and the gout. The eighteenth-century father is a pagan bursting a blood vessel in the ripeness of time; the nineteenth-century father is a Jehovah dictating an inexhaustible Deuteronomy. Money, as Butler saw, makes the difference; and money, in the nineteenth century, is very different from money in the eighteenth century. Fortune, the speculator's goddess—not money—pours out its plenty from the South Sea bubbles and the slave trade in the eighteenth century. Sacks of gold descend from heaven by fantastic parachute, and are stored in the gloating caves, and trade is still spacious and piratical. How different is the nineteenth century, when Economics appears as a regulated science. With the rise of industrialism, Fortune has given place to cash, cash has become Consols and debentures. Investment does not float down from on high. It seeps in, it is secreted, it accumulates. Its accumulation gives birth to new laws of property and these become moral laws and obtain divine sanction. Investment is a token of energy and a huge will to power, and the fathers who exerted this will expected their families to run like the machines that were making their money.

The Way of All Flesh struck this system at its most vulnerable points: its sentiment, its priesthood and their myth. Butler ignored questions of justice and went for the enfeeblement of religious life and the paralysis which crept upon the emotions. The Musical Banks of *Erewhon* pour out a useless coinage, and when Ernest Pontifex kneels in prayer he fails to save either the souls of the poor, who have no time for him, or his own investments. He is useless to God and Mammon, and to offend Mammon is as serious, for Butler, as to offend God, for Mammon is so much richer in vitality and meaning than the stuffed Anglican God. But what Butler really opposed to Victorianism was not the sort of responsibility we would oppose to it; Butler opposed a system and its myth not with another system but with the claims of human personality. Against Victorianism he placed himself; himself with both feet on the ground, telescope to blind eye and in perverse self-possession, against people whose dreary will to power—and whose hold on spiritual and material property as well—had dried the sap of sense and life.

We cannot think of Butler without the Butleriana. We always come back to Butler as a man. We come back to the undigested slice of rebel egotism. Full of theories himself, he is constantly leaving the ranks of the specialists and joining the amateur ranks of the human beings. George Eliot may be all very fine, but he has bought a dictionary in order to read *Daniel Deronda* in the original! Now this is not nineteenth century at all. To start with, there is no ambition in it; and the more one thinks of him and his failure to fit in, the more one feels he is not a prophet, or at any rate not the prophet of Mr. Shaw's invention. On the contrary, he is a sport or throwback. He looks more and more like a throwback to the eighteenth century. His science—with its affection for Buffon—smacks of it.

That science, one suspects, is a rather literary science. His literary antecedents suggest the eighteenth century, too. *The Way of All Flesh* by its egocentricity, its very flatness and discursiveness, calls to mind the autobiographies of the eighteenth century, things like the *Autobiography* of Gibbon.

The genius of that age was to display a man to the full and yet to contain him within some intellectual assumption. The worldliness, the curiosity, the plainness, the tolerance, the irony, the comeliness of the eighteenth century are qualities which *The Way of All Flesh* revives. Not wholly so, for he was kicking irritably against the pricks; but he leapfrogs over the backs of the Victorians to alight beside the author of *Jonathan Wild* and *Amelia*—those novels in which Fielding was especially concerned with the moral and financial illusions of the virtuous. Butler would be at home in the cudgeling matches of Johnson or in Swift's dry and incinerating indignations. *Erewhon* is a straight descendant of *Gulliver*—a poorer book because it lacks savagery and the sublime, plain figure of Gulliver himself—it is no fellow to a mild book like *News from Nowhere*. Where, but in Swift or Fielding, shall we find the suave parallel to this passage from *The Way of All Flesh*:

> "It seems to me," he continued, "that the family is a survival of the principle which is more logically embodied in the compound animal—and the compound animal is a form of life which has been found incompatible with high development. I would do with the family among mankind what nature has done with the compound animal, and confine it to the lower and less progressive races. Certainly there in no inherent love for the family system on the part of nature herself. Poll the forms of life and you will find it in a ridiculously small minority. The fishes know it not and they get along quite nicely. The ants and the bees, who far outnumber man, sting their fathers to death as a matter of course, and are given to the atrocious mutilation of nine-tenths of the offspring committed to their care, yet where shall we find communities more universally respected? Take the cuckoo again—is there any bird which we like better?"

Shooting out his hatred and his contradictions, taking back his hatred with laughter, begging us, like Montaigne, to get our dying done as we go along, Butler is certainly an attempt at a rotund man, even though we know that the common-sense view of life is so often a refuge of the injured and the timid, and is neighbor to the conventional.

One's criticism is that the priggishness of Butler, rather than the roundness, gets into the characters of *The Way of All Flesh*. We must except Butler's working-class characters, those collector's pieces, like Mrs. Jupp, the landladies, charladies and servants. A novelist picks those up as he goes along. It is the great weakness of *The Way of All Flesh* that the characters are dwarfed and burned dry by Butler's argument. They are often very tedious. He chose them for their mediocrity and then cursed them for it. They can't stand up to his tweakings. Here Miss Savage was a sound critic when she pointed out the dangers of his special pleading; and although one can feel the years ripening the book, one ends with the feeling that Ernest Pontifex does not amount to much. Why should he come into his fortune? Merely that the unrighteous should have their reward? One does not feel that Ernest has very deeply developed because of suffering or fortune. He has escaped only. And he seems rather lost without his enemy. The weakness is that Butler is doing all the talking. There is no contradictory principle. Ultimately the defense of orthodoxy, even an orthodoxy as dim as Theobald's, is the knowledge of human passions. The strange thing is that Ernest does not give us the impression of a man who enjoys himself; he sounds like a man whose hedonism is a prig's hygiene. He looks like becoming the average bachelor of the room marked Residents Only.

One would give anything to have met Butler. For Ernest, Butler's shadow, one cares very little. Unlike Butler he does not act; because of the necessities of the book he is acted upon. His indiscretions are passive. He has no sins; he has merely follies. Still, Butler made more of a hand of self-portraiture in this reminiscence than Thackeray made of Arthur Pendennis and Butler seems to have learned from Thackeray's disquisitional method. These two misfit novelists, born 100 years too late, have many things in common. Christina is another Amelia from the latter pages of *Vanity Fair*, but filled out with richer comic truth. Her ruthless day-dreams are wonderful, her play-acting diplomacy is observed with wicked affection. She is one of those mothers whose right breast never lets on what the left breast is feeling. We are given the great Jekyll and Hyde masquerade of the female bosom:

> As regards Ernest, the suspicions which had already crossed her mind were deepened, but she thought it better to leave the matter where it was. At present she was in a very strong position. Ernest's official purity was firmly established, but at the same time he had shown himself so susceptible that she was able to fuse two contradictory impressions concerning him into a single idea and consider him as a kind of Joseph and Don Juan in one. This was what she had wanted all along, but her vanity being gratified by the possession of such a son, there was an end of it; the son himself was naught.

"The matter" she was "leaving," as the reader will remember, was a maternal plot to make him betray his friends. The paragraph goes on just as penetratingly into the male version of this kind of humbug:

> "No doubt if John had not interfered Ernest would have had to expiate his offence with ache, penury and imprisonment. As it was the boy was 'to consider himself' as undergoing these punishments. . . ."

One is made to feel the pathos of human jealousies, hatreds and humbug. One is tricked into forgetting that they are inevitable. Butler believed that living, like money, should be in the foreground of human life and not an anxiety in its background. He hated the efficient mechanic doctrine, the mechanistic science and (as one sees in *Erewhon*) the machine with its stereotyped response. He pitied the conscious Ernest who toes the line and tried to inflame in Ernest the healthy sabotage of the unconscious. What, strangely enough, Butler failed to find, in this early introduction of the unconscious into English fiction, was the passion. It was odd going to the unconscious and finding there—what? That chronic perversity: common sense.

A PLYMOUTH BROTHER

THE reaction from puritanism has been so strong and general in the last forty years or more that we too easily assume the extreme forms of it are dying. I do not believe they are. One kind of puritanism goes, after a long battle, and a new one takes its place. In an irreligious age, puritanism simply becomes scientific or political. Or it becomes a severe, exclusive addiction to psychological method. We may suppose that the Plymouth Brethren are a declining sect; but their place is taken by new international sects like the Jehovah's Witnesses, and this group is manifestly on the increase. It is not difficult to see why. The attack on science, the attack on social and political effort, does not affect the educated alone; it is eagerly followed by the ignorant and powerless. And then there are more intimate attractions. Extreme puritanism gives purpose, drama and intensity to private life. One of the greatest mistakes which the genial critics of puritanism make is to suppose that puritanism seen from the outside is the same as puritanism seen from the inside. Outwardly the extreme puritan appears narrow, crabbed, fanatical, gloomy and dull; but from the inside—what a series of dramatic climaxes his life is, what a fascinating casuistry beguiles him, how he is bemused by the comedies of duplicity, sharpened by the ingenious puzzles of the conscience, and carried away by the eloquence of hypocrisy. He lives like a soldier, now in the flash of battle, now in the wangling of camp and billet. However much he may bore others, he never suffers from boredom himself.

That distress eats into the lives of the children of the puritans. Puritanism burns up the air and leaves a vacuum for its descendants. When we read Edmund Gosse's *Father and Son* which describes the remarkable life of a family of Plymouth Brethren, we see that an insufferable ennui drove the son from his father's faith. Extreme peculiarity in a religious sect is exciting, even stimulating and enlarging to a child; it isolates him, and in doing so gives him a heady importance, an enormous lead (in some respects) over his more orthodox fellows. But the experience is too fierce. It creates that "chaffiness"—so quickly burned out—which the early Quakers were always talking about. The real reason for the boredom to come lies in that war against the imagination which all puritan sects—the political and scientific it should be observed, as well as the religious—have undertaken. Sir Edmund Gosse's parents would not allow their child to read or hear stories. Fact, yes; but stories were not true, therefore they were lies. The young Gosse, whose father was a scientist, was familiar with birds, insects, the creatures of the sea, and with books of scientific travel; but he had never heard of Jack the Giant Killer or Little Red Riding Hood.

> So far as my "dedication" was concerned (he writes) I can but think that my parents were in error thus to exclude the imaginary from my outlook upon facts. They desired to make me truthful; the tendency was to make me positive and sceptical. Had they wrapped me in the soft folds of supernatural fancy my mind might have been longer content to follow their traditions in an unquestioning spirit.

Yet it would be hard to call the elder Gosse a totally unimaginative man. As a scientist he was unimaginative, and so nipped the promise of his own intellect and career; but as a religious man he was riotously imaginative. He lived in the Eastern imagery of the Bible; he believed in it literally; he apprehended the instant end of the world and prepared himelf for a literal flight upwards into the air toward the arms of the angels. His was simply an intense and narrow imagination. And there is a comment by the son here which is very suggestive. We might assume that Gosse senior was a typical middle-class Victorian scientist and Nonconformist, presumably conditioned by his class and his age and bent on the general purpose of practical self-improvement; but, as the son points out, the father's religious life really sprang from a far earlier period. Gosse senior was not a nineteenth-century man; his Calvinism had survived, one might say intact, from the seventeenth century. Conduct, which meant everything to the nineteenth-century man, meant little to the elder Gosse; vision, the condition of grace, was everything. Later on, when the boy grew up and went to live in London, the father was worried very little by what the boy did; but was in agony about what he might think or feel. Was he still a dedicated soul, had he fallen from grace? To such questions the elder Gosse might bring the exhausting and pettifogging inquiry of a lawyer, rather than the imaginative anxiety of the religious mystic; but the attitude, as the son says, is nearer Bunyan's or Jeremy Taylor's than it is to the nineteenth century.

In our talk about environment we too easily assume that people living in the same time, in the same place, under the same conditions, are alike in their responses. We forget the time-lags, the overlaps, the sports and faults of history. It is surprising to find that American travelers to London in Victorian times saw an eighteenth-century city. We detect such lags and fixations in nations which are far enough away, in the Germans, the Spaniards, the Irish. We do not so easily detect them in private life. What was it that prolonged the seventeenth-century stamp upon the elder Gosse? A possible explanation is that, on both sides, the family was a genteel one of steadily declining fortune, and no family is more tenacious of the past, more prone to fixation than the declining family. We have only to compare Gosse's quarrel with Butler's to see the difference between two contemporaries. Gosse was fortunate; for Butler's nineteenth-century father had become a kind of practical Jehovah who thrashed prayer and Latin into his son indifferently. Gosse never hated his father. There was a break, a tragic and passionate break, not a clash of wills so much as a division of principles; and, since the breach was tragic, its agony was without resentment. Butler and his father, in their common hatred, were vituperative to the end; the Gosses gazed helplessly, emotionally across the gulf of history between them. Centuries separated them. The violence of the revolutionary nineteenth century did not possess them; and so it was the scorn, the satire and hatred of Butler and not the scrupulous, unavailing sympathy and impartial regret of Gosse that were to whip up the violent reaction against the Victorian family, and especially the Victorian father.

Gosse's attitude to his father is acquiescent and almost Gibbonian. If Gosse's imagination had been fed in childhood he might have used his father as a starting-point for one of those imaginative libels, like Dickens's portrait of Micawber, which are fatherhood's vicarious and unwilling gift to literature. But from Gosse, the ex-puritan and melodious prig, we get instead a positive, literal, skeptical document. What an incredible story the mere facts make. Nothing fixes the fantastic note like the episode of the moth. The naturalist, his wife and his child were at prayer one morning in 1855:

> . . . when through the open window a brown moth came sailing. My mother immediately interrupted the reading of the Bible by saying to my father, "Oh, Henry, do you think that can be *Boletobia?*' My father rose up from the sacred book, examined the insect, which had now perched, and replied "No! It is only the common *Vapourer Orgyia antiqua!*" resuming his seat and the exposition of the Word, without any apology or embarrassment.

I said earlier that Gosse senior could not be called unimaginative, but as the son points out, he was certainly deficient in sympathetic imagination. In one sense his fanatical religion was scientific, an exhaustive classification and checking up.

There was, for example, the question of Prophecy. The father said that no small element in his wedded happiness had been the fact that he and his wife were of one mind in the interpretation of Sacred prophecy. They took to it as profane families take to cards or the paino. They played with the Book of Revelation as if it were Happy Families or Snap:

> When they read of seals broken and of vials poured forth, of the star which was called Wormwood that fell from Heaven, and of men whose hair was as the hair of women, and their teeth as the teeth of lions, they did not admit for a moment that these vivid mental pictures were of a poetic character, but they regarded them as positive statements, in guarded language, describing events which were to happen, and could be recognized when they did happen. It was the explanation, the perfectly prosaic and positive explanation, of all these wonders which drew them to study the Habershons and the Newtons whose books they so much enjoyed. They were helped by these guides to recognize in wild Oriental visions direct statements regarding Napoleon III and Pope Pius IX, and the King of Piedmont, historic figures which they conceived as foreshadowed, in language which admitted of plain interpretation, under the names of denizens of Babylon and companions of the Wild Beast.

The conviction that the last days of the queenly arrogance of Rome had come so affected Gosse's mother that her husband wrote in his diary that it "had irradiated her dying hours with an assurance that was like the light of the Morning Star." As the years went slowly by—and how slowly they passed for the bored and ailing child who was expected to live at this pitch—it began to dawn on him that there was something incredibly trivial about such convictions. The elder Gosse could swallow one Eliot's stuff about prophecy and yet reject Darwin. He was an educated man, yet he could say that Shakespeare, Marlowe and Ben Jonson endangered the soul and that Dickens was preferable to Scott "because Dickens showed love in a ridiculous light." The child of such a man was obliged to develop two selves. One assented, got itself publicly baptized and dedicated at the age of ten, and confounded the wise with his

theology and unction; the other quietly built up a very different mind—and as the sons of puritans will—an inveterate irony.
This came out at the time when his father was thinking of
marrying again. The father (the child sharply detected) was
put, for once, in the position of the penitent. One was required,
the child remembered, "to testify in season and out of season."
Was the lady (he therefore asked) "one of the Lord's children"?
Had she, he pressed, "taken up her cross in baptism"? The
father had to admit that the lady had been brought up in the
"so-called Church of England." "Papa," said the little prig,
wagging his finger, "don't tell me that she's a pedobaptist?"

Gosse was encouraged to draw this portrait by the revolt of
the times. He was faced by the difficulty that at the moments
when narrow or peculiar religion is behaving most ludicrously,
it is also providing its adherents with emotions or intentions
that one must respect. Nothing could have been more intellectually disgraceful and spiritually disastrous than the boy's
public dedication; nothing more dingily farcical; or more humiliating when one considers that Gosse's father was, after all,
an educated man. Yet one must respect the emotions that the
participant felt. There is, as Gosse said, something comic and
tragic, really tragic, in the theme. On a similar subject Mark
Twain became savage; he was driven to a kind of insulting
nihilism. Gosse, in the end, was rather more bored than out-
raged by his father, for he understood the defect of character
that had caused the malady. He saw that the sin was the denial
of the imagination and the pestering of the judgment. He saw
that, at the time of the Darwin crisis, his father had really sold
his intellect and perhaps his soul. That flight to Devonshire
was a flight from the society of his equals, who would challenge
his faith every day, into a society of rustics who could be guar-
anteed to swallow everything he said. We smile with amusement and irony at the two figures; the father examining his
insects under the naturalist's microscope, the son applying the
lens of the biographer and producing one of the most brilliant
specimens of his century.

THE SCIENTIFIC ROMANCES

A CLOUD of dust travels down the flinty road and chokes the glossy Kentish greenery. From the middle of the moving cloud come the ejaculations of an unhandy driver; the clopper of horses' hoofs, the rumble of a wagonette or trap. One catches the flash of a top-hat or a boater. One smells horse manure and beer. And one hears that peculiar English spoken by the lower middle class, a language in which the syllable "-ing" either becomes "-ink" or loses its final "g," and which is enlivened by cries of "Crikey" and "Golly." The accent is despairing, narrow-voweled yet truculent, with something of the cheap-jack and Sunday League in it, and it is broken by a voice, not quite so common, which says things like, "We're not the finished thing. We're jest one of Nature's experiments, see. We're jest the beginning." And then—I don't quite know why—there is a crash. Over goes the wagonette, the party inside hit out with their fists, noses bleed, eyes are blackened. Most surprising, a nearby house catches fire. Do not be alarmed. The time is the late 'nineties and you have simply been watching the outing of a group of early H. G. Wells characters who have become suddenly aware that science is radically changing the human environment. No Frenchified or Russianized fiction this, but plain, cheerful, vulgar, stoic, stupid and hopelessly romantic English. It is as English as the hoardings.

There are always fist-fights and fires in the early Wells. Above all, there are fires. They occur, as far as I remember, in all the scientific romances except *The Island of Dr. Moreau*— a very pessimistic book—and are an ingredient of the Wellsian

optimism, an optimism whose other name, I fear, is ruthless-
ness. I have lately read all those scientific books from *The Time
Machine* to *The War in the Air* and it has been a refreshing
experience. There was a time, one realizes, when science was
fun. For the food of the gods is more entertaining than the
prosaic efficacy of vitamins; the tripods of the Martians are
more engaging than tanks. And then, here you have Wells at
his best, eagerly displaying the inventive imagination, first with
the news and at play, with an artist's innocence. Here you see
his intoxicated response—a response that was lacking in his
contemporaries—to the front-page situation of his time, and
here you meet his mastery of the art of story-telling, the
bounce and resource of it. Above all, in these early books, you
catch Wells in the act, his very characteristic act, of breaking
down mean barriers and setting you free. He has burst out himself and he wants everyone else to do the same. "Why," cries the
engineer in *The Food of the Gods*—the poorest of these books—
"Why don't we do what we want to do?"

For that matter, I have never read any book by H. G. Wells,
early or late, which did not start off by giving me an exhilarating
sense of personal freedom. Every inhibition I ever had faded
from me as I read. Of course, after such a high, hard bounce
one comes down again. The answer to the engineer's question is
that we do not do what we want to do because we want to do
opposite things at the same time. Yet that infectious Wellsian
sense of freedom was not all anarchy, romantic ebullience or
Utopian uplift. That freedom was a new fact in our environment; one pays for everything—that is all. I do not know what
date is given to the second scientific revolution, but one has to
go back to the great centuries of geographical discovery for a
comparable enlargement of our world; and it is a suggestive fact
that we have to go back to Swift, the Swift of Lilliput and La-
puta, before we find another English novelist going to science
for his data and material as Wells has done. (The influence of
science, in the one hundred fifty years that lie between those

two writers, is philosophical, not factual.) Wells's eager recognition of the new environment is one of the sources of the sense of freedom we get from him. I make no comparison of the merits of Wells and Swift—though the Beast-Men of *The Island of Dr. Moreau* are derivatives of the Yahoos and are observed with Swift's care for biological detail—but in his best narratives Wells does go back to the literary traditions of the early eighteenth century, the highest traditions of our narrative literature. The ascendancy of Swift is a question of imaginative range and style; above all it is due to a humanity which is denied to Wells because he arrived at the beginning, the crude beginning, of a new enlargement, whereas Swift arrived toward the end of one. None of Wells's narrators, whether they are South Kensington scientists or people, like the awful Bert, who appear to be suffering from an emotional and linguistic toothache, is capable of the philosophical simplicity and sanity of Gulliver; for Wells has only just spotted this new world of agitating chemicals, peculiar glands, and obliterating machines. The sense of wonder has not grown far beyond a sense of copy. He is topical and unstable, swept by eagerness yet visited by nauseas sudden and horrifying. Suppose we evolve into futility or revert to the beast from which we have arisen? Such speculations are alien to the orthodox eyes which were set in Swift's mad head; he had no eye to the future; the eighteenth century believed in a static world. The things Swift sees *have happened.* To Wells—and how typical of an expanding age—the things he sees have *not* happened. They are possibilities. In these scientific romances one catches occasionally the humane and settled note: in *The Time Machine,* in *The Island of Dr. Moreau* and in *The War of the Worlds,* which are the most imaginative stories of the group and are free of the comic Edwardian horseplay. The practical experiment has been detached from the practical joke; the idea is untainted by the wheeze. The opening sentence of *The War of the Worlds* suggests a settled view of humanity, besides being an excellent example of Wells's mastery of the art of bouncing us into belief in anything he likes to tell us:

> No one would have believed in the last years of the nineteenth century that human affairs were being watched keenly and closely by intelligences greater than man's and yet as mortal as his own.

It is not surprising that the passages of low comedy, which elsewhere are Wells's excellence, should be a failure in the scientific romances. Naturally they break the spell of the illusion with their clumsy realism. And if love is born, Wells is Walt Disney at his worst. The love scenes between the giants in *The Food of the Gods* are the most embarrassing in English fiction, and one wonders that the picture of the awful Princess, goggling in enormous close-up and fanning herself with half a chestnut tree, did not destroy the feminist movement. But except for faint squirms of idyllic petting in *The Time Machine,* none of these aberrations misdirects the narratives of the three books I have mentioned. I cannot include *The War in the Air* among the best; it *is* an astonishing piece of short-term prophecy and judgment. One remembers the bombing of battleships and the note on the untroubled mind of those who bomb one another's cities; but the book is below Wells's highest level. So, too, is *The Invisible Man,* which is a good thriller, but it develops jerkily and is held up by horseplay and low comedy. Without question *The Time Machine* is the best piece of writing. It will take its place among the great stories of our language. Like all excellent works it has meanings within its meaning and no one who has read the story will forget the dramatic effect of the change of scene in the middle of the book, when the story alters its key, and the Time Traveler reveals the foundation of slime and horror on which the pretty life of his Arcadians is precariously and fearfully resting. I think it is fair to accuse the later Wells of escaping into a dream world of plans, of using science as a magic staircase out of essential social problems. I think the best Wells is the destructive, ruthless, black-eye-dealing and house-burning Wells who foresaw the violence and not the order of our time. However this may be, the early Wells of *The Time Machine* did not escape. The Arcadians had become as pretty as flowers in their pursuit of personal happiness. They had dwindled and would be devoured because of that. Their happiness itself was haunted. Here Wells's images of horror are curious. The slimy, the viscous, the fetal reappear; one sees the sticky, shapeless messes of pond life, preposterous in instinct and frighteningly without mind. One would like to hear a psychologist on these shapes which recall certain surrealist paintings; but perhaps the biologist fishing among the algæ, and not the unconscious, is responsible for them. In *The Time Machine*—and also in the other two books—Wells is aware of pain. None of his investigators returns without wounds and bruises to the mind as well as the body, and Dr. Moreau is, of course, a sadist. *The Island* is hard on the nerves and displays a horror more definite and calculated than anything in Wells's other books. Where *The Time Machine* relieves us by its poetic social allegory, *The Island of Dr. Moreau* takes us into an abyss of human nature. We are left naked at the end of the shocking report, looking with apprehension at the bodies of our friends, imagining the tell-tale short legs, the eyes that shine green in the dark, the reversion to the wolf, the hyena, the monkey and the dog. This book is a superb piece of story-telling from our first sight of the unpleasant ship and its stinking, mangy menagerie, to the last malign episode where the narrator is left alone on the island with the Beast-Men. Neither Dr. Moreau nor his drunken assistant is a lay figure and, in that last episode, the Beast-Men become creatures of Swiftian malignance:

> The Monkey Man bored me, however. He assumed, on the strength of his five digits, that he was my equal, and was forever jabbering at me, jabbering the most arrant nonsense. One thing about him entertained me a little: he had a fan-

tastic trick of coining new words. He had an idea, I believe, that to gabble about names that meant nothing was the proper use of speech. He called it "big thinks," to distinguish it from "little thinks"—the sane everyday interests of life. If ever I made a remark he did not understand, he would praise it very much, ask me to say it again, learn it by heart, and go off repeating it, with a word wrong here and there, to all the wilder of the Beast People. He thought nothing of what was plain and comprehensible. I invented some very curious "big thinks" for his especial use.

The description of the gradual break in the morale of the Beast-Men is a wonderful piece of documented guesswork. It is easy enough to be sensational. It is quite another matter to domesticate the sensational. One notices, too, how Wells's idea comes full circle in his best thrillers. There is the optimistic outward journey, there is the chastened return.

It would be interesting to know more about the origins of *The Island of Dr. Moreau,* for they must instruct us on the pessimism and the anarchy which lie at the heart of Wells's ebullient nature. This is the book of a wounded man who has had a sight of sadism and death. The novelist who believed in the cheerful necessity of evolution is halted by the thought of its disasters and losses. Perhaps man is unteachable. It is exciting and emancipating to believe we are one of nature's latest experiments, but what if the experiment is unsuccessful? What if it is unsurmountably unpleasant? Suppose the monkey drives the machine, the gullible, mischievous, riotous and irresponsible monkey? It is an interesting fact that none of Wells's optimistic contemporaries considered such a possibility. Shaw certainly did not. Evil, in Shaw, is curable. He believes in the Protestant effort. He believes that men *argue* their way along the path of evolution, and that the life force is always on the side of the cleverest mind and the liveliest conscience. When he reflects on the original monkey, Shaw cannot resist the thought that the monkey was a shrewd animal going up in the world, and Shaw feels a patronizing pride in him which the self-made man may feel about the humble ancestor who gave him his start in life. There is certainly no suggestion that he will ever lose his capital, which is civilization, and revert. There is no thought, in this quintessential Irish Protestant, that the original monkey may be original sin. Nor could there be: the doctrine of original sin is a device of the emotions, and about our emotions Shaw knows absolutely nothing at all. But to the emotional Wells, the possibility of original sin in the form of the original monkey is always present. The price of progress may be perversion and horror, and Wells is honest enough to accept that. Shaw appears to think we can evade all painful issues by a joke, just as Chesterton, the Catholic optimist of his generation, resolved serious questions by a series of puns.

Wells can be wounded. It is one of his virtues. One is reminded of Kipling, another wounded writer—was Wells satirizing Kipling in that chapter of *The Island of Dr. Moreau* where the Beast-Men are seen mumbling their pathetic Law?—and Kipling and Wells are obviously divergent branches of the same tree. Wells the Utopian, Kipling the patriot—they represent the day-dream of the lower middle class which will either turn to socialism or fascism. Opposed in tendency, Wells and Kipling both have the vision of artists; they foresee the conditions of our time. They both foretell the violence with a certain appetite. Crudity appeals to them. They are indifferent or bad-hearted, in human relations. They understand only personal independence which, from time to time, in their work is swallowed up in mass relationships. In the final count, Kipling—like Wells's man in the sewer in *The War of the World*—falls back on animal cunning. It is the knowing, tricky, crafty animal that survives by lying low and saying nothing. Kipling, for all his admiration of power, believes in the neurotic, the morbid and defeated mind. This strain is in Wells also, but he has more private stoicism than Kipling has, a stocism which blossoms from time to time into a belief in miracles and huge strokes of luck. Impatient of detail, mysteriously reticent about the immediate practical steps we must take to ensure any of his policies, Wells believes—like Kipling—in magic: a magic induced by impudence or rebellion. Wells and Kipling—these two are light and shadow to each other.

Wells's achievement was that he installed the paraphernalia of our new environment in our imagination; and life does not become visible or tolerable to us until artists have assimilated it. We do not need to read beyond these early scientific works of his to realize what he left out. The recent war, whose conditions, he so spryly foresaw, has made that deficiency clear. When we read those prophetic accounts of mechanized warfare and especially of air bombardment, we must be struck by one stupendous misreading of the future. It occurs where we should expect it to occur: in the field of *morale*. Wells imagined cities destroyed and the inhabitants flying in terror. He imagined the soldiers called out to keep order and the conditions of martial law and total anarchy. He imagined mass terror and riot. He did not reckon with the nature, the moral resources, the habits of civilized man. Irresponsible himself, he did not attribute anything but an obstructive value to human responsibility. That is a serious deficiency, for it indicates an ignorance of the rooted, inner life of men and women, a jejune belief that we live by events and programs; but how, in the heyday of a great enlargement of the human environment, could he believe otherwise? We turn back to our Swift and there we see a mad world also; but it is a mad world dominated by the sober figure of the great Gulliver, that plain, humane figure. Not a man of exquisite nor adventurous spirituality; not a great soul; not a man straining all his higher faculties to produce some new mutation; not a man trying to blow himself out like the frog of the fable to the importunate dimensions of his program; but, quite simply, a man. Endowed with curiosity, indeed, but empowered by reserve. Anarchists like Wells, Kipling, Shaw and the pseudo-orthodox Chesterton, had no conception of such a creature. They were too fascinated by their own bombs.

THE FIVE TOWNS

I T IS a long time now since the earth seemed solid under the feet to our novelists, since caprice, prophecy, brains and vividness meant less than the solid substance of time and place. And Arnold Bennett, in books like *The Old Wives' Tale* and *The Clayhanger Family,* seems to be the last of the novel's four-square gospelers. I return to him often and always, once I get into him, with satisfaction. A book like *The Clayhanger Family* has the sobriety as well as the tedium of a detailed engraving; and there is, oddly, enough of the connoisseur in Bennett to induce our modern taste. He is not a dilettante in the ego's peculiarities and he is without interest in elegance; he is the connoisseur of normality, of the ordinary, the awkward, an heir—one might say—of the makers of the Staffordshire figures who thought Moody and Sankey as good a subject as equestrian princes of the blood. We speak of the disciplines of belief, of art, of the spirit; Bennett speaks of the discipline of life itself, reveres its frustrations, does not rebel against them; kneels like some pious behavior to the drab sight of reflexes in process of being conditioned. He catches the intolerable passing of time in our lives, a passing which blurs our distinctiveness and quietly establishes our anonymity; until our final impression of him is as a kind of estate agent's valuer walking with perfunctory step through the rooms of our lives, ticking his inventory and treating us as if we were long deceased. He cannot begin— and I think this is his inheritance from the French naturalists— until we are dead, until we and our furniture have become indistinguishable evidence. I find this very restful. Frustration

—*pace* Mr. Wells—is one of the normal conditions of life, and calming is the novelist who does not kick against the pricks.

Fidelity and sincerity are the words one puts first to Arnold Bennett's work. Some years ago there appeared an anthology called *The English in Love,* containing love passages from the English novelists, and I was much struck by the superiority of Bennett's contribution to the work of specialists like Meredith and D. H. Lawrence. Bennett was not describing passion; but against his quiet exactitude and sincerity, the lyricists looked forced and trite. The very matter-of-factness of Bennett made him one of the best portrayers of women we have had. The vices of romanticism or of misogynist satire passed him by in his best work completely. What other words come to mind when we think of him? They are his own words: "detracting" is one, "chicane"—a great favorite—is another; but there is a sentence in the early pages of *The Clayhanger Family* which contains a volume of criticism on him. He is writing of young Edwin Clayhanger coming home from his last day at school in the Five Towns: "It seemed rather a shame," Bennett says of Edwin, "it seemed even tragic, that this naïve, simple creature, immaculate of worldly experience, must soon be transformed into a man wary, incredulous and detracting." The essence of Bennett's mind is packed into that awkward sentence with its crick in the neck at the feeble beginning and the give-away of its three final words. Bennett had borrowed the manner and methods of the French naturalists without being seriously formed by the scientific, political and philosophical ideas which made them naturalists and gave them their driving force. Timidity rather than conviction is behind the brevity of his address. The result is that the apostle of will, efficiency and success appears to us hesitant and uncertain; he is between two stools; he cannot make up his mind whether life is "rather a shame" or "tragic." And when you compare *The Clayhanger Family* with the contemporary French *Les Thibaults*—which, like *Clayhanger,* contains a prolonged study in fatal illness and is also concerned with the relation of father and son—you feel at once, though you recognize the conscious artist, Bennett's lack of imaginative stamina and resilience. What Bennett observes will be truthfully, almost litigiously, observed. Hazard will set the points wrongly in the lives of humdrum people and push them off the rails. Time will get its teeth into them more deeply year by year. We shall feel, as Edwin felt, that we must "brace ourselves to the exquisite burden of life." We shall feel we are interpenetrated "by the disastrous yet beautiful infelicity of things." What we shall miss is the sense that life is conceived of as anything in particular, whether it be the force that makes the Five Towns or forms the bleak impetuosity of Hilda Lessways. We shall not feel that life is much more than a random collection of *things*.

Admitting the absence of a frame, allowing for some lagging of narrative which the modern novelist would speed up, everything else in *Clayhanger* is good. Bennett, as I have said, was the connoisseur of the normal, the ordinary and the banal. Where other novelists add, he—as he said—detracted. For example, how easy for the novelist to identify himself with the sixteen-year-old Edwin and to exaggerate that sense of being alone with the universe which the boy had when he sat in his room alone at night. Bennett collects that emotion, astutely yet compassionately—but he collects it, labels it—it becomes part of the collection of human samples which make up Edwin Clayhanger's life. Bennett's pursuit of the normal is even better illustrated by his treatment of the character of the hard, impulsive, passionate figure of Hilda Lessways. Here he uses a characteristic device: he makes two full-length portraits of her from two different points of view, a method which gives a remarkable suspense to the story. The first portrait of Hilda is romantic and mysterious outline. In the second, with enormous dramatic effect, he fills in the plain reality of her life. That second appearance of hers, as she cleans the house and quarrels with her mother about money, is a remarkable portrayal of the relationship of two women. As spectators of Hilda's character we might easily exaggerate, romanticize and misread her disaster; but Bennett's gift as a novelist is to abolish the role of spectator. He almost painfully domesticates the reader, puts him in the slow muddle, murmur and diurnal perturbation of a character's life, so that the reader knows no more than Hilda knows, where she is going or why she is going there. Where most novelists live by a sort of instinct for imaginative scandal, Bennett—by some defect of imagination which he is able to turn to advantage—clings like a cautious puritan to sober likelihood. He doesn't bet: "It's a mug's game." The result, in the portrait of Hilda, is a staggering probability. There is a passage when she discovers her husband is a bigamist and a crook, that the child she is expecting is illegitimate, and that she will be left penniless in their boarding-house at the mercy of bailiffs. She is faced by ruin. How do people face ruin? Variously, unexpectedly; they traipse, protected by conviction, through their melodramas. Bennett seems to reply:

> Hilda in a curious way grew proud of him. With an extraordinary inconsequence she dwelt upon the fact that was grand—even as a caterer, he had caused to be printed at the foot of the menu forms which he had instituted the words: "A second helping of all or any of the dishes will willingly be served if so desired." And in the general havoc of the shock she began to be proud also of herself because it was the mysterious power of her individuality that had originated her disaster.

The determination to avoid the dramatic has led to something far more dramatic: revelation, a new light on character, the unexpected vistas in ordinary life.

Bennett's characters have three dimensions; the slow but adroit changing of the light that is thrown upon them makes them stereoscopic and gives them movement. And this movement is not the swift agitation of the passions but the dilatory adjustment to circumstance.

One of the reasons why bad novels are bad is not that the

characters do not live, but they do not live with one another. They read one another's minds through the author. In *Clayhanger,* we feel at once that the characters are living together because, quite without prompting and entirely in the course of nature, they misunderstand one another. Edwin never understands his father because he does not know his father's past. The father cannot understand the son because the father's whole attitude to life is that his rise from barbarous poverty is a primitive miracle. He is primitive, the son is rational. Each one bumps awkwardly along in the wonder of his own nature. When the father is stricken by fatal illness the son becomes the tyrant. Their emotions about each other are strong; but the two men do not feel these emotions for each other at the same time. The fierceness of the father's battle for life in the long, gray death scene startles the son—and yet he feels how strange it is that a dying man should be strong enough to return again and again to the struggle, whereas he, the son and slave, should be at the point of collapse. A writer with little poetic feeling, Bennett thinks of our awkwardness with each other, of the unbridgeable gaps of time, experience and faculty which separarate us, and not of our ultimate isolation. That is why he is a pathetic and not a tragic writer; one who feels uncertainly that "it is rather a shame," that we have to bear time's burden of "beautiful infelicity."

Bennett's collector's passion for ordinariness is a kind of poor relation of Meredith's passion for the fantastic. It is amusing to make an irreverent comparison between Meredith's chapter *On an Aged and Great Wine* with Bennett's fervent hymn to building materials and plumbing in *Clayhanger.* This tedious literalness of Bennett's culminated in that nightmare of deified gadgets, *Imperial Palace.* But the virtues of Bennett lie in his patient and humane consideration of the normal factors of our lives: money, marriage, illness as we have to deal with them. Life, he seems to say, is an occupation which is forced upon us, not a journey we have chosen, nor a plunge we have taken.

Such a view may at times depress us, but it may toughen us. Bennett really wrote out of the congenital tiredness of the lower middle class, as Wells wrote out of its gambling spirit and gift for fantasy; and in the end, I think, Bennett's picture, with its blank acceptance of the Sunday School pageants, the Jubilees, the Band of Hope, the fear of the workers, the half-baked attempts at culture, is the more lasting one. It is history. History presented—when we glance back at Bennett's French masters—with the dilettante's and collector's indifference to any theory of what history may be about.

SONS AND LOVERS

WHAT of the writers who emerged after the last war? D. H. Lawrence, for example—can he tell us anything; how does he seem now? A great influence, like Wells was, on ordinary conduct; a whole generation dropped the puritan tradition and made love after the fashion of Lawrence's new puritanism. The cult of sex was also a protest against the ignoble atmosphere of city life. Wells supplied the blue print for free-love; Lawrence replied with the content. It was a new content for marriage. Free-love awakens Lawrence's irony; he admires the restlessness of it but sees that it is governed by the law of diminishing returns. Like Wells, too, Lawrence is one of the journalist-novelists. He writes a novel a year about his travels and the mistakes of his friends, a religious journalist where Wells is political. Has Lawrence had any influence on contemporary writers? Yes, he is responsible for the fact that no living writer has any idea of how to write about sexual love. Lawrence's phallic cult was a disaster to descriptive writing. The ecstasies of sexual sensation are no more to be described than the ecstasies of music which they resemble. The realism of the Chinese *Golden Lotus,* for example, makes Lawrence look silly. But above all, it was fatal for imitators of Lawrence to pick up his contagious manner and leave the beliefs that did so much to create the manner; on the other hand, no one could possibly believe what Lawrence believed, and Lawrence hated people if they tried, because he believed in the inviolable, personal contradictions. One day when Lawrence and Frieda were out riding in Mexico, Frieda cried out, "Oh, it's wonderful, wonderful to feel his great thighs moving, to feel his powerful legs!" "Rubbish, Frieda," Lawrence shouted back. "Don't talk like that. You have been reading my books. You don't feel anything of the sort." Quite rightly and consistently Lawrence allowed no one to believe what he believed. All the same, Frieda persisted; she did feel like that! Certainly she *wanted* to feel like that. Lawrence's teachings are interesting because they are a compendium of what a whole generation wanted to feel, until Hitler arose, just after Lawrence's death, and they saw where the dark unconsciousness was leading them. Seen in this light, Lawrence represented the last phase of the Romantic movement: random, irresponsible egotism, power for power's sake, the blood cult of Rosenberg. And Lawrence was representative, because tens of thousands of people in England and Europe were uprooted people, like himself.

Still, that was only one of the lights in which Lawrence could be read. The man of genius is a melting-pot and everything that came to the surface in the English soul between 1910 and 1940 can be found in Lawrence. We are interested now not in what he taught—if it *was* teaching—but in his disposition: and that is vivid the moment we pick up any of his writings. First of all, *the whole of England,* before and after the last war, acted upon Lawrence's imagination. His angry paganism of demigods released a repressed religious imagination in English literature. He reintroduced the direct apprehension of experience. He wrote from within—from inside the man, the woman, the tree, the fox, the mine. His people and his scene, whether it is a German road, a Nottingham kitchen or a Mexican village, are no longer fingered with one hand in the manner of naturalistic writers; they are grasped with both hands, with mind and senses. The impersonal novelist, the god with the fountain-pen, has gone; the people, the trees, the mines, the fields, the kitchens come physically upon the page. And although Lawrence is the most personal of novelists, quite as personal as Thackeray or Meredith were, yet he does not continually obtrude. At his best, he puts the reader instantly in the scene; instead of drawing it up neatly to be considered with all the feeling left out.

"He saw the whitish muddy tracks and deep scores in the road where part of the regiment had retired. Now all was still. Sounds that came, came from the outside. The place where he stood was still, silent, chill, serene; the white church among the trees beyond seemed like a thought only."

To you, who are not a writer, the white church *would* have been exactly that: a thought, a mark on the skin of your mind. Or:

"He, in his semi-conscious sleep was vaguely aware of the clatter of the iron on the iron stand, of the faint thud, thud on the ironing board. Once roused, he opened his eyes to see his mother standing on the hearth rug with the hot iron near her cheeks, listening, as it were, to the heat. Her still face with the mouth closed tight from suffering and disillusion and self-denial, and her nose the smallest bit on one side and her blue eyes so young, quick and warm, made his heart contract with love. When she was quiet so, she looked brave and rich with life, but as if she had been done out of her rights."

"Listening to the heat"; "Done out of her rights"—those are instantaneous, intimate, non-literary observations. They are natural, personal and not considered. Personal to Lawrence, they become personal to us. The greater part of our observation of the world has no conscious purpose; from the point of view of the good life, society, our work and so on, it is refractory. It feeds the unorganizable soul. And the soul cannot be ordered about and cannot compromise: see the miner in *Jimmy and the Desperate Woman*:

"I'm nothing but made use of," he said now talking hard and final to himself, and staring into space. "Down the pit I'm made use of, and they give me a wage, such as it is. At the house I'm made use of, and my wife sets the dinner on the table as if I was a customer in a shop."

"But what do you *expect*?" cried Jimmy, writhing in his chair.

"Me? What do I expect? I expect nothing. But I tell you what . . ." he turned and looked straight and hard into Jimmy's eyes.—"I'm not going to put up with anything either. . . . If I give in to the coalface and go down the mine every day to eight hours' slavery more or less, somebody's got to give in to me."

He is an impossibilist: one of the stock comic characters or simply the obstinate brute; but he is a piece of nature and it is useless to argue with him. Lawrence writes of that part of our nature with which it is useless to argue. He shows us things carelessly, as they cannot help being:

"A flat, shallow, utterly desolate valley, wide as a bowl under the sky, with rock-slopes and grey stone slides and precipices all around, and the zig-zag of snow-stripes and ice-roots descending, and thin rivers, streams and rivers rushing from many points downwards, down in waterfalls and cascades and threads, down into the wide, shallow bed of the valley, strewn with rocks and stones innumerable, and not a tree, not a visible bush."

It is interesting to contrast a very consciously made novel like Bennett's *Old Wives' Tale* with Lawrence's *Sons and Lovers*. Both novels cover a life-time of family life and truthfully recreate English sentiment. Bennett feels from the outside. He puts down what he has known. He sympathizes, pities and invents. And he condescends. In the mind's eye the characters of any novel can be measured for height, and Bennett's characters always seem to me small people, miniatures seen from a height as Bennett looks down upon them on the writing-table. The characters of *Sons and Lovers* are less complete in their detail, there is a blur in many of them so that we are not always sure of the focus; but they are life-size. They are as big as Lawrence is. He has got inside them until they have grown to normal size. We *follow* Constance in *The Old Wives' Tales*; we walk *with* Mrs. Morel in *Sons and Lovers*. We are as uncertain as she is, from day to day. The very muddle of the narrative in this book with its puzzling time sequences, its sudden jumps backward and forward, gives us a sensation that is familiar and real; the sensation that life sprawls, spreads sideways, is made up of re-minders and recapitulations, and sags loosely between one point of definition and the next. The Russian novelists had this inter-est in the loose texture of life whose crises begin so far away from their overt moment, and sometimes clean off the track of the expected drama. Not only that, they and Lawrence see that what we call a crisis in human relationships is a collection of crises, a rumbling and grumbling, a gabble and to-ing and fro-ing of human intercourse. Rarely does a crisis come to its final decisive outburst; nothing is final; we do not boil over, we leak away. Lawrence's sense of the life-size of people is his gift; it is also his weakness; but if we are to look for the virtues of a novelist we shall find them in those places where he is wrig-gling his way round his weaknesses. Lawrence is a muddling narrator, totally unskilled in construction; all right, he seems to say, let the living people drag on as best they can. They will move and compel because they live, because he will make us share their life in the collier's cottage, in the factory where Paul Morel works, on the farm where he spends his holidays. Instantaneously we shall breathe with them. And it is this power to make the reader's chest rise and fall, as it were, with the breathing of the characters in all the off moments, the lost hours, the indecipherable days of their life, that gives *Sons and Lovers* its overwhelming intimacy. There is no novel in English literature which comes so closely to the skin of life of working-class people, for it records their feelings in their own terms. The description of the older son's death, the many scenes describing the father's halting resentment or remorse, little moments of daily life when the children hang round the father's chair, are beautifully done. Common English life wears the habit of things gone wrong, of awkwardness and frustration, and Law-rence touches this quality with faithful hands. To the fidelity

and the submissive spirit of the early part of *Sons and Lovers,*
he returned in only a handful of short stories of which the
Odour of Chrysanthemums seems to me the most impressive.
He wrote unanswerably well—and this is true of so many English novelists—only of the environment of his childhood.

Sons and Lovers goes wrong when Lawrence begins telling
lies, that is to say when he starts arguing, as in the Miriam
episode which is often boring and obscure. English novelists
are afraid and ashamed of adolescence because, later in life, to
be serious about oneself is considered priggish and conceited.
The young prig is taken at his own valuation in French literature—see Stendhal and Flaubert's *Sentimental Education*—and
is generally admired because the French respect the gradual
formation of the mature nature. They are also interested in the
formation of artists. But Lawrence grew up in a community
and indeed in a country where the biography of an imagination
embarrasses and is despised. I have always liked the Clara
Dawes episode in *Sons and Lovers,* partly because it begins well,
and partly for the grotesque scene where Clara's mother sits up
belligerently determined to prevent the lovers from going to
bed together. There is a guilty hang-dog humor and great
truth of observation in this episode, although the character of
Clara Dawes is overglorified by her sexual attraction to the
author. Certainly *Sons and Lovers* is patchy—it was much re-
written—and English novelists who write autobiographical
novels seem to plunge in and have no idea where to bring
their life story to an end. Lawrence cheats about the story of
his adolescence; the spirit of rebellion brought with it a shame
not only of his shames but of his happiness. The suppressed
secret is that the pressure of Paul's environment made him a
snob. He half admits it, but only in discussion. It is never enacted. Imagine Stendhal, the supreme portrayer of very young
men in European literature, missing that.

To the English novel as a form Lawrence made one or two
important contributions. He brought in new subject matter. He

put the reader more or less in the position of writing the novel for himself, by giving him instantaneous observation and by slackening the strings that move the puppets. Like the Russians, he made the days of his characters' lives more important than the plot. From Meredith he developed the notion that people are not individual characters, but psychic types, flames lit by the imagination. They do not (after *Sons and Lovers*) develop, but leap higher and higher until they strike their certain fate. This conception of character was used in another sense by Marxist satirical writers who followed him. Lawrence gave novels a subject instead of a plot. Especially in his short stories, Lawrence used a summary, stand-still description of character, so that the whole story (see *The Prussian Officer*) is a series of dramatic assertions and reiterations about two men, culminating in the tragedy. This tense and even frenzied method was made tolerable by the colloquial sound of his own voice, i.e. the reader believes he is instantly saying it all himself. This manner arises because Lawrence is often clumsy and commonplace in straight narrative and because he is too egotistical and lacking in humility to know what people are really like; it accounts for much that is boring incantation. But to the short story, which can support the *tour de force,* these dramatic summaries are an excellent addition, though we must allow, as in Meredith, for a certain air of theater. Like Meredith (and Hall Caine) Lawrence writes at the top of his voice and is railing against his subject. Only his extraordinary sense of physical life and his lapses into accidental nature, save these rhetorical stories. In the end, the mining stories, things like *The Fox* and the rich irony of pieces like *The Rocking Horse Winner* survive whole. For the rest, we must dip for his descriptions. Once he was uprooted from the Midlands and his class, he ceased to be a novelist; he was a traveler, a remarkable letter writer, brilliant in discoveries which he buried under pulpit-loads of nonsense about people and a life he could not tolerate.

A POLE IN THE FAR EAST

A GOOD deal of our culture as well as our capital is locked up in the Far East. Looking at those investments again, one fingers the script with the last-minute love of a nervous shareholder. They have acquired an unreasonable personal value, even though the bottom may have fallen out of the market. Stevenson, Conrad, Maugham—we read them in the bleak perspective that opens in the dirty wake of the Pacific war. Literature has followed the flag. What sort of literature? The answer is—hopelessly romantic literature, that is to say romantic literature without hope, literature filled with guilt.

What about Conrad? I have been reading some of the Malayan novels again, after a lapse of twenty years—books like *Almayer's Folly, The Outcast of the Island, The Rescue, Lord Jim* and shorter pieces like *Youth, The Secret Sharer* and *Freya of the Seven Isles.* What struck me was how vague and even falsified these books were in my memory. The atmosphere one remembered, of course. But even stories like *Almayer's Folly* were muddled in my mind like the memory of a dream. They *are* dreams, these books. Their color, their unreal major characters, their insectile minor ones, their tortuous action, live in the compelled twilight of a hypnotic dream, a dream that slows down to the intense heat of nightmare. Here and there the temperature becomes colder and, as in the yacht episode of *The Rescue,* you touch that *Tatler*-like actuality of the Maugham subject; but it is only for a moment. The half-light comes down, the shadow and the sun-shot fog of Conrad's ruminations cloud the obvious issue, and the dream thickens in the head. After-

wards it will be difficult to say once more what *was* the issue
Conrad had in his tentative, evasive, suspicious and rather ex-
asperated imagination.

This is not true of Conrad's best work. *Youth,* for example,
is one of those stories where elaboration did not get to work.
It is a story of sunrise and not sunset in the East; and I think
all Conrad's best work is in what may be called his straightfor-
ward daytime manner. *Youth* has little of the famous Conrad
atmosphere and mystification. It is not written in sackcloth and
ashes. In *Youth* one is led only to the frontiers of that fog which
possesses so many of the writings whole. (I put *The Secret
Sharer, The Nigger of the Narcissus* and *Typhoon* in the *Youth*
class.) That *Youth* leads you to the edge and does not engulf
you is, of course, Conrad's intention. It is a story of travel, not
of arrival. The capture of a first marveling glance of the longed-
for East, the song of an immaculate delusion is all its object.
The wrecked sailors have arrived exhausted at Bangkok:

> Further out old Mahon's face was upturned to the sky,
> with the long white beard spread out on his breast, as though
> he had been shot where he sat at the tiller; and a man, all
> in a heap in the bows of the boat, slept with both arms em-
> bracing the stem-head and with his cheek laid on the gun-
> wale. The East looked at them without a sound.
> I have known its fascination since [Conrad never knew
> when to stop, but as the next passage foreshadows the rest
> of his Malayan work, it needs to be quoted]. I have seen the
> mysterious shores, the still water, the lands of brown nations,
> where a stealthy Nemesis lies in wait, pursues, overtakes, so
> many of the conquering race, who are proud of their wisdom,
> of their knowledge, of their strength. But for me all the
> East is contained in that vision of my youth. It is all in that
> moment when I opened my young eyes on it.

Destiny, Nemesis, those dirty inquisitorial familiars who turn
up on the deck lifting their hierophantic palms behind the
backs of Conrad's simple Devonshire sailors or half-cracked

traders in the jungle of the archipelago, do not appear until the last page of *Youth*. I often wish it could have been the same in books like *The Outcast* or *The Rescue*. For though Destiny is a laconic conception, it is one which encourages wordiness in novelists; and the reader of Conrad feels a baffled irritation, as if he were a commercial traveler getting heavy admonitions every day from an importunate head office. One ought not to feel like this, and I am convinced that one would not do so in Conrad if one felt that Conrad's Destiny was endowed with the sublime and indispensable gift of inevitability. Conrad's Destiny seems to be an idea poisoned by exile, dwarfed by a bad temper and embittered by a failure to meet great men worth destroying. To characters like Willems, in *The Outcast*, or Almayer, Destiny can only be nasty, as the police are nasty to tramps.

The valuable side of Conrad's conception of Destiny is that it is a sense of history—a sense of history which the Slavonic imagination has made theatrical. Conrad seems to have turned the Polish exile's natural preoccupation with nationality, history, defeat and unavailing struggle, from his own country to these Eastern islands. The natives are a defeated people. They remember massacre. They live under the Dutch and English overlords, swindled by the Arab traders, with eyes and hearts in the past. They turn, as the conquered must, to intrigue, which is relieved on rare occasions by sudden ecstatic, despairing loyalties. They turn from corruption to nostalgia for the sublime virtues. Babalatchi, the one-eyed scoundrel, diplomat and philosopher who wrecks the outcast, and shakes but does not break the fortunes of Lingard, is one aspect of the temperament of the defeated; Hasim, its aspect of fierce hope, poetic loyalty and timeless experience of evil. It has been said that Conrad does not draw the Malay as he really is, and that his Malays are idealizations. They are really transplantations from Polish history. They are an exile's interpretation of the bloody history of the islands, and of the historical situation at the time he was writing. And knowing the situation, he knows the intrigue—how it is something which goes far deeper than human idiosyncrasy and private jealousy or ambition, but is the ferment of a defeated society itself. Conrad's gift for handling intrigue in his novels is at its best when it has real intrigue to work on—such as can be seen in *Almayer, The Outcast* or even in the stodgier *Rescue;* when this gift of his is turned from society to psychology, that is to say, to a man's intrigue with himself, as in *Lord Jim,* then Conrad is less successful. The sense of intrigue grinds down human motive too fine.

I say "less" and then hesitate. As Conrad exhausted his early material, his imagination naturally turned to improvization. He who had been, in the sense of my earlier use of the word, an historical novelist, now became a prophetic one. What is a prophetic novelist? He is hard to define, but I should say he is one to whom human beings are timeless; they are souls and not persons, and good and evil and fate fight for the possession of their future. This element had always been in Conrad's work and gave his realism the distorting stamp of a spiritual vision. But, on the whole, in England we reject the prophets; it is so obvious that they are disappointed men. We find this in D. H. Lawrence, whose affinity with Conrad is very close. Lawrence is angry about sex; Conrad is angry about honor. They are both inordinately conscious of failure, the one of the failures of sex, the other of the failures of loyalty. An undertone of guilt runs through their writing. When we consider Lawrence's diatribes about sexual failure we answer that there are a lot of other things to do besides going to bed; and when we consider Lord Jim, running away from job after job, on the waterfront, because of his treachery to himself, or Tom Lingard confused by the crassness of human nature, we feel that human nature has quite enough on its hands without crying because it isn't perfect. The soul may be marred by the evils its commits, but is far more commonly marred by the failure *to admit* that it has committed evil, or by the mania of admitting too much. Conrad's problems are esoteric. Lord Jim was not a good man gone wrong, but, like the outcast, a compulsive neurotic. The charge of morbidity originally brought against Conrad must be sustained; his morbidity was in fact the irritant which created the Conrad fog.

The excellencies of Conrad do not lie, in my opinion, in that dubious Romantic over-world, but in his real observation, in his feeling for real life. In the big elaborated books he is always avoiding his climaxes, and on principle—when he doesn't, you get the impossible dialogue between Lingard and Aissa at the crisis of *The Outcast*—in the daylit stuff he is never worried by these false climaxes. They are mixed in with the stream of life: the captain going into his bathroom in *The Secret Sharer;* the "old man" admitting the existence of the fire in *Youth*. The normal portraiture is astonishing. Conrad's eye for the soul, before the soul ran away with him, is tremendous. Here is the first glance at a City man; not Conrad's best at all, but how percipient he is:

> His clear pale face had under its commonplace refinement that slight tinge of overbearing brutality which is given by the possession of only partly difficult accomplishments; by excelling in a game, or in the art of making money; by the easy mastery over animals and over needy men.

Or the portrait of the "old man" in *Youth*:

> He was 60 if a day; a little man, with a broad, not very straight back, with bowed shoulders and one leg more bandy than the other, he had that queer twisted-about appearance you see so often in men who work in the fields. He had a nutcracker face—chin and nose trying to come together over a sunken mouth—and it was framed in iron-grey fluffy hair, that looked like a chin-strap of cotton wool sprinkled with coal dust. And he had blue eyes in that old face of his, which were amazingly like a boy's, with that candid expression some quite common men preserve to the end of their days by a rare internal gift of simplicity of heart and rectitude of soul.

The genius of Conrad was directed to intensifying the life of a man or a woman and to contrasting that intensity with the slacker, ragged commentary of their real circumstances. His characters live on the edge of a great anxiety, an unbearable exasperation, a threatened loss. They are faced by the sardonic refusal of life to play up. He got this last effect even in his picture of native life. Take this scene from *The Outcast,* in the native compound where Babalatchi has been talking about the tragedy of his race. He is sitting among the domestic noises:

> From under the house the thumping of wooden pestles husking the rice started with unexpected abruptness. The weak but clear voice in the yard again urged, "Blow up the embers, O brother!" Another voice answered, drawling in modulated, thin sing-song, "Do it yourself, O shivering pig!" and the drawl of the last words stopped short as if the man had fallen into a deep hole.

That slackening of the tension, that anti-climax is typical Conrad. It is the grimace of the bear with the sore head; but, when it is done in terms of real life, it is dramatically perfect.

THE IRISH R.M.

*"Did you ever eat my grandmother's curry?" said Flurry,
to me, later, as we watched Bernard Shute trying to back
his motor into the coach house.*

I said I had not.

*"Well, you'd take a splint off a horse with it," said Mrs.
Knox's grandson.*

*The Aussolas woods were full of birds that day. Birds
bursting out of holly bushes like corks out of soda-water
bottles. . . .*

YES, there is no doubt about it: the *Experiences of an
Irish R. M.* are your grandmother's curry. They are a
light literature which takes the skin off your tongue, the breath
out of your lungs and—to quote a favorite phrase of the authors
—"puts your eyes on sticks." And then, even those sentences I
have quoted have a horse in them. There are horses on nearly
every page of this book, malicious and heroic creatures of deep
character which seem to be out on a perpetual hunt. It is indeed hard to know which are the people and which are the
horses. Perhaps they are all horses. Flurry Knox would willingly
have become one. So would his grandmother. Most of the
Somerville and Ross women, with their rain-fiercened complex-
ions, their long heads and box-like bodies, their sprained ankles
and strained shoulders and their frightful high spirits, are un-
imaginable without their whites and their bays. Their pace is
spanking, their talk flies out like froth. It was not a freak of
satire that in the beginning of Anglo-Irish literature, Swift

149

drew the Houyhnhnms as the master race; he was simply recording the national religion.

With a malice and madness that match the Somerville and
Ross characters, the Irish climate acts as a mirror to their antics.
The frost is crisp on the fallen leaves in the bare woods, the
woodcock rise out of the trees or the snipe zip away over the
frozen bogs into a sky of Neapolitan enamel; but within an
hour rain is spouting off the hat brims of the sportsmen, and
days of mugginess or downpour jail the mind and drive it to
thoughts of the whisky bottle, the long meditated intrigues of
tribal life, the treacheries and despondencies of the lonely colonial wits. A world that was on the verge of becoming Turgenev's turns into a jumble of Surtees, Tom Moore and *The
Fall of the House of Usher;* and half the farce lies not in the
horseplay, but in the ingredients themselves. We begin to
laugh before we start reading and that is apt to mean that we
stop laughing before the end, and wonder why the authors
dare not be quiet for a moment. What would happen if they
were quiet? What did the Major do when he was not trying to
keep pace with Flurry Knox's mare or (far more complex) follow Flurry's mind? There were mornings, we are told, when he
spent the time in the gentlemanly task of writing letters. What
was he writing? Or what was old Mrs. Knox thinking as she sat
with her stockinged feet in the fireplace, oblivious of the good
feed for poultry which always lay under the Louis Quinze
chairs on her drawing-room floor at Aussolas, and lulled by the
pompous cooing of the doves which flew into the room and
perched on the picture frames of the smoke-kippered portraits
of her ancestors? Unless there is an answer to these questions
there is force in the criticism of Somerville and Ross that used
to be made in the sour, wan yellow dawn of the Irish revival,
when it was a crime for anyone to laugh in Ireland, unless
they laughed for the right party: the criticism that these ladies
were simply purveying the stage Irishman to English maga-
zines and winding up the old parish hurdy-gurdy of Irish farce.

And, of course, they were. The tradition of Irish farce is permanent. The stage Irishman is permanent. He is as permanent as the Irish narrative gift and the use of words as an intoxicant. The puritanism of Maynooth and Merrion Square cannot put its gooseflesh on the warm native fancy. But there is more than one Somerville and Ross. An early novel, written before the *R.M.* made them popular, does attempt to say what the Anglo-Irish were like between one View Hallo or one petty sessions and the next. That book is *The Real Charlotte*. I don't want to be a spoil-sport, especially now the *R.M.* has been canonized by *Everyman*, and I write as a foreigner, but *The Real Charlotte* did something which had not, up to the 'nineties, been done in Irish literature. It portrayed the Anglo-Irish with the awful, protracted mercy of the artist. It "placed" them as no novelist had thought of "placing" them before; as surely, for example, as Mrs. Gaskell knew how to place her world in *Wives and Daughters*. I do not mean that *The Real Charlotte* is as sound or as accomplished a novel as Mrs. Gaskell's. It was a first novel, awkwardly built, and, like so many Anglo-Irish writers, the authors never got rid of an amateur, almost a juvenile streak; but *The Real Charlotte* was a beginning of great promise. One went to Ireland looking for the characters of the Irish R.M.; one found oneself, thirty years after it was written, surrounded by the disquieting people of this one serious novel.

The scene is Galway and the long loch beyond it. There is the big estate on the lake. There is the agent's modest place nearby. There are one or two absurd houses. And then, back in Dublin or the worst end of Bray, there is the genteel squalor of Francie Fitzpatrick's life. In England Francie would be a lower middle-class beauty on the make; in the Ireland of the 'nineties she is a beautiful hoyden, a tomboy and a flirt, coarse-grained yet childishly unaffected. If she ceases to be prim she will be a mess, a noise without innocence. She goes to Galway to hook a husband, preferably a mindless young officer who will mend her family fortunes. Too ingenuous to be called an adventuress, too beguiling to be thought entirely vulgar in her man-hunt or her manners, Francie will never find her place.

In England, the class system would provide repose for Francie's soul; in Ireland the tribe system, with its withering snobberies, punishes her at every point of her social climb. She is doomed to be second-rate, to attract second-rate behavior. And though *The Real Charlotte* is a novel about jealousy and the never-ceasing intrigue and treachery of Irish life, its main stuff is this snobbery. Not a plain, excluding snobbery that tells us where we may go and where we may not, but a snobbery that is in the blood. Not a snobbery versed in distinguished ancestors only, but a snobbery bedeviling the character with the pretensions of second cousins and the mildewed memories of better times. It is a snobbery that has become the meaning of life. It permeates everything: good sense, idealism, hatred, tenderness, religion—even pity. We must allow something for the fact that this book is written in the 'nineties; and when the Dysarts wince because Francie keeps her gloves on at tea, we are charmed by the comedy of the manners of a period. Anglo-Irish snobbery was pretty genial about such quaintness. But underneath this are the inturned passions of a small, defensive and decaying colonial society: Francie is a social casualty in the everlasting skirmish with the other Ireland. Only by exaggerating their exclusiveness and creating low comedy around them can the Ascendants keep their ascendancy.

Of course, we may read in the Dysarts a devotion to manners, sensibility and excellence; but the devotion is so defensive that it becomes negative. It has become a mania like Lady Dysart's acrostics. And the mania spreads downwards. So Lambert, the land agent, wishes to impress as much as the Dysarts do, and his desire turns to self-destructive hatred of them. He ends by trying to cheat them. Francie's cousin Charlotte, who is half peasant and whose clumsy mind can yet devise labyrinthine schemes, bids too high on Francie's behalf, hopes to capture a Dysart for her, and is betrayed by the girl. In a curious pas-

sage, the young Christopher Dysart feels a mingled envy and
pity for Francie's vital but ill-judged insouciance; and Francie
to whom he is incomprehensible because he is too far above
her, rubs her low breeding into him in order to cause him pain
and, by causing pain, to bring him nearer to her understanding. Again, Lambert enjoys making a fool of Charlotte by
arousing her feelings in order to exploit her purse and cut a
figure. Snobbery creates victims to pity, and all these characters
discover the strange pleasure of forgiving the people they have
injured. If they all only knew it, the logical end of their mania
was the sensitive, tedious ineffectuality of Christopher Dysart.
In him there is a masterly portrait of the lifeless, hopelessly
neutral, decent young aristocrat of the period.

Cousin Charlotte has been compared to Cousine Bette and,
allowing for the change to the raw Irish scene, there is something in the comparison. The money motives, the class structure, are there. To these elements one must add a peculiar
psychological quickness to catch the perversity of human feeling and the cross-ruffing of Fate: for example, in her jealous
plottings Charlotte cannot bear not to give herself away. Feeling presents itself as intrigue. Francie is not the only flirt; they
are all flirting with every dream and issue. They cross one
another and double-cross themselves. Pity becomes hatred,
hatred turns into tenderness, tenderness into cruelty. We watch
with fascination while the dull, irritable land agent with his
debts, his horses and his ailing wife, ingeniously plots his own
downfall.

All this must be visualized against an animated scene which
is broken by some of the *R.M.* comedy that was to come. The
absurd pleasure launch on the lake, tooting away at the least
convenient moment, and its inane comment on the people is a
delightful invention. The awful English officer and Don Juan
is an excellent cad. The middle-class carpet dance is a fearful
romp. A hundred small touches keep this small world in a continual ripple and change of color. On the other hand, the

chorus from peasant life is boring. Fifty years of politics lie between us and these skirling *commères,* with their high-pitched
domestic life and the loquacity of distressed Elizabethans. But
the narrative writing has the Irish visual gift, so bold in its
metaphors, so athletic in its speed, as if tongue and eye were
racing against each other. There is the native animism:

> Tall brick houses, browbeating each other in gloomy re-
> spectability across the street.

The shrewd is punched home by the baroque:

> She was losing hold of herself; her gestures were of the
> sort that she usually reserved for her inferiors, and the cor-
> ners of her mouth bubbled like a snail.

And then, though there is hardly a breath of Irish politics in
the story, they are there by implication. For the characters are
exclusively the Irish Protestants and their isolation gives a
strength to the strokes in which they are drawn.

The faults of *The Real Charlotte* are obvious. The national
malady of not "letting on" what you are up to enables the novelist to catch the changeableness of human character; but
toward the end the elusive becomes the frantic. It is unforgiv-
able that Francie is killed out riding; especially as her death,
one is pretty sure, is due to the profound snobbery of the
authors. There is no way of making a lady of her, so she had to
be killed. But after one has removed the old-fashioned trap-
pings, the irony, the insight and portraiture of this novel, show
that Anglo-Irish society might have got its Mrs. Gaskell, if the
amateur tastes of the discursive colonial had not breezily rid-
den the chance off the page.

AN EAST END NOVELIST

" AND the effect is as of stables." My eye has been often
baffled by lack of the word which would define the poor
streets of the East End, as they used to be before the war; and
here in Arthur Morrison's *Tales of Mean Streets* which were
written in 1894, I find it. Those acres of two-story houses which
lie below the level of the railway arches of Bethnal Green and
which stand like an alien stretch of unfeatured plowing beyond
the Commercial Road, are particularized at last. The mind has
won a foothold in a foreign city.

For, east of Aldgate, another city begins. London flattens and
sinks into its clay. Over those lower dwellings the London sky,
always like a dirty window, is larger; the eyes and hands of
people are quicker, the skins yellower, the voices are as sharp as
scissors. Every part of London has its smell, and this region
smells of rabid little shops, bloated factories, sub-let workrooms
and warehouse floors; there is also the smell of slums, a smell of
poverty, racy but oftener sour; and mingling with these working odors, there arises an exhalation of the dirty river which,
somewhere behind these streets and warehouses and dock walls,
is oozing toward the flats of the Thames estuary like a worm.
The senses and the imagination of the stranger are so pricked
by this neighborhood that he quickly gets a fevered impression
of it; it will seem dingier or more exotic than it really is. And
when we turn to literature for guidance, we are even less sure
of what we see. For the literature of the East End is very largely
a stranger's literature. It lies under the melodramatic murk
and the smear of sentimental pathos, which, in the nineteenth

century, were generated by the guilty conscience of the middle classes. They were terrified of the poor who seethed in an abyss just beyond their back door. The awful Gothic spectacle of hunger, squalor and crime was tolerable only as nightmare and fantasy—such as Dickens provided—and the visiting foreigner alone could observe the English slums with the curiosity of the traveler or the countenance of the anthropologist. And there was another difficulty. Philanthropy, for all its humbug, did slowly have its effect on the public conscience in every generation, so that it was genuinely possible to say "things have changed." The Ratcliffe Highway went. Limehouse had been purged, and there arose a romantic literature of the East End, based on a riotous evocation of the bad old times. The stranger's literature was the literature of a time which first strengthened morale by giving the reader a fright, and then went on to make the fright pious, sentimental and picturesque.

But what of the literature written from within the East End, the really saturated literature which has been lived before it has been written? For many years now, in accounts of the realism which came into fashion at the time of Gissing, I had noticed a recurring title: *Tales of Mean Streets,* by Arthur Morrison, and lately I have been put on to *The Hole in the Wall* and *Child of the Jago* by the same author. They are written from the inside and they have extraordinary merit; *The Hole in the Wall* strikes me as being one of the minor masterpieces of the last forty years. It has the kind of fidelity to scene that the modern documentary writers have sought, yet is never flattened, as their work is, by concern for conditions; let us not allow "conditions" to deflate the imagination or argue away the novelist's chief delight and greatest difficulty: the art of constructing and telling a story complete in itself. For unless he learns this art, a novelist neutralizes his power of observation, his power to observe more than one thing at a time, his power of writing on different planes and varying perspectives, and discriminating among the accumulated incrustations of fact that clog an impressionable mind. Arthur Morrison had this power. "Conditions" were in his bones; his books stand apart from the worthy and static pathos of Gissing, from the character albums of the writers of low comedy, from the picturesque and the nightmare schools. Mr. Morrison's early novels and sketches are often modest in their art, like the work of someone learning to write, but they have an anthropological drama of their own, and, at any rate, are not more awkward than Bennett's *Tales of the Five Towns*. What is missing from these novels is the modern novelist's sardonic exposure of the economic rackets which make the poor man poor; the brutality of poverty is subject enough for Mr. Morrison. A book like *Child of the Jago,* the story of a young thief in Bethnal Green, shows a sharp-eyed and intimate knowledge of how East End society used to behave as a society, of how it used to deploy its cunning and uphold its customs. Injustice is done and the President of the Immortals has already abandoned the hopeless scene to the human instinct of self-preservation when Mr. Morrison comes in to record it. Out comes the cosh, the street wars begin, the half-naked harpies run at each other with broken bottles, the pimps and fences step over the bodies of the drunks who lie, pockets turned inside out, in the gutters. It's a world of sullen days in backrooms with the baby lying half dead on the bed and the hungry women gaping listlessly at the empty cupboards, while the men go out in search of loot and drink and come back with their eyes blackened and their belts ready to flay the undeserving family. I have picked out the seamier side of *Child of the Jago* not to gloat over the horrors but to indicate the material. Such incidents are not raked into the book without discrimination; these novels are not pools of self-pity in the Gissing manner; nor are they worked up with that sadistic touch of angry ecstasy which Dickens brought to his pictures of poverty. In Mr. Morrison's book slum life is the accepted life, a dirty but not a turgid stream. In their position, you say—as one ought to say of all human beings—

THE LIVING NOVEL

these people have lived, they've kept their heads above water for a spell. Man is the animal who adapts himself.

Child of the Jago describes the brutal, drunken, murderous London of the late nineteenth century which used to shatter the visiting foreigner and send him home marveling at English violence and English hypocrisy. Its picture of the street wars is unique. *The Hole in the Wall* raises this material to a far higher plane of narrative. Here is a thriller set in Dockland, where the filthy river, its fogs and its crimes, stain the mind as they did in *Our Mutual Friend*. Every gas-lit alley leads abruptly to some dubious business. The average thriller takes us step by step away from probability. It strains away from likelihood. *The Hole in the Wall* belongs to the higher and more satisfying kind, which conducts us from one unsuspected probability to the next. Mr. Morrison has employed what is, I suppose, the classical method of writing this kind of book; he shows us the story mainly through the eye of a young boy. The child goes to live with his grandfather who keeps a pub at Wapping and there he gradually discovers that his heroic grandfather is really a receiver of stolen goods. The old man comes by a wallet containing £800 which has been robbed from a defaulting shipowner—who has been murdered—and the plot is made out of the attempts of various criminal characters to get this money back. The merit of the book lies in its simple but careful reconstruction of the scene—the pubs and gin-shops of the Old Ratcliffe Highway, the locks and swing bridges, the alleys and gateways of Dockland with their police notices, the riverside jetties and their lighters, the way over the marshes to the lime kilns. I take it to be a mark of the highest skill in this kind of novel that nothing is mentioned which will not have, eventually, an importance to the tale; and that the motives for action arise in the characters and are not imposed on them by the need of working up a mystery and creating suspense. We do not know what their next step will be, because these people are still ruminating upon it themselves. Marr, the absconding

shipowner, disguises himself as a sailor, but forgets that he
will blab if he gets drunk; Dan Ogle who merely intends to
take his watch, gradually sees that murder will be necessary if
the £800 is to be taken; the blind fiddler who does not mind
very much being double-crossed, thinks otherwise when he is
assaulted and ridiculed as well as cheated. And Mr. Morrison
succeeds with them because he shows them to us, first of all as
ordinary shady characters muddling along the path of shifty
illegality, and then suddenly faced by a new, a more terrible
temptation and jumping at it.

The Hole in the Wall moves calmly from one major scene
to the next; there is no sagging of the narrative. We see Marr,
stunned and tottering, led like a broken marionette between
his murderers. They are bawling at the tops of their voices so
that, in the night, passers-by will think they are drunken sailors
helping a pal, instead of murderers, dragging an almost lifeless
body to the river. We see the body fished out—and what a remarkable piece of description that is. It "tells"—as Henry James
used to say—because of the very homeliness of the boy's narrative. (There is a lesson to the modern tough writers here. They
lose their effect because they are tough all the time. They do
not allow us to have the homely, frightened, law-abiding emotions. They do not allow us the manly fear, and they lose the
interest of moral conflict.) And then there is the tremendous
scene where the blind fiddler takes his revenge on Ogle, the
murderer. He is hiding in a lime-quarry. At night the fiddler
gropes across the marshes to the shed where Ogle is sleeping:

> He had been gone no more than a few seconds, when the
> snore stopped. It stopped with a thump and a gasp, and a
> sudden buffeting of legs and arms; and in the midst arose a
> cry; a cry of so hideous an agony that Grimes the wharf-
> keeper, snug in his first sleep fifty yards away, sprang erect
> and staring in bed, and so sat motionless for half a minute
> ere he remembered his legs and thrust them out to carry
> him to the window. And the dog on the wharf leaped the

length of its chain, answering the cry with a torrent of wild barks.

Floundering and tumbling against the frail boards of the shed the two men came out at the door in a struggling knot; Ogle wrestling and striking at random, while the other, cunning with a life's blindness, kept his own head safe and hung as a dog hangs to a bull. His hands gripped his victim by ear and hair, while the thumbs drove at the eyes the mess of smoking lime that clung and dripped about Ogle's head. It trickled burning through his hair and it blistered lips and tongue, as he yelled and yelled again in the extremity of his anguish.

The blind man had blinded his persecutor.

One puts the book down looking back on the ground it has covered, seeing how economically it implanted that sinister Dockland of the 'eighties on the mind, with a simple warmth and precision; how it mocked the little criminals, and then, suddenly, struck out into the squalor behind the drink in the snug bar and the bawling songs in the upper room; and how finally it pierced one with human fear and horror, without once cutting adrift from probability and an identifiable daily life. It is a masterly course, sustained, calm and never exaggerated. The style is a little old-fashioned, but it never scuttles away for safety into period dress. There was a London like this —we are convinced—mean, clumsy and hungry, murderous and sentimental. Those shrieks were heard. There were those even more disturbing silences in the night. Dockland, where the police used to go in threes, has its commemoration.

AN AMATEUR

THE businessman who is a novelist in his spare time, an occasional and amateur novelist, is a character who must always be envied by professionals. For here is a man who has avoided the treadmill of talent and the catastrophes which lie in the path of genius. The businessman who is a novelist is able to drop in on literature and feel no suicidal loss of esteem if the lady is not at home, and he can spend his life preparing without fuss for the awful interview. There need be no last-minute slapdash à la Dostoevski; no years of painful groping among the hallucinations of the intellect, such as Flaubert suffered; no spiritual crises which will split a masterpiece in two; no flagging hackwork to patch the interval between one work and another. The amateur can afford to be thorough, and he usually is thorough precisely in those places where the professional slurs, skimps, and hopes for the best. But there is yet another advantage to be envied. I am not thinking of the solid income of the businessman whose leisure really *is* leisure and not a haunted escape from contracts and creditors; I am thinking of the businessman's solid character. To have that and yet also to have the gift, to know that the gift can never play the devil with his life—those seem to be outrageous advantages.

The novels of J. Meade Falkner, an almost forgotten writer of the late 'nineties, brings such reflections to the mind. Falkner was not a businessman novelist of the Italo Svevo size; but he has his small place. *The Nebuly Coat* and *The Lost Stradivarius* are mystery stories tinctured by scholarship and are now, I think, too slow and unmysterious for our taste—the last war hurried the pace of these things—but in *Moonfleet* he wrote a story of adventure that will have a permanent place among the minor *genre* pieces of our literature. A word about Falkner, first of all. He was a most remarkable man. By taste and education a scholar whose researches in archeology, folklore, paleography, architecture, church music and medieval history earned him a papal medal and many honors at the Universities, Falkner spent all his life in Armstrong Whitworth's, whose chairman he was during and after the last war. He was a brilliant diplomatist and negotiator with foreign Governments. He traveled all over the world for his firm. He said that he owed his versatility to his medieval mind, and in her preface to the abridged Penguin edition of *The Nebuly Coat,* Lady Longford says that he applied the same minute care to his reports for Armstrong Whitworth and his researches in the Vatican library. In the Civil Service the various mind has been common; in the bustle of industry it is rare. And during his packed career, Falkner wrote works of learning and these three novels.

The Nebuly Coat and *The Lost Stradivarius* recall the books of Sheridan Le Fanu, but they are not on the level of the Irish master. Falkner lacked Le Fanu's psychological curiosity and the uneasiness of his imagination. Where Le Fanu was skilled in disturbing the mind, Falkner, with the habits of research, spoiled things by setting our minds at rest. It is true that the character of Westray, the young architect in *The Nebuly Coat,* is peculiar, and that he is distressed about the morality of shielding an impostor who is possibly a murderer; but the episode is so obscure that I cannot help suspecting Westray's real motive was snobbery. He thought it blasphemy to expose a lord or to throw doubt upon the records of Somerset House and the College of Heralds. Again, In *The Lost Stradivarius,* there is a suggestion of wicked practices in the occult. Le Fanu would never have descended to anything so gentlemanly and so scholarly as the suggestion that the habits of Medmenham Abbey had had a secret revival. When Le Fanu's characters are haunted by guilt, the guilt is guilt, not a connoisseur's lucky historical find. If either of these two novels of Falkner's are attractive light reading, it is because of their antiquarianism and because of the precision of their setting. We are at the beginning of that passion for antiques which started in the nineteen-hundreds, I suppose, and which so oddly foreshadowed the genteel auctioning off of heirlooms which swept Britain and Europe after the last war. *The Nebuly Coat* is an antique in itself. With wonderful verisimilitude, Falkner invented a cathedral town and worked out a carefully documented and imaginary catalogue of its family stains and historical dilapidations, and he hinged his plot on no less a matter than the technical delicacies of architectural restoration. There is also some heraldry in this book and, in *The Lost Stradivarius,* a good deal of musical scholarship. This material and his use of it to create an atmosphere, interest us a little now, for he wrote with clarity; but Falkner showed up to this point small sense of character or narrative. This is a mark, so often observed, of the diligent amateur. No professional would document his work so well; but no professional would throw it all away on uninteresting people.

Moonfleet is another matter altogether. Here is a novel which has the sustained excitement, if not the richness of character, of the best work of Stevenson. It is a brilliant *pastiche* of eighteenth-century adventure, limpid, tender and running over the complicated score of its great detail without ever striking a wrong note or a superfluous one. How true the note always is. Pedantry has vanished. Now when Falkner is describing the history of the wicked Mohunes and the legends of their wickedness and burial in the church beside the sea; when he describes how the tides flood the crypt and the evils that come from it; and later on, when he troubles us with an account of the disused marble quarries of Dorset and the habits of the quarrymen, he pours these things into a story which flows more swiftly on, because of them, to fresh eddies of excitement. The elements of detection and mystery are multiplied. We want to know about those quarries as badly as we want to know about the escaping smugglers who have gone to earth in them. A whole coast with its cliffs, its marshes and its shingle roaring in the storms, has become urgent to us, such is the life which Falkner can impart to topography. These descriptions cannot be skipped, for Falkner achieved here, with an apparent ease, the art of gradual revelation. It was the eighteenth century's great lesson to narrators who had not yet been disorganized by the cult of nature, and who therefore did not throw in a ton of scenery for emotion's sake. Nature was used and useful, and the gradual disclosure of its usefulness was an invaluable accompaniment to the voice of narrative. This is apparent in writers as widely different as the circumstantial Defoe and the melodious Abbé Prévost. There is something of the latter's tone in Falkner's writing, a modest candor, which sets the young hero a little apart from the too stalwart ranks of boy heroes, and gives a tenderness to the circumspect descriptions. Here is Falkner's picture of the country into which the boy and the smuggler escaped after their climb up the cliff face. They are on the edge of the abandoned quarries:

> We had left the stony tillage fields, and the face of the country was covered once more with the closest sward, which was just putting on the brighter green of the spring. This turf was not smooth, but hummocky, for under it lay heaps of worthless stone and marble drawn out of the quarries ages ago, which the green vestment had covered for the most part, though it left sometimes a little patch of broken rubble peering out at the top of a mound. There were many tumble-down walls and low gables left of the cottages of the old quarrymen; grass-covered ridges worked out of the little garden-folds, and here and there still stood a forlorn gooseberry bush or a stunted plum or apple tree with its branches all swept eastward by the up-channel gales. As for the quarry shafts themselves, they too were covered round the tips with the green turf, and down them led a narrow flight of steep-cut steps, with a slide of soapstone at the side, on which the

marble blocks were once hauled up by wooden winches. Down these steps no feet ever walked now, for not only were suffocating gases said to beset the bottom of the shaft, but men would have it that in the narrow passages below lurked evil spirits and demons. . . . We waited a few minutes and then he took me in his arms and began to descend the steps, back first, as one goes down a hatchway.

That is a fairly static description, a breathing space in the action of the story. Yet how it moves, how it flows and coils like the water receding along the snaky course of one of those southern estuaries that Falkner liked to write about. And the same, simple, inevitable movement is in the passages of action. This is the scene at the end where Elzevir loses his life in trying to rescue the boy on the terrible Chesil Beach.

I saw the string of men lashed together and, reaching down as far as man might, to save any that came through the surf, and heard them shout to cheer us, and marked a coil of rope flung out. Elzevir was by my side and saw it too, and we both kept our feet and plunged forward through the quivering slack water; but then there came an awful thunder behind, the crash of the sea over the wreck, and we knew that another mountain wave was on our heels. It came in with a swishing roar, a rush and rise of furious water that swept us like corks up the beach, till we were within touch of the rope's end, and the men shouted again to hearten us as they flung it out. Elzevir seized it with his left hand and reached out his right to me. Our fingers touched, and in that very moment the wave fell instantly, with an awful suck, and I was swept down the beach again. Yet the undertow took me not back to sea, for amid the floating wreckage floated the shattered maintop and in the track of that great spar I caught, and so was left with it upon the beach thirty paces from the men and Elzevir. Then he left his own assured salvation, namely the rope, and strode down again into the very jaws of death to catch me by the hand and set me on my feet.

But the secret of the success of *Moonfleet* does not lie first of all in its ingenious and masterly unveiling of an adventure; nor even in the naturalness of it all. The secret, I think, is that

Falkner makes us feel for the church and village of Moonfleet something of that touching emotion which we have had for a place we have lived in and unaccountably loved in its smallest particular. He has hit upon our love for place and on the feeling that, in such a place, great happenings may start as innocently, but as irreparably, as spring water bubbles up from the earth to start a river. And once he had struck this note he sustained it. Not once does it falter. It grows clearer and stronger like a rising wind, like the high note of *Treasure Island*, which never loses its eagerness, or the grave and ominous accent of *The Fall of the House of Usher*.

I do not rank *Moonfleet* with these tales, for it has not their scope. Falkner was no great maker of characters. The boy-narrator and Elzevir the smuggler, who slowly adopts him in place of his dead son, are simple beings; not wooden, not lay figures indeed, but simple. They grow a little, experience makes them, and the dumb growth of their affection into an austere and self-sacrificing love is a moving undertone to the story. Theirs is not the conventional relationship of partners in adventure. One sees the passage of time reversing, or at least modifying, their attitude to each other. But outside of these two there is nobody. In this book, Falkner does not attempt what he could not do excellently; and like one of those small academic paintings in which we detect the flash of a minor master, *Moonfleet* arrests the mind because it has satisfied the eye. We have seen something that is small, perhaps, but exquisitely, affectingly well done.

TWO WRITERS AND
MODERN WAR

"And so good-bye to the war. I know not how it may have been or may be to others—to me the main interest I found (and still in recollection find) in the rank and file of the armies, both sides, and in those specimens amid the hospitals and even the dead on the field."

THIS passage comes from *Specimen Days*, from those pages where Whitman described his work in the hospitals during the American Civil War. The interest of Whitman's pages about this war lies in the fact that he is the first to reveal the modern attitude. He stands at the breaking point with the past.

The American Civil War was the first modern war. It is true that the Crimean War, some eight years earlier, has resemblances with the American conflict. There is the awakening of public concern for the care of casualties, a concern which had grown with medical knowledge. But the Crimean War was fought in a small area. It was fought by professional soldiers—the British commander-in-chief directed operations from his private yacht to which he returned to dine and sleep every night —and the casualties, though heavy, were less than half of those suffered in America, where a million men died in the field, the hospitals and the prison camps. The Civil War involved everyone, the armies became conscript armies almost at once. The professional soldiers were put to the task of training the man in the street. Similar conditions, it will be said, existed in the

Napoleonic wars—for Napoleon was the first to use conscription on a great scale. But the Napoleonic army was the Grande Armée. The conscript was transformed by the professional and national notions of Glory and the impulse of the Revolution. He was, in a sense, a party man and not a citizen in military dress. And then, when we read the memoirs of those wars, in English or in French, we notice that they are the work of men bent on the military career. They have the professional officer's outlook. Gleig—a subaltern of Wellington's—who wrote an account of his adventures in the Peninsula, is typical of them. One can imagine Gleig reborn in the 'sixties and exclaiming at the moral deterioration of his profession, once it is overweighted by every Tom, Dick and Harry. There is a loss of style and manner, both in action and in the narratives written afterwards. The precise horrors of war are sometimes mentioned in the classical records but, generally, rhetorical clichés are preferred: carnage, slaughter and so on.

If Gleig were to return and read Whitman's notes, he would first be struck by the importance given to the casualties and the hospitals; and then by the unprotected nakedness of human feeling. The classical manner was not inhumane; but it put military dignity and professional virtue first. It was the manner of leaders. War, the most lawless of activities, was given a frame of decorum; you might not always fight by the code of honor, but a code of honor existed and, above all, you spoke and wrote in accord with it. The British troops sacked San Sebastian and fired at the officers who tried to stop them; but Gleig in *The Subaltern* speaks in the voice of a gentleman when he describes and deplores the event. There is no suggestion that war is a human tragedy. This suggestion is not made until the civilian fights. He cannot shrug his shoulders and say, "C'est la guerre." He is stunned by his own fears, stupefied by his own atrocities, amazed at his happiness, incredulous at the point of death. When all people are at war, no code, no manner, can contain the experience. The nearest writers to Whitman are Tolstoy and Erckmann-Chatrian—it is interesting to note that they were all writing about war at the same time—but Tolstoy's ironical pacifism and Erckmann-Chatrian's mildness and peace-ableness are a branch of the main stream of popular feeling. They are not, like Whitman, the stream itself. The *The Histoire d'un Conscrit de 1813* was written in 1864. It has been called *l'Iliade de la peur* and it portrays the pathos of the conscript's situation. The tragedy of the conscript is a passive one: that a quiet, peaceable man like himself should be killed. But in Whitman—as in Wilfred Owen—the tragedy is not passive; it lies not only in what is done to a man but in what he himself does and in what happens to him inside. When we compare these things with the sentiment of Erckmann-Chatrian we see that these authors are propagandists concerned with society. The freshness of their document is deceptive. They describe the Napoleonic wars with wonderful verisimilitude; but the wars are not taken direct from life. These writers have digested the moving simplicities of old men's hearsay. They are propagandists with an uncommonly delicate ear. They write to warn opinion in the fond domestic parlor behind the little shop.

Compared with them, Whitman does not know his mind. He is all over the place. He is the public. It is typical of *Specimen Days* that its first picture of the war is of the news spreading in the streets at night. The emotion of the street catches him. He is not intoxicated with patriotism but he does not deny the message of the pennants and the flags in the street. He is the man in the parlor who goes out into the street and loses his head. He feels the herd instinct. Two great wars have made us guarded, and when we read *Specimen Days* and especially the poems called *Drum Taps,* we resist that old-fashioned war. The sun has faded the defiant and theatrical photograph, and paled the headlines to a weak-tea brown. The uniforms are shabby. We suspect Whitman's idea that out of this a nation is born; it sounds like the cracked bugle and slack drum of propaganda. And yesterday's propaganda puts no one in a flurry. Yet, in all this, the loquacious Whitman is right. It is the bewildering thing in all his work, that this dressed-up egotist with all the air of a ham actor, is always half-right when he is most dubious. He is the newspaper man who reflects the ambiguous quality of public feeling. His virtue is that he begins on the pavement and that, like the streets, he has no shame and no style. Excitement and incantation take the place of it. The soldiers straggle into Washington after the defeat at Bull Run:

> The men appear, at first sparsely and shame-faced enough, then thicker, in the streets of Washington—appear in Pennsylvania avenue, and on the steps and basement entrances. They come along, in disorderly mobs, some in squads, stragglers, companies. Occasionally, a rare regiment, in perfect order, with its officers (some gaps, dead, the true braves), marching in silence, with lowering faces, stern, weary to sinking, all black and dirty, but every man with his musket, and stepping alive; but these are the exceptions. Side-walks of Pennsylvania avenue, Fourteenth street, etc., crowded, jamm'd with citizens, darkies, clerks, everybody, lookers-on; women in the windows, curious expressions from faces, as those swarms of dirt-cover'd return'd soldiers there (will they never end?) move by; but nothing said, no comments. . . . Amid the deep excitement, crowds and motion, and desperate eagerness, it seems strange to see many, very many, of the soldiers sleeping—in the midst of all, sleeping sound. They drop down anywhere, on the steps of houses, up close by the basements or fences, on the sidewalks, aside on some vacant lot, and deeply sleep. A poor seventeen- or eighteen-year-old boy lies there, on the stoop of a grand house; he sleeps so calmly, so profoundly. Some clutch their muskets firmly even in sleep. Some in squads; comrades, brothers, close together—and on them, as they lay, sulkily, drips the rain.

All that effort to produce one last remarkable phrase—that is Whitman.

After this the reality begins. And the reality, as the first modern war drags on, is the casualty list. In the classical narratives men are merely shot. Sometimes they are blown up. The aftermath was not minutely described. "Bloodshed," "carnage," generalize it. Whitman, too, uses those words but with all his voice. And he went round the hospitals and saw the gangrene, the amputations, the unspeakable wounds. He smelt the ether. Saw the tiptoe walking. The screens put round. He saw the stretcher cases lying out in the rain and glad to be cooled by it. He knew men crawled under bushes to die by inches. He took down the last words and wrote letters for men too weak to write. The men were not sorry for themselves. They talked very little. They had become detached and incredulous. Thousands, he knew, died and were never identified. It struck him, when he saw the burial trenches, that the typical soldier of this first modern war was "unknown."

That discovery marks the beginning of the modern attitude to war. We write as followers, not leaders. And though Whitman likes the heroic act, the message in the leader's eye, enjoys seeing the President ride past with his escort of cavalry and feels the public emotion of the "great convulsive drums," he writes more surely when he goes back to the rank and file, when he recovers his sense of anonymity. (Odd that this huge and often so flaccid egotist should be able to puff himself large enough until he is identified with all the people and lost in them: it is his paradox.) It is his paradox, too, that doggerel and the real thing trapes along together like the blind leading the blind, unable to see, unable to stop. In avoiding literary jargon, he easily wallowed in the tear-jerking stuff of small town In Memoriam notices—to emerge from the bathos with perhaps one line or two worth writing:

"Grieve not so, dear mother" (the just-grown daughter speaks through her sobs,
The little sisters huddle around speechless and dismay'd)
"See, dearest mother, the letter says Pete will soon be better."

Alas, poor boy, he will never be better (nor may-be needs to be better that brave and simple soul),

While they stand at home at the door he is dead already,
The only son is dead.

But the mother needs to be better,
She with thin form presently drest in black,
By day her meals untouch'd, then at night fitfully sleeping,
  often waking,

In the midnight waking, weeping, longing with one deep
  longing,
O that she might withdraw unnoticed, silent from life escape
  and withdraw,
To follow, to seek, to be with her dear dead son.

Blake could be simple, but he was never maudlin.

And there are the curious parallels with the poetry of the
last war, the same mixing of the romantic note with the realism.
We turn from Wilfred Owen's

> I am the enemy you killed, my friend,
> I knew you in this death.

to Whitman's

> Word over all, beautiful as the sky,
> Beautiful that war and all its deeds of carnage must in time
>   be utterly lost,
> That the hands of the sisters Death and Night incessantly
>   softly wash again, and ever again, this soil'd world:
> For my enemy is dead, a man divine as myself is dead,
> I look where he lies white-faced and still in the coffin—I
>   draw near,
> Bend down and touch lightly with my lips the white face in
>   the coffin.

Well, there it is. The set piece has gone, the full-bottomed
formal patriotism of the eighteenth century, the episodic poetry
of the early nineteenth. The sense of occasion has gone. There
are no more "incidents from the French camp," there is no
loss of the *Revenge,* no *Charge of the Light Brigade,* no *Burial
of Sir John Moore.* The serving soldier has been outnumbered

and swamped by the civilian soldier. The profession has been drowned in the classes. Nor can we attribute the change to a decay of the love of country—as some critics tried to do at the beginning of this war—for Whitman was a bombinating patriot, yet he wrote no pieces of occasion of that kind. *Drum Taps* describe the general scene, what the unknown and anonymous man did and saw and how filthily he died. Patriotism has not decayed; but the human being has emerged. He emerged first of all, it is interesting to observe, in a civil war, a war of ideas; and in the country which, to so many people, had seemed the Promised Land, where no formal tradition of war existed. Whitman himself observed, in his confused groping way, that a new way of warfare was necessary to America. A new way of writing about war certainly emerged; perhaps that is what he was trying to say.

It is worth while turning at this point to an American novelist who is the child of the Tolstoy-Whitman movement, the child of the Crimea and Bull Run. I am thinking of Stephen Crane and his book *The Red Badge of Courage* which was published in the 'nineties. The achievement of Crane was individual and high, but in placing it we must now confess that it came in on the Tolstoy wave; and that but for Tolstoy, it would never have been written. There is an important difference of experience between Tolstoy and Crane. In writing respectively about the Napoleonic and the American Civil Wars, both writers were reconstructing wars they had not seen; but Tolstoy *had* seen the Crimea, he had been a soldier, whereas Crane had seen war only as an intrepid journalist will see it, and the journalist does not go through the mill of soldiering. However adventurous he may be, he is not fully-conditioned. He does not, in the end, feel this is his inescapable fate. He does not look mildly into the blank expressionless features of death; but, dramatically, with face half-averted. One feels that Crane stands apart from his scene and that a great skill has to take the place of an innured contemplation of the subject. Crane is simply the specialist and expert who has narrowed his interest to the relation of a man with himself or a crowd's relation with other crowds in the battle; whereas Tolstoy in his wide survey saw that war was a continuation of peace. One curious common emotion nevertheless unites the master and the disciple. They reject the formal, the professional and rhetorical attitude to war; they reject the illusions of the profession and the traditional litanies of patriotism; but they cannot quite conceal a certain sadness at the passing of these things. In Tolstoy one so often suspects the secret longing of the repentant, the too-repentant soldier; in Crane the faint harking back to romance expresses, I suppose, the reporter's hidden regret that he has not a profound and comprehensive point of view.

The Red Badge of Courage is a *tour de force*. Crane starts a bugle call and sustains it without a falter to the end of the book. The scene is a single battlefield in the American Civil War, and the purpose of the novel is to show the phases by which a green young recruit loses his romantic illusions and his innocence in battle, and acquires a new identity, a hardened virtue. War has ceased to be a bewraying and befogging dream in his mind; it has become his world and he derives virtue from his unity with it. There is a second element in the story. To Crane a battlefield is like a wounded animal. The convulsions of its body, its shudders, its cries and its occasional repose, are the spasmodic movements and dumb respites of the groups of soldiers. There is not only the individual mind in the battlefield, but there is the mass mind also. Crane watches the merging of the individual with the herd. There is no plot in this book; it is a collection of episodes. We do not know which battle is being described or what are its objects. The rights and wrongs of the war itself are not discussed. No civilian and hardly a sight of the work of man, like a house or a cultivated field, comes into the picture. Few of the characters are named; the central figure is known simply as "the young man." The enemy are just the enemy, something fabulous and generally invisible in the blue smoke line of the engagement, terrifying and dragon-like at the worst, and at the best a singularity to be mistrusted. Who wins or loses is obscure. The whole thing is almost as anonymous as a poem or a piece of music and has the same kind of tension and suspense. For we are not specially interested in the mortal fate of the boy. We do not specially fear that he will be killed, nor do we privately hope he will cover himself with glory. Our eyes are fixed on something different in him; on each adjustment in his character as it comes along. At the end of this book, we say to ourselves, we too shall know how we shall behave when we discard our illusions about war and meet the reality. Romantically we fear or hope for battle as a way of singling ourselves out and dying; but underneath this day-dream is the awe of knowing that battle is a way of living before it is a way of dying, and one in which we cannot calculate our behavior in advance. It was one of the discoveries of the unrhetorical attitude to war in literature, that even the men on the right side and in the just cause are afraid; and to Crane—an adventurous man who died young from the effects of going to see trouble all over the earth—the deep fear of fear was a personal subject.

This comes out in the first chapter of *The Red Badge of Courage,* where the young man is seen in the camp listening to the rumors and torturing himself with questions. He feels courageous but will courage stand? Will he stay or will he run in panic? These are overmastering questions. The first dead do not scare him, nor does the early uproar. He can stand the first attack and face the fear hidden in the wall of forest where the enemy lie, and after the frenzy of the first onslaught he lies for a few moments in the trench overcome by a sense of fellowship with his companions and experiencing with astonishment "the joy of a man who at last finds leisure." But, fixed on their intense personal problem, his heart and mind have not yet understood that while the imagination expects decisive and single answers, reality does not deal in such simplicities. The attack, to everyone's despair, is renewed. The second phase has begun. It is too much. The youth throws down his rifle and runs. Here Crane shows his power as a novelist, for in this part of the story he writes those dramatic scenes and draws those portraits which have given the book its place in the literature of war. This is where the dying soldier, walking white and erect like a rejected prince among his broken court, goes stiffly toward his grave. Crane was an observer of the ways of dying, but this death is one of the most terrible, for it is a progress to death:

> The spectral soldier was at his side like a stalking reproach. The man's eyes were still fixed in a stare into the unknown. His grey, appalling face had attracted attention in the crowd, and men, slowing to his dreary pace, were walking with him. They were discussing his plight, questioning and giving him advice. In a dogged way he repelled them, signing to them to go on and leave him alone. The shadows of his face were deepening and his tight lips seemed holding in check the moan of great despair. There could be seen a certain stiffness in the movement of his body, as if he were taking infinite care not to arouse the passion of his wounds. As he went on he seemed always looking for a place like one who goes to choose a grave. Something in the gesture of the man as he waved the bloody and pitying soldiers away made the youth start as if bitten. He yelled in horror. Tottering forward he laid a quivering hand upon the man's arm. As the latter slowly turned his wax-like features toward him the youth screamed:
> "Gawd! Jim Conklin!"
> The tall soldier made a little commonplace smile.
> "Hello, Henry," he said.

If the boy's horror and quivering seem conventionally over-emphatic in that passage, the rest is not. Writers are always faced by two sets of words before they write; those which will draw a literary curtain over reality, and those which will raise the veil in our minds and lead us to see for the first time. Crane's gift for raising the veil is clear. The presence of "spectre" and "commonplace smile" in that portrait is imaginative observation at its best.

The book is filled with observation of this kind. Some is placed there by poetic intuition:

> The sun spread disclosing rays, and, one by one, regiments burst into view like armed men just born of the earth. The youth perceived that the time had come. He was about to be measured. For a moment he felt in the face of his great trial like a babe, and the flesh over his heart seemed but thin. He seized time to look about him calculatingly.
>
> But he instantly saw that it would be impossible for him to escape from the regiment. It enclosed him. There were iron laws of tradition and law on four sides. He was in a moving box.

This inner sensation of the experience is matched by wonderful, small phrases of verisimilitude: "His *forgotten feet* were constantly knocking against stones or getting entangled in briars." Or there is this picture—how common it has become in modern realism, which Crane anticipates by thirty or forty years:

> Once the line encountered the body of a dead soldier. He lay upon his back staring at the sky. He was dressed in an awkward suit of yellowish brown. The youth could see that the soles of his shoes had been worn to the thinness of writing paper, and from a great rent in one the dead foot projected piteously. And it was as if fate had betrayed the soldier. In death it exposed to his enemies that poverty which in life he had perhaps concealed from his friends.

The only word a modern reporter would not have written in that passage is the word "piteously."

Toughness, that is to say fear of facing the whole subject, as Crane faced it, has intervened to make the modern writer's picture purely visual and inhumane—one remembers the turned-out pockets of the dead in Hemingway and his bravado about writing a natural history of the dead. The pathetic fallacy abounds in Crane's prose and we hear of "the remonstrance" and "arguments" of the guns; but for all the artiness—which belongs to the 'nineties—there is pity, there is human feeling. There is a background of value and not a backdrop gaudy with attitudes. There is a quest for virtue—what else is the meaning of the young boy's innocent odyssey among his fears, his rages and his shames?—and not as one sees in Kipling, the search for a gesture or some dramatic personal stand which avoids the issue and saves the face. Crane ignores the actor in human beings, the creature with the name on the personal playbill; he goes—at any rate in *The Red Badge of Courage*—for the anonymous voice in the heart.

CAVALLERIA RUSTICANA

"*Growling still, he went off at an ambling pace of his mule, under the burning sun; a sun which split the stones now, and made the stubble crackle as if it was catching fire. At the gully between the two mountains he seemed to enter into a furnace; and the village on top of the height hanging above the precipices, scattered between enormous rocks, mined with caverns which made it seem suspended in the air, blackish, rusted, appeared abandoned, without a shadow, with all the windows open in the heat, like so many black holes, the crosses of the church towers trembling in the sun-dark air.*"

THIS is a description of the country north of Catania in the summer. I have taken the paragraph from one of the few descriptive passages in Giovanni Verga's Sicilian novel *Mastro-Don Gesualdo*. Soldiers who have fought in that heat-hammered island will appreciate the exactitude of Verga's eyes and perhaps the jolting of D. H. Lawrence's translation. The critic will observe how the phrases which do not directly describe heat, most intensely convey the sensation of it. "Furnace" is, of course, direct enough, and if you have looked down an industrial furnace, one of those long, ochreous, silent and unsurpassably intent corridors of short flame, the word will not be simply a conventional literary metaphor. Furnace is indeed the only word for a mountain gully under a vertical sun. But the thought of summer in Sicily brings back to my memory those black holes in the stone houses and the darkening, smoked-glass effect of tyrannical light. The sun is an enemy; earth and sun are at war with each other, and the candor of the Mediterranean scene is not disclosed until the evening when the battle has its sudden southern end or in the early morning, before it has begun.

Those are the hours when we can think of Theocritus and the Greeks. But in the middle hours of the day images of violence come into our minds. We think of earthquakes, the *mafia,* the bombs and shots of the factions and all those tales of boiling jealousy, the Judas kiss of the duelist and the long knife lying in the flat of the hand. It was, after all, upon Verga's story, *Cavalleria Rusticana,* that Mascagni built his opera. The story was not romantic, southern hyperbole. We saw Sicilian violence transplanted in Chicago a few years after Verga's death, a violence still naïve, spontaneous and quite outside the range of our moral judgments. It belonged to an earlier culture than ours, and strangely enough to that pastoral world of the delightful Theocritus. The sweet notes of the reed were drawn from the lips of men enjoined to kill in certain psychological situations. But what went on behind the violence? What was life like in the broken streets of the mountain towns and villages? Verga, who had been born near Catania in the 'seventies, came back from Naples when he was about forty to find out. His journey was one of those returns to the source which are commonly fruitful in the lives of artists. He was tired of writing novels about leisured people who make love to one another's wives and who go on chewing over the really not very astonishing sensations which they have detached from the meat of living. He had nothing new and certainly nothing brilliant to say about the subject. He came to Sicily to get back to something more important, which was going to be stark in the manner of Zola. And, first of all, Verga was very stark. *Cavalleria Rusticana* is an admirable, naked story, ruthlessly economical and as plain a piece of surgery on the passions as you could ask for. It is more than surgery; the more terrible Sicilian knife is at work.

La Lupa, the story of a man-devouring peasant woman who has
to be killed by her son-in-law, is another of the same kind.
There is something superb, an excess which amounts to the
poetry of pride, about these acts of transcendent psychological
justice among people who are blinded by the rage of honor,
amid starvation, crippling toil and rags.

Unlike Mérimée who looked at the violent and idyllic rem-
nant of pastoral culture in the Mediterranean with the eyes of
a connoisseur, Verga was committed. The Sicilians were his own
people. He got back inside them. There was not much inside
them, in our sense anyway, for they were southerners without
introspection, black and white in their souls, like their light;
but as a society they had a great deal. Verga planned to write
five novels, each one to deal with a class in Sicilian society. The
first dealt with the poor. (An American translation exists.) The
second dealt with the people who are just above the masses; and
this one, *Mastro-Don Gesualdo* was translated by D. H. Lawrence, who was just the man to feel an idiom. In this book we
find what it is that lies behind the Sicilian violence. The answer,
according to Verga, is more violence. Violence of tongue, violence of will, greed, push, scramble, gossip, the awful ruthless,
comic, bitter, incorrigible barnyard belligerence of family life;
fights for money, fights for food, fights for possession. Misery is
the basis of it, the misery of poor land, the misery of the isolated
towns where the nail-scratches of scandal and contempt are
scrawled over everyone's life. The beautiful are the humble and
submissive who refuse to join the fight; worse luck for them,
they are kicked out and trodden on and their poor-spiritedness
is a byword. So we should describe the people in Verga's novel
and yet they do not distress us. Only the suburban townsman
idealizes the countryman and is shocked by the malignance of
country life and its poisoned solitudes. Only the suburban
townsman conveniently forgets that the countryman must fight
for money and property like the rest of the world. Far from
distressing us, Verga's people gradually take possession of our

minds, seize us with their grasping hands, harangue us about their case until we are forced to see the point of it, and to see that here, in this ludicrous family screeching about pride, money, marriages, and ownership, something elemental is taking place. His people are able to convince us of this not merely because it is true but because Verga is a very considerable novelist. He has a rich range of mood, a pungency of metaphor; something in him is equal to the clamor of the heart; he has a comprehensive grasp of scene; and without being naturalistic he seems to be able to pull up people by the roots straight out of nature and put them, rife as they are, upon the page. They come out with such vocal, physical emphasis that at first one is stunned and deafened. Verga depends on the crackle of his dialogue and on an allusive atmosphere which each sentence creates. You have to watch that and keep your senses keen or you will miss his transitions. And then these Sicilians think and feel at the tops of their voices. Their bellies are "full of poison," their mouths "spit bile"—a vast amount of bile is spat in this book; Lawrence must have loved the anger of it—and in a few pages you will see people compared to vipers, wolves, hounds, tigers, wasps, pigs, cows, donkeys, scorpions and vampires, a whole menagerie. All this makes the early chapters trying until you acquire a kind of sardonic animal grin yourself; then things go splendidly.

You notice that Verga is not a regional novelist in the provincial sense of the word. *Mastro-Don Gesualdo* is no more regional in this rather derogatory meaning, than Turgenev was in *Lear of the Steppe*. No, Verga is European and modern. His visual power, which is heightened by his constant use of peasant metaphor and his identification with the peasant mind, is very modern. This visual quality is one which literature has developed, I think, to fill the place previously taken by traditional, moral and religious generalizations; the traditional Catholic novel, for example, about Sicily had no need of this physical vividness. Verga, no doubt like Cézanne, supposed he was being scientific. Now the visual, oral style becomes monotonous, unless the human heat of the book grows until it becomes convulsive and momentous. And Verga's story does grow. We see Mastro-Don Gesualdo, a common worker on the roads, in his first rise in the world. First his fight against his own family over their petty trade; then his marriage and the fight against his wife's aristocratic relations—they are a scarecrow lot of decayed aristocrats but not too grand to smell the main chance a long way off—then his fight against the town's jealousy of his wealth. And finally his fight against his daughter and her husband who is a duke. In that last fight Don Gesualdo attains the rigor of spiritual agony. The struggle begins when the cholera has driven his patriarchal family to the mountains. It develops when revolutionaries from Palermo incite the peasants to get back the common lands which he has taken. It gets the better of him when he has to fight for command not merely of his property but of his wife and daughter. He defeats his daughter but loses the wife who has never loved him. The whole world rises against him. They see his weakness. He is not a monster but, searching for power, he has forgotten he is capable of sorrow; and meaner people spring upon the shoulders of this man whose will has been exorbitant. There, it occurs to me, is the Sicilian subject as one sees it in Verga; exorbitance. A man must carry his passions to the extreme, and fate, like a counter logic, will come down the road to meet and defeat him, not with one clean blow but a long, slow bludgeoning, beating him to his knees and then down into the dust of the greedy generations from which he sprung.

The intensity of Verga is achieved by dense detail. He is totally without rhetoric. Of a suspicious man he writes: "Don Ferdinando, always after them, sewed to their heels, silent . . ." Of the Duke's servants in Palermo in the wonderful final scene when Gesualdo lies dying among the idle footmen in his daughter's grand house: "An army of lazy rascals, lackeys and chambermen, yawning with their mouths shut, walking on tiptoe

and serving you without saying a word. . . ." Those phrases take
one back to Browning's *Ring and the Book*. But thinking about
this intensity has led me to forget Verga's comic gift. Verga
saw the fantastic comedy of the family struggle. He saw the
sardonic farce of Sicilian politics, and how much they depended
upon local personality. The intruding priest, for example, who
gets the men of property on to the revolutionary side so that
they can save their property, is a real, slippery beauty. Who has
not met that busy little ferret? Then there is the young Baron
seducing the awful touring actress by sending her food to guz-
zle from his mean mother's larder; and there is the christening
scene where all the relations get in their digs at the right point.
They all hate Don Gesualdo, and very likely, they point out,
the child is not his. An important point to notice in Verga's
dialogue is that people do not always talk to one another. They
declaim out of themselves.

> Don Gesualdo kept on chatting with Cousin Zacco, each of
> them with his heart in his hand, oh so friendly! Then the
> baroness spat out the question that was boiling inside her:
> "Is it true that your husband lends him money—on the
> quiet?—Have you seen him come here to him? Tell me, what
> do you know?"
> "Certainly, certainly," replied Don Gesualdo at that mo-
> ment. "You must take children as they come."
> To confirm this Zacco pointed to his own girls ranged in a
> row like so many organ pipes, modest and pleasing.
> "Look you. I have five girls, and I'm fond of them all
> alike."
> "Why, of course," replied Limoli. "That's why you don't
> want to marry any of them off."
> Donna Lavinia, the eldest, threw an ugly look behind her.
> "Ah, are you there?" said the baron. "You are always ready,
> like the devil, in the litany, you are!"
> All at once down in the square below there exploded the
> deuce of a noise of crackers. . . . It was Santo, Don Gesualdo's
> brother, celebrating the baptism of his niece in that fashion,
> in his short sleeves, on all fours down there below, with a

lighted fuse. Don Gesualdo opened the window to pour out a sackful of abuse.

"Fool! You'd have to be doing something! Fool!" The friends calmed him.

"Poor chap! Let him alone! It's one way of showing his pleasure."

A novelist is tested by his power of sustaining long scenes and large groups of people and by his power of continual dramatization. It is his duty to break a marriage, a birth, a death, or some enterprise into living fragments. This gift of fragmentation is given only to the greatest novelist; lacking it, the glib, second-rate ones are perhaps more quickly read. They are certainly quickly forgotten. But Verga is one of the great in this novel, a Balzacian. He sees a society, and that society working in men and women. Perhaps, like the Sicilian sun, he hammers his words too pitilessly on our heads and batters us with the theme of self-interest; but he has the space of the masters. I would say to any young novelist who wanted to shake himself into a fresh consideration of the art of the novel, to get hold of Verga quickly. When Italians boasted about him in Paris before the war they were not far wrong.

POOR RELATIONS

THE small house on the cliff of Passy hanging like a cage between an upper and lower street, so that by a trick of relativity, the top floor of the Rue Berton is the ground floor of the Rue Raynouard, has often been taken as a symbol of the life of Balzac. The custodian of the house—now a Balzac museum with the novelist's eternal coffee-pot, his dictionary of universal knowledge and with his appalling proof sheets framed on the wall—shows one the trap-door by which Balzac escaped to the lower floor in the Rue Berton. Down it the fat breathless novelist of forty-one went stumbling and blurting, like his own prose, to the Seine. Two houses in one, a life with two front doors, dream and reality; the novelist, naïve and yet shrewd, not troubling to distinguish between one and the other. Symbol of Balzac's life, the house is a symbol of the frontier life, the trap-door life of the great artists, who have always lived between two worlds. There Balzac wrote his letters to Madame Hanska in Poland, the almost too comprehensive, explanatory and eloquent letters of a famous and experienced writer who has the art, indeed the habit of self-projection at his fingertips; there, when the letters were posted, he went to bed with the docile housekeeper who was finally to turn round and blackmail him, and so provide him with the horrifying last chapters of *Le Cousin Pons*. At this house in the worst year of his life, the least blessed with that calm which is—quite erroneously—supposed to be essential to the novelist, Balzac wrote this book and *La Cousine Bette,* respectively the best constructed and the most fluent and subtle of his novels.

A new life of Balzac was published in Paris in 1944. It is called simply *Vie de Balzac* and is by André Billy. This biography contains nothing new, but it gathers all the immense biographical material in a couple of volumes. Its detail is as lively and exhaustive as a Balzac novel; the manner is warm but skeptical, thorough but not dry. Very rightly, M. Billy looks twice and three times at everything Balzac said about his life, for he is dealing with the hallucinations of the most extraordinary egotist in the history of literature. One can imagine a less diffuse biography; one in which the picture of his time played a greater part and where every detail of a chaotic Bohemian career was not played up to the same pitch. But given the gluttony of Balzac's egotism and the fertility of his comedy, one is not inclined to complain.

Like the tones of bronze and antiques—Balzac estimated the weight and value of himself with the care of an auctioneer's valuer—with which he darkened the house he finally took for Madame Hanska when he had got his hands on some of her fortune, the novels of Balzac weigh upon the memory. The reader is as exhausted as the novelist by the sheer weight of collection. One is tempted to see him as the stolid bulldozer of documentation, the quarrying and expatiating realist, sharpening his tools on some hard view of his own time. He seems to be stuck in his task. Yet this impression is a false one, as we find whenever we open a novel of his again. Balzac is certainly the novelist who most completely exemplifies the "our time" novelist, but not by his judgments on his society. He simply *is* his time. He is identified with it, by all the greedy innocence of genius. The society of rich peasants brought to power by revolution and dictatorship, pushing into business and speculation, buying up houses and antiques, founding families, grabbing at money and pleasure, haunted by their tradition of parsimony and hard work, and with the peasant's black and white ideas about everything, and above all their weakness for fixed ideas, is Balzac himself. He shares their illusions. Like them he was humble when he was poor, arrogant when he was rich. As with them, his extravagance was one side of the coin; on the other was the face of the peasant miser. The cynic lived in a world of romantic optimism. We see the dramatic phase of a century's illusions, before they have been assimilated and trodden down into the familiar hypocrisies. To us Balzac's preoccupation with money appears first to be the searching, scientific and prosaic interest of the documentary artist. On the contrary, for him money was romantic; it was hope and ideal. It was despair and evil. It was not the dreary background, but the animating and theatrical spirit.

Balzac learned about money, as M. Billy says, at his printing works in the Rue du Marais. He expected to find that fallen aristocrat, the goddess Fortune of the eighteenth century; instead he found that in the nineteenth century the goddess had become a bourgeois bookkeeper. His laundry bills, his tailor's bill, his jeweler's bills were mixed with the printing accounts. The imagination of the businessman is always governable; Balzac's was not. Financially speaking, Balzac was out of date. Like his father, who also was willing to work hard enough, he sought for Fortune, not for Profit; far from being an example of Balzac's realism, his attitude to money is really the earliest example of his Romantic spirit. Balzac's attitude to money was that of a man who did not understand money, who could not keep it in his hands, the plagued spendthrift and natural bankrupt. His promissory notes were a kind of poetry in his early years; later on they became articles of moral indignation; in the end—to quote M. Billy's delightful euphemism, he lost all "pudeur morale." The creation of debts began as exuberance; it became an appetite, one of those dominant passions which he thought occurred in all natures, but which really occur only among the most monstrous egotists. Madame Hanska's fortune did not calm him. He went on buying here and there, incurring more debts, scheming without check. And the last people he thought of paying were his wretched relations and especially his mother. To her, he behaved with the hypocrisy and meanness of a miser and the worse he treated her the more he attacked her.

At this point it is interesting to compare Balzac with Scott whom he admired and consciously imitated. Madame Hanska's estate in Poland was for many years his visionary Abbotsford; the passion for antiques, the debts, and the crushing labor, the days and nights of writing without sleep, were Abbotsford too. Balzac saw himself as an aristocrat; Scott saw himself as a laird: they are by no means the first or last writers to provide themselves with distinguished ancestors. He went to the length of traveling to Vienna as a Marquis, with coronets on his luggage; it was ruinous, he discovered, in tips. But the honorable Scott was broken by debts; they drove him to work as a duty; they wore out his imagination. Balzac, on the contrary, was certainly not ruined as a writer by his debts. His debts were a natural expression of a voracious imagination. One may doubt whether any of his mistresses moved his inspiration—though clearly their maternal sympathy was necessary—but one can be certain that Balzac's imagination was ignited by the romance of purchase, by the mere sensual possession of things. The moving impulse in his life was, as he said, the discovery of the "material of civilization," the literal materials; and although he considered this a scientific discovery, it was really a mysticism of things. Every object he bought, from the famous walking-stick to the museum pieces, represented an act of self-intoxication that released the capacity—so vital to the creative artist—to become unreal.

It is easy, as M. Billy says, a hundred years after, to blame Madame Hanska for delaying her marriage with Balzac and for adding the afflictions of reluctance and jealousy to his life of appalling labor, but obviously he was possessed by a kind of madness, and he would have stripped her of all her property. One understands her hesitation after reading his later and maniacal letters about money and things.

> "Je suis sûr qu'au poids il y aura, dans notre maison, trois
> mille kilogrammes de cuivres et bronzes dorés. C'est effrayant,
> le bronze! Cette maison est, comme je te le disais, une mine
> de cuivre doré, car mon ébéniste me disait qu'il y en a mille
> kilogrammes. À huit francs le kilo, à vendre aux chaudron-
> niers, c'est trente-deux mille francs de valeur réelle. Juge de
> la valeur, en y ajoutant le valeur d'art."

Ruinous. There was no "valuer d'art." His brain gave way
under the strain of his schemes and combinations. Yet, *Le
Cousin Pons* and *La Cousine Bette* were written in that year;
and when Pons makes the fortune of his persecutors with his
collection of antiques which they had despised, one sees Balzac
avenging himself for the complaints of his mistress. No; he was
not weighed down by debts, in the sense of having his talent
ruined by them. His extravagances floated him on the vital
stream of unreality. He was the Micawber for whom things
were only too continuously "turning up," a Micawber who
worked. Balzac and Micawber are, it is interesting to note, contemporary financiers of the period.

The ox-like groans, the animal straining and lamentation of
Balzac, his boasting, his bosom-beating letters to women like
Madame Carraud before whom he parades in the role of the
indomitable martyr of circumstance, have created an imaginary
Balzac. One sees—his own phrase—"the galley slave of fame." A
rather different impression was formed by his contemporaries.
Once he had put his pen down he was childishly gay:

> Naïveté, puérilité, bonté, ces trois mots reviennent sous
> la plume de tous les contemporains. Le portrait de Balzac
> que nous a laissé le poète des *Meditations* se trouve con-
> firmé en tous points par celui qu'a tracé George Sand: puéril
> et puissant, toujours envieux d'un bibelot et jamais jaloux
> d'une gloire, sincère jusqu'à la modestie, vantard jusqu'à
> la hâblerie, confiant en lui-même et dans des autres,
> très expansif, très bon et très fou, avec un sanctuaire de
> raison intérieure où il rentrait pour tout dominer dans son
> œuvre, cynique dans la chasteté, ivre en buvant de l'eau, in-

tempérant de travail et sobre d'autres passions, positif et romanesque avec un égal excès, crédule et sceptique, plein de contrastes et de mystères. . . .

Some indeed found him grubby, ill-kempt and uncouth. Hans Andersen hardly recognized the dandy of the evening party in the tousled Bohemian of the following day. There was a Rue Raynouard and a Rue Berton in his appearance and in his nature.

Instant in his admirations and schemes, Balzac was like a child for whom everything happens *now* and in a *now* that is connected with no future. Certainly with no future of incurred obligations. The burden of Balzac's life is not apparent until one sees him at work; and then we see that not debt but his method of writing was the fatal aggravation.

In a sense Balzac is a made, or rather re-made writer. There were times when he rushed down to the printers at eleven o'clock at night and they took the chapter of his novel page by page as he wrote it. But such moments of inspired exhibitionism were rare. In general Balzac strikes one as being the gifted talker whose mind congests when he sits down to write what he has just spoken. No doubt he could have turned out the cheap thrillers of his early period as easily as he spoke; but with his other books the process was agonizing. There would be several versions of the text, each one smothered with erasures and additions; chapters were put into different places, more chapters were sandwiched in between. Pages and pages scrapped, more pages added. The historian of the contemporary scene had only to go out of his door to see a new thing to squeeze somewhere into the text. And this was not the end of the confusion and the struggle. Once the printers had sorted out the manuscript and had produced their galleys, the ungovernable author began a hardly less drastic process of destruction and reconstruction. Night after night, from midnight until seven—and these were merely regular hours. There were days and nights of almost continuous labor without sleep. "Il ne savait pas sa langue," said

Gautier. The time spent and the printers' costs would have eaten seriously into earnings not already mortgaged by extravagance.

Let us return to the double house in the Rue Raynouard and look once more at the two great novels Balzac wrote in that small room above the trap-door, when his brain was already breaking under the appetites he imposed upon it. Open *Le Cousin Pons*. There is the expected chapter, that roughly and in a domineering way generalizes and clears a space for the characters in the Parisian scene. And then, like a blow in the face, comes the brutal sentence: "On n'a jamais peint les exigences de la gueule." One stops dead. What on earth has poor Pons done that his fastidious habit of dining at the expense of his better-off relations should become a treatise on the trough? Comically treated, of course; Balzac examined the dossier of human nature with the quizzical detachment of some nail-biting, cigar-stained Chief of Police who is going rapidly up in the world; who has seen so many cases; who thanks heaven that he does not make the moral law and that a worldly Church stands between himself and the Almighty. Passion, even when it is a passion for the best food, always becomes—in the experience of the Chief of Police—a transaction; Pons trades the little errands he runs on behalf of the family for the indispensable surprises of the gourmet. In the pursuit of that appetite he is prepared to ruin himself where other men, more voluptuously equipped by nature, will wreck themselves in the capture and establishment of courtesans. Sex or food, money or penury, envy or ambition—Balzac knows all the roads to ruin. If only men and women were content with their habits instead of craving the sublimity of their appetites.

But *Pons* is a type. He is a poor relation. In that isolation of a type, one detects the main difference between the French and English novels. The English novel has never lived down its early association with the theater, and has always had to wrestle with a picaresque or artificial plot. But even if this had not been so, we could never have been a nation of moralists. Our instinct is to act; our interest in morals is a practical interest in results. The French novel—and how obvious this is in Balzac —is dominated on the contrary by a sense of law. Behind the individual lies the type, behind the act lies a law governing the act. The French novelists are the lawyers of the passions; they proceed from the prototype to the particular and then carry it back for comparison. Subtle and litigious in tactic, they conclude that human experience, however bizarre, however affecting, can never escape the deep inscription of its category or evade the ordinance of some general idea.

To an English taste there must always be something arbitrary in such a structure. Natural Protestants, we resist a determinism so Roman and so Catholic. But we must be abashed by the double reference in which French fiction is so rich. Look at the delightful Pons. His character has so many departments. He is an old man, an ugly man, an outmoded but respected musician, a dandy survived from an earlier period, a collector of antiques, a poor man, a careful man, a simple man who is not quite so simple—see his valuable collection of pictures and bric-à-brac cunningly picked up for next to nothing—a sexless man, a gourmet, a hanger-on, shrewd in his own world, lost in the society into which he has grown up. Pons is the kind of character who, inevitably, becomes fantastic in the English novel simply because no general laws pin him down. He would become a static "character." Instead Balzac takes all these aspects of Pons and mounts each one, so that Pons is constructed before our eyes. We have a double interest: the story or plot, which is excellent in suspense, drama and form—this is one of Balzac's well-constructed novels, as it is also one of the most moving—and the exact completion, brick by brick, of Pons and his circle. There are the historical Pons—he is an *incroyable* left-over from the Directoire—the artistic Pons, the financial Pons, the sociable Pons, the moral Pons, and in the end Pons dying, plundered, defiant, a man awakened from his simplicity and fighting back, the exquisitely humble artist turned proud, sovereign and dangerous in his debacle. Pons is a faceted stone, and part of the drama is the relation of each facet with the others. Thus his fantastic dress is related, via dandyism, to his small, esteemed, but out-of-date position in the world of art. That adjoins his love of good living—picked up in smarter days —which links up with the solitariness and social spryness of the bachelor, his timidity and his sexual innocence. We have the portrait of a man who in every trait suggests some aspect of the society in which he lives. The history of his time is explicit in him. Yet he is not a period piece. A period piece is incapable of moral development and the development of a moral theme is everything in the novels of Balzac, who facilitates it by giving every character not merely a time and place, but also an obsession. Among English novelists it is only Henry James and, on occasions, Meredith, who move their drama not from incident to incident, but from one moral situation or statement to the next. (In Meredith's *The Egoist* one recalls the tension, tightening page by page, that precedes the accusation: "You are an egoist.") So it is with the story of Pons. He is snubbed by his ignorant relations who do not realize even the financial value of his collection of antiques and pictures. In consequence, rather than be dropped or ridiculed, he gives up his beautiful dinners and retires to taste the blessings of the concierge's motherly cooking and pure friendship with the delightful Schmucke, a man even more simple than himself. At that point an English novelist might have given up. The lesson was clear. But Balzac, like Henry James, saw that drama lies in the fact that there is no end to moral issues. For him—recomplication, further research. And so, just as Pons is getting a little tired of his land-lady's cooking, society tempts him again. His relations apologize, and Pons is one of those good men who cannot bear other people to say they are in the wrong. He conceives a grandiose scheme for returning good for evil. He will find a husband for the unmarriageable daughter. He will announce the enormous value of his collection and leave it to her in his will. Result, gratitude? Not a bit of it. The family is longing to wipe out the memory of their humiliating apology by vengeance, and when the marriage scheme collapses, they finish with Pons. Once more we have come to a natural end of the novel. But once more Balzac recomplicates. Pons falls into the grip of his concierge, who has suddenly become covetous now that she has two harmless, childless, womanless old men in her power; and his downfall is ensured by the very innocence of Schmucke, who cannot believe evil of anyone.

Balzac is the novelist of our appetites, obsessions and our *idées fixes,* but his great gift—it seems to me—is his sense of the complexity of the human situation. He had both perceptions, one supposes, from his peasant origins, for among peasants, as he was fond of saying, the *idée fixe* is easily started; and their sense of circumstance overpowers all other consideration in their lives. A character in Balzac is so variously situated in history, in money, in family, class and in his type to begin with; but on top of this, Balzac's genius was richly inventive in the field least exploited by the mass of novelists: the field of probability. It is very hard to invent probabilities. This simple means that Balzac knew his people as few novelists ever know their characters. The marriage scene in *Le Cousin Pons* for example: there we have the rich German all set to marry the daughter of the family. The awful facts of the "régime dotal"—a phrase repeated in pious chorus by the family with the unction usually reserved for statements like "God is Love"—have been accepted by him. He has merely to say the word. At this tense moment the German electrifies everyone by asking the unexpected question: Is the girl an only child? Yes, she is. Then he must withdraw. A man of forty is an idiot who marries a girl who has been spoiled in her childhood. She will use the fact that he is so much older than herself to prove she is always right. That way lies hell. The respectability of the institution of marriage is in itself no satisfaction.

But *Le Cousin Pons* moves from one surprising probability to the next, backed by the massed ranks of human circumstance. The change in the character of the charming, motherly landlady of Pons who suddenly takes on the general professional character of the concierges of her district creates another powerful situation—powerful because so isolated are we, so obsessed with possibility and hope, that the probable is unperceived by us. The last thing we care to believe is that we are governed by type and environment. Balzac believed nothing else.

I do not know that I would put anything in *Le Cousin Pons* above the first part of *La Cousine Bette,* though I like Pons better as a whole. Pons is the old bachelor. Bette is the old maid. The growth of her malevolence is less subtly presented than the course of Pons's disillusion, because Balzac had the genius to show Pons living with a man even simpler than himself. One sees two degrees of simplicity, one lighting the other, whereas Bette stands alone; indeed, it may be complained, that she is gradually swamped by the other characters. She is best in her obscurity, the despised poor relation, the sullen peasant, masculine, counting her humiliations and her economies like a miser, startling people with her bizarre reflections. They laugh at her and do not conceive the monstrous fantasies of her painful virginity. And we are moved by her in these early pages when she is hiding her Polish artist, shutting him in his room like a son, driving him to work; or, later, when Madame Marneffe gives Bette the shabby furniture. Bette is a wronged soul; and when her passion does break, it is, as Balzac says, sublime and terrifying. Her advance to sheer wickedness and vengeance is less convincing, or, rather, less engrossing. It is a good point that she is the eager handmaid and not the igniting cause of ruin; but one draws back, incredulously, before some of her plots and lies. Acceptable when they are naïve, they are unacceptable when they fit too efficiently the melodramatic intrigue of the second part of the book. But the genius for character and sitiuation is here again. La Marneffe, rooted in love's new middle-class hypocrisy and growing into a sanctimonious courtesan, is nicely contrasted with the besotted baron who had grown up in an earlier period—"between the wars" in fact—when the fashion of love was brisker and more candid. That situation alone is a comic one. The diplomatic farce of La Marneffe's supposed pregnancy is brilliant. The lies and short repentances of the sexagenarian Baron are perfect. Only Adeline does not, to my mind, come off in this novel; and here we come upon Balzac's rather dubious advocacy of marital fidelity. He sounds as little convinced as a public speaker haranguing his way to conviction. Adeline's pathetic attempt to sell herself, in order to save her husband's fortunes, is embarrassing to read; are we to admire virtue because it is stupid? Balzac protests too much.

No one has surpassed Balzac in revealing the great part played by money in middle-class life; nor has anyone excelled him in the portraits of the parvenu. Henry James alone, coming at the zenith of middle-class power, perceived the moral corruption caused by money; but money had ripened. It glowed like a peach that is just about to fall. Balzac arrived when the new money, the new finance of the post Napoleonic world was starting on its violent course; when money was an obsession and was putting down a foundation for middle-class morals. In these two novels about the poor relation, he made, it seems to me, his most palatable, his least acrid and most human statements about this grotesque period of middle-class history.

THE BOHEMIAN

THE English visitor to the Continent is always surprised by the part played by students in society and in politics. They have even become the subjects of music and literature by a sort of natural right which, I believe, has never existed in England since the time of Chaucer. The drinking songs and the tales of Heidelberg, a book like Murger's *Scènes de la Vie de Bohême,* have no parallel in England; and the explanation seems to be that the English universities preserved the monasticism of the Middle Ages but cut themselves off from the medieval spirit. A student tradition, one that goes back to Abélard and Villon, is not nurtured in seclusion; it depends upon poverty and mingling with the ferment of the town. This has not been in the character of any of our older universities; for us the student does not exist. We have never idolized youth. Our idol, oddly enough, has been the Public School boy, and when a Frenchman asks us for the parallel to Murger's book, we are forced to hush up the fact that *Charley's Aunt* is the only play about an undergraduate, and to divert his attention to the enormous importance of *Tom Brown's Schooldays.* Among the Anglo-Saxons it was the unsecluded Americans, rather than ourselves, who took to the Quartier Latin as ducks to water in the last twenty years.

Like most English readers, when I was young I owed my first notions of the Quartier Latin to the sentimental and watered-down works of Thackeray, Du Maurier and W. J. Locke. These fanciful imitators of Murger were said to be harmless; while the sentiment, the tears and the picaresque farce of Murger were condemned as misleading. A Bohemia like his had never existed. Or, if it had, it certainly existed no more. Only lately I have read his *Scènes de la Vie de Bohême,* and I regret, as usual, that I did not go to the fountain head before. Some of it is tedious, but the sketches have very amusing moments. Murger had that acute Parisian sense of comic pose, a kind of wit of situation as well as a wit of words and ideas, that crisply feathers the surface of life as he skims along. But the interesting thing about *La Vie de Bohême* is less the story than its success. Not entirely does Murger owe that to the accident of Puccini's opera. Murger had already made a very successful play of the book before Puccini took it up. A suggestive light is thrown by a remark of the Goncourts which they put down in their *Journal* in 1856:

> "When Murger wrote La Vie de Bohême," they said, "he had no notion that he was writing the history of a social world which was to become a power within five or six years, yet that is the fact today."

The Bohemians, they say, bar the way to the well-born who are damned as amateurs. "The advent of Bohemia means the domination of socialism in literature." They should have written "the domination of that new uprooted class 'the intelligentsia.'"

If socialism does owe something to Bohemia, what Bohemia really did to artists and writers in the long run was, of course, to isolate them from society. Not socialism, but art for art's sake came out of that fruitful myth and produced in figures like Gauguin, Verlaine and Modigliani an isolation more haggard and stark than anything the frittering Murger and his little circle ever knew. Murger went to seed among the obliging tears of a small Parisian clique. The Goncourts maliciously note his first tailcoat, and his official break with the hungry past when he set up at the Café Riche. He became a journalistic slave, and in the words of his own Rudolphe honestly said, as we all have:

"Je veux bien consenter à regarder le passé, mais ce sera au travers d'une bouteille de vrai vin, et assis dans un bon fauteuil. Qu'est-ce-que tu veux?—je suis un corrompu. Je n'aime plus que ce qui est bon."

He had, the Goncourts remarked, one of the largest funeral processions of his time, and among the mourners of the poet of hunger was Théophile Gautier, who talked, not very suitably, of the influence of cattle-cake on the flavor of steak, all the way to the cemetery.

Where the Goncourts' sharp nose for tendency was right was in detecting the enormous potential of publicity in the early idea of Bohemia. Murger, who was half-German, had given a halo to romantic disorder and, by the end of the century, Puccini and English best-sellers like Du Maurier and W. J. Locke, had carried the idea triumphantly into every vicarage and suburban villa. If you sat on the floor or boiled an egg unassisted you became a Bohemian. The romance of the 'fifties had become the myth of the century. The English Bohemians of Du Maurier and Locke are no longer poor students. They are the sons of rich parents. The famous Trilby is a model, but she comes from a distinguished Irish family! Du Maurier's Laird— the only agreeable character in a dreadfully coy book—has his Broadwood and his furniture sent over from England to the Quartier Latin; and Locke's heroes always belong to the best county families and are tired of their clubs. The strange thing is that we are shown the lives of poor artists no more, but the lives of people whose ambition is to throw up everything and become poor in order to be artists or to live near them. Middle-class society is kicking over the traces. It is in conflict with itself. Yet the conflict is, so far, not very profound. The illusion of the new Bohemia was that it could preserve the middle-class amenities while throwing over the irksome conventions that protected them. And by the 'twenties we had arrived at a paradoxical situation which would have soured the faces of Murger's circle at the Café Riche: the bourgeois had been converted to art. All the world was bent upon becoming artistic. The Quartier Latin and Montparnasse had become the quarters of the rich. I remember my own early bewilderment in Paris. Brought up to believe that my intellectual emancipation depended on my finding a cheap room to live in on the left bank of the Seine, and that damnation awaited those who dwelt on the right, I gloomily remember I could not afford to be a Bohemian. Life was cheaper in Passy; one went to Montparnasse or the Rue de Seine to borrow money and to wonder what spirit of perversity and masochism had possessed the sons of rentiers that they must put on fancy dress and live among the worst drains of Europe. The Goncourts were right—Bohemia had become a racket, a greater racket than they could have guessed.

No doubt I exaggerate. My nose, insufficiently Bohemian, has many times led me out of the pensions of the Mont St. Geneviève and so closed a world to me except as a spectator. I recognize my own facial expressions in Murger's picture of the bourgeois who used to go night after night to the café to watch with a craving he dreaded to reveal. There is, and will always be, the temporary Bohemianism like that of Murger's Rudolphe; and always, no doubt, what Murger called the Bohemianism of the *impasse*. That gaunt man with the Christ-like face and the invalid's straggling beard, who sat all day over his cup of coffee and who looked as if he were starving, was a one-time silk salesman despite his "artistic" appearance. But he was in fact starving, God knows why, and they picked him up half dead in the street. The Bohemians of the *impasse* were, as Murger said, chronically unproductive and garrulous. If I wish to visualize a Bohemian of this kind I always think of a middle-aged man who, as an alleged fashion journalist, spent his days with the manikins of the Rue de la Paix and played the harmonium on Sundays at a Methodist chapel. Murger knew his subject. It was his only subject. He knew and illustrated in his own life and work the drift into finicking which the life of the clique encourages. The frenzied hunt for the *piéce de cent sous,* the strangling estimate of whether the next meal lies north, south, east or west as you leave the door, are not the only enemies of the Bohemian; nor the hospital its final dread. The dreaded enemy is self-discovery. The inner terror which Murger described in another of his books is the fear not that the talent for which one suffers is insufficient, but that it simply is not there at all.

Socialists—the most respectable of men—have come to attack Bohemia for its disorder and its philosophy of isolation; but I wonder whether those who do so really attack it from a rival Bohemia of their own, the equally ancient Bohemia of the exile and refugee. Political Bohemia from the time of Herzen and through the life of Marx, offers a story no less wretched and picaresque than the lives of students and artists. If the Bohemia of the artist had been taken over wholesale by middle-class society in 1931, and had gone, its place was taken by this revived Bohemia of the refugee. Colorless and despondent, watchful and suspicious, whispering in groups over the backs of chairs at the Coupole or the Dôme, the exiles sat waiting for news from home, where the gaudy and gregarious figures of the earlier decade hoped they'd heard the last of it. And perhaps that is a portent. Mr. E. M. Forster has lately recommended a return to Bohemia for writers; but tomorrow independent political thought, not art, may be one of the seven deadly and unremunerative sins. Du Maurier's Little Billee turned "deathly pale" when he saw Trilby, a lady of one of the best Irish families, posing for "the altogether"; his grandson may crumple up if he catches her indecently exposing the charms of a minority mind to oblige a few friends.

I have said very little about Murger's sketches themselves. They have a boulevard wit and when, later on in life, Murger decided to give up the fastidiousness of art and to go after money in the theater, he made the right decision. He was not a natural highbrow. His melancholy temperament was that of the clown, not of the poet; he was a born writer of farce, and his young men have that too eternal youth of the theater. His student wit is exact. And his sense of *blague* never fails him. The youth who paints a luxurious room on screens in lieu of furniture, the expert borrower who has noted down where he can get a free meal for every day of the money and, going out for it, discovers his host has left and is on his way to see the borrower on the same mission—these are the brainwaves of the theater. The light sentiment, the conventional Parisian irony, punctuated by an occasional real phrase taken from life, are agreeable enough in short snatches. And the Mimi of the book, whose life with Rudolphe is frankly, if rather cosily, described as a hell of jealousy and injudicious expense—hats and boots were Mimi's weakness—is a good deal livelier than the Mimi of the play or the opera. The ornately facetious style is not the journalese of the comic writers, though I don't know that makes it any better. Really, there is no serious reproach which can be fairly made against Murger. He is simply a little writer, a brilliant dabbler in unreality, high spirits and sadness, whose very melancholy, as it ripples along, reveals a fundamental lack of seriousness. His letters with their outcry against hunger and their hard tale of work, describe with bitter dignity a Vie de Bohême which he glossed over with a phrase or two in the sketches. His own horrible death—his flesh was decaying; shortly before he died his lip fell off when he was shaving—and the death of the real Mimi, were the end of a story very different from his light elegy of lost youth.

THE ENGLISH FRENCHMAN

"He counted on a certain repugnance in those who most admired him, as men of his disposition count on the help of a certain instinctive dislike in those of whom they are most anxious to make themselves masters."

SO WROTE Arthur Symons in an acute preface to a collection of Prosper Mérimée's stories. Repugnance certainly disturbs our admiration of them; indeed, between Mérimée and the reader one might say that repugnances are exchanged like the names of seconds in a duel. We open *Colomba* or *Mateo Falcone* with the feeling that it is sunrise, that presently our infinitely accomplished adversary will come coolly through the woods and in a couple of minutes put a bullet through our lungs. We shall have died for God knows what, though Mérimée himself will suggest that our fate was no more than the icy flash of a diamond on the dark finger of death. For Mérimée a life is a campaign.

For us who have two wars in our blood such a writer has a peculiar interest. He can count on our repugnance and our attraction still. As a writer of *nouvelles* he is, without question, a master; and in the construction of stories of action or, perhaps one should say, in stories of the consciously active man, he is inhumanly exact. "I have spent my nights lately writing for posterity," he wrote in the *Lettres à une Inconnue*. It is true. As bodies are preserved endlessly in ice, or the fly forever printed flawlessly in amber, so his stories appear new to the minds of every generation, and we cannot imagine a time when

Carmen is forgotten or *Colomba* unreadable. It is an effort to approach and read many of the overwhelming figures of literature. But Mérimée remains crystalline, exact, apparent; he can be approached at once. The interesting thing is his refusal to be great; I mean his refusal to be a great man in the histrionic manner of the nineteenth century. Where his contemporaries in France and England seem to have gone to the wigmakers to dress for the character-part of prophet, thinker and visionary, and to prepare the long oration of their careers, Mérimée steps back. Where they are positive and aggressive, he is negative and critical. They, in the manner of the century, are going to be great men. Their role and their audience will be everything to them. But when we look at Mérimée it appears to us that the sight of so many vibrant egotisms, warming up their engines and preparing to take off with a roar, must have produced in him a perverse decision, a decision without modesty, to stay isolated on the ground. And we know that it was his aim—a singular one for a writer—not to be a great man, but to obtain regard as a scholar and a gentleman; an English gentleman, of all things, as romantic Frenchmen conceive that character to be. In this, Mérimée was just as much an actor, just as much an heir of the Romantics and just as much a prophet as the rest of his contemporaries. He was simply the reverse of the medal. Like Stendhal, he discloses that the other side of Romanticism is the quest for personal power and for a primitive justification of it. He is not an aristocrat who inherits power in some sense as a trust; he is the intellectual, the clerk or servant of aristocrats, who becomes the libertine of the will to power, pursuing it, inciting it, probing it, and in the story of *Colomba,* exalting it. The themes of *Carmen,* of *Tamango,* of his superb historical novel, the *Chronicle of Charles IX,* of *Mateo Falcone,* and even of that ironical little comedy of manners, *L'Abbé Aubain,* are all alike in this respect: they indicate ruthless private wars; his people are goaded by pride or vanity to seek dominion. And when one side or the other has won, or when both have de-

stroyed each other—what is left? Mérimée is too honest an artist
and too clear-minded to suggest that anything can be left for
people like this but the emptiness of conquest. War in the heart
and mind destroys as infallibly as war on a continent. It is an
absolute evil. A shocking laugh there may be, like Colomba's
derision when she sits back well-fed by her revenge; but in
general Mérimée leaves us abruptly and we see an empty stage
where pity cannot tread. For pity has not been born.

In this attitude of mind Mérimée was prophetic. He foreshadowed one kind of writer who would succeed the prophets.
His critical intelligence, the hard rapier-like sound of an intellect without heart, evokes an echo in ourselves. He is the
scholar, the artist, the poet of insensibility. He is—one hardly
likes to breathe the suggestion—tough. We have often thought
that the visions, the sentiment, the complacencies of the nineteenth century deluded us; we turn for respite to Mérimée who
encases his heart, prepares to repel by a skilled display of
strategy and marksmanship, and declares that the aim of man
must be a self-control so established, a mistrust so masked, that
he can never be duped. That decision of his, "not to be duped,"
is famous. The word recalls a fashionable contemporary word:
disabused.

And yet how refreshing Mérimée is! What brilliant uses may
be made of an arrested development! The shock does not come,
after all, until the ends of his stories: when Tamango's broken
glory fades into a Governor's anecdote, or when Carmen's death
is merely a gloss on the customs of the gypsies. And that final
shock is wiped out by the memory of the first shock we get
when we begin a new story; the shock of pleasure and exhilaration in something new and strange. Mérimée is never boring.
He writes like a gifted raconteur who is nonchalant, entirely at
ease, but always alert in the presence of his circle. A bore has
been defined as a man who tells us everything, and Mérimée
never falls into the trap. He rewrote *Colomba* sixteen times to
be sure of avoiding it. His economy of narrative is native to his

guarded and scholarly mind. One may resent a curtness which was the fruit of mistrust, and one may add that the man who is not duped does not live to the full—"life is time's fool"—but if Mérimée is curt, he also has the rare gift of order, which I take to be the first essential of good narrative. Mérimée's gift of order enables him to place his scenes, as Turgenev and Pushkin placed theirs, briefly but infallibly before our eyes; to know, in *Colomba,* for example, how much of Corsica to describe, how far to dilate on local custom, how far to build up his anecdotes about the vendetta until the main vendetta of the story looms over us like an iron cloud, impassable and momentous on a mountain road. A great part of the pleasure of reading his stories comes from our awareness of their construction. At each phase we are conscious of being set free from the irrelevancies by which other writers mystify the reader, and of being directed by a mind that knows how to eliminate. One of the many difficulties the novelist has is to discern the situation clearly and many greater writers than Mérimée fail to do this; whatever Mérimée may lose by his gift of isolating certain elements of character, he gains by the clarification of issues. So that we are able in *Colomba* simultaneously to hold in the mind many contrary things. We watch Colomba's will to revenge working on her brother's mind, but we do not lose sight of the civilization he has, or the difficult nervous English girl he has left in Ajaccio. Even at the crisis of the book, when Colomba's conspiracy breaks and murder, somehow and somewhere, is inevitable, we never lose sight of the sunlight and the fog on the maquis and of the chattering Colonel and his daughter ambling cheerfully toward the awful hour when—as the bandit says—there will be fresh meat for sale in the town. Mérimée, of course, gets his effect by a lucid prose style which deliberately lowered the emotional temperature in order to heighten the intellectual excitement. He excels in his skill at rendering the depths by keeping to the surface, by attending to the beguiling and untrustworthy smile of life. His own emotions abstain from the narrative and, as I said before, we are free—that sense of freedom is the great gift of the Romantic tradition. With him we are free, also, of the Romantic burden. And even at the end, when the shock comes, as it always does in Mérimée, when we see him going too far and Colomba jeering at the broken father whose sons have been murdered, we are left reluctantly admiring the wicked perfection of the scene, the injurious irony. In the same way the end of *Tamango* is perfect.

In their dissociation of power and energy and pride from the rest of life, Stendhal and Mérimée are prophetic of an aspect of fascism. And Mérimée added a predilection for primitive types. He is saved from the complete accusation by his scholarship and by his detachment. Mérimée does not desire to return to the primitive or to a world without mercy. He declined to have an organic conception of history. He was an anthropologist, not a mystic. Even his Byronism was moderated to the temper of what became a gentleman with the spleen. He has a little in common with Pushkin, whom he translated, a harder, frozen Pushkin always on guard. His mind was skeptical. There is a clear statement of his skepticism in his historical novel, *The Chronicle of Charles IX,* where he extracts the utmost irony out of the religious wars and the massacres of St. Bartholomew and detaches himself from the tale half-way through in order to explain his method of writing history to the reader. "This is not the last time brothers will kill each other in France," says the dying convert to his Huguenot brother; and Mérimée excels in describing the ambiguities of conscience in an age when professions of faith do violence to the soul. This novel set out to undermine the laden and stolid histories of Sir Walter Scott, and it reads as if it were written, not in the first half of the nineteenth century, but in the last twenty years. There is a succession of incomparable scenes, and there is no dead wood. Again, our pleasure is a double one; we are watching the building of the characters and the story while we are borne along by it. And again we are struck by another aspect of Mérimée which brings him close to us: what he passes off as his belief in anecdote is really his perfunctory name for documentation. Unfeeling he may be, but he can reconstruct an environment, a period, the corner of a battlefield, a gaming table, a Corsican hut or a house of rendezvous in Seville, with a fidelity to their normal condition which many a more profuse writer, and more humane, has failed to achieve. He has the patience, the grace, the exactitude if he has also the perfunctoriness of the amateur. A writer might learn his art from him and dread the perfection he had learned.

THE CENTENARY OF
ANATOLE FRANCE

A NATOLE FRANCE was born on April 16th, 1844. He
ripened with the century and died (over-ripe, the critics
said) in 1924. His centenary comes too soon, for it has caught
his reputation floating indeterminately in the trough that always follows a wave of fame. We find it hard to face the elders
whom we admired when we were young and who dominated
our scene, for they contain too much of our discarded life. Reading them again we find them mocking us with our own image,
like a parent or a brother who is ourselves yet not ourselves.
And yet it is not hard to disentangle oneself from Anatole
France. Despite his artifice, his epicureanism, his air of ripeness
and skepticism, he is at heart an adolescent writer. His world—
as he says toward the end of his last autobiographical book,
The Bloom of Life—is the world of desire and illusion. His
way is the primrose path of nostalgia, sensual pessimism and
self-love. The famous irony is the artful weapon of the bookish
man who never grows up, who tastes life and history. They are
a gourmet's dish, sweetened by the senses, salted by horror. He
observes, but does not experience; and, beginning as a dreamer,
a writer of historical *pastiche,* a faun-like comedian of the mu-
seums and the libraries, he ends in moral nihilism. One is reminded of his own phrase about Van Dongen's portrait in his
old age: "It makes me look like a Camembert that is running."

The notes of tenderness and the naïve which appear in both
the sentimental and the savage writings of Anatole France led

many critics to feel that, if he was appalled by human nature, he also pitied it. But now one begins to doubt. One does not pity men until one understands their dignity. As one reads his life and re-reads his books one builds a picture of Anatole France shut up in a day-dream world, protected by all the authority of a superb culture, tortured by self-pity and not by pity for mankind. His reminiscences of childhood and youth, his essays in the archaic improprieties of history, and his two or three realistic novels reveal a man who chooses to exploit the pleasure, the terrors and the final anarchy of a personal solitude. He became a kind of Gibbon who has lost the love of liberty in the love and hatred of himself and who, tactfully withdrawing from the battle of history, contents himself with the footnotes. It is the course of the bookish man, the man who has tippled the illusions of the library and whose irony scarcely conceals the complacency of the non-combatant. One might suppose, after reading his novel about the Terror, *The Gods are Athirst,* that the French Revolution was an idle piece of human sadism caused by boredom or some northern incursion of the sirocco, and that the forces of history are really nothing but the agglomerated aberrations of human character. The complacency of this view is as shocking as the Terror. It is not a cold complacency; it is the complacency of the day-dream and self-love.

To this passive and cunning view of life, Anatole France brought the genial resources of his unorganized reading, the power to crystallize it in anecdote and to link the anecdotes together, with the subtlety and wit of the French tradition. One is rummaging in a second-hand bookshop—and, of course, he was the son of a famous bookseller—and each volume has its human habit and voice. As a novelist Anatole France was less a creator of characters than a compressor of them. He squeezed them out of books, as wine drips out of the press. His naïve priests and his fanatics, his trenchermen and his sluts, his always bedable girls, his politicians gulled by their own corruption are the fantasies of the library, jocosely or morbidly removed from the treadmill of life. There is scathing diagnosis —see his handling of the Dreyfus case in *Penguin Island*—there is art. But a heavy price is paid for this intellectual high-coloring of France's characters: we cannot take them seriously. They have wine instead of blood; sex but not vitality. The Terror in *The Gods are Athirst* does not terrorize except as a theory about the Terror. We are engaged by the sensational notion that hundreds offered themselves voluntarily to the guillotine, that the Moscow confessions were anticipated, that a woman would cling to her lover with a wilder ardor and attain an even more powerful satisfaction, when she knew he had that morning condemned innocent men peremptorily to death. For we know that some women do offer themselves to murderers with special zeal. And yet, in the end, we put down this novel which was to blast the puritan out of us and to replace him by the mellow and stoical reader of Lucretius—we put it down with the feeling that we have been tricked. Surely, we say, huge scenes have been left out. Surely it is perverse to personify the Revolution in a narrow prig like Gamelin and to treat the Terror as an outburst of selfrighteousness or to isolate it as a clinical instance of insanity. Is it enough to regard the Terror merely as one of the frenzies of human nature? Was it not inevitable and therefore tragic? Is it not an insult to those cart-loads of human beings jolting toward the guillotine, to give them the pathos of marionettes, to treat them as a cat treats a mouse, to use them as a psychiatrist's anecdote? The sadism and pity of Anatole France are certainly powerful and unrelenting in this book; but, in the end, one comes to regard it as a piece of erotica, while its judgment—that after revolutions have done their worst, life eventually goes on exactly as before —relies on an obvious confusion of ideas.

I see nothing humane in this book. On the contrary, it seems to me a plea for human isolation, and it has paid the price of such pleas; it has missed the sight of human dignity. Irony has made horror trivial. One sees it through a keyhole. Anatole France professed to recover something of the eighteenth century, but the humanity of the eighteenth century was not the fruit of a philosophy of contemplation. Gibbon recorded the crimes and follies of mankind, but his History was imbued with a hatred of tyranny; and Voltaire, that "chaos of clear ideas"—was driven by the same passion. The humanity of the eighteenth century was an active faith, enlarged by the variety, not desiccated by the absurdity of human nature; and men like Gibbon and Voltaire did not suppose themselves to be standing on some magically stationary point in history. A mystic like Blake did not think of the Terror as chiefly an example of the savor of human cruelty.

The purely literary critic would say that the talent of Anatole France was the talent of annotation. He was, like so many of his characters, a collector of bric-à-brac, a *bouquiniste* of the quays, a conversationalist. He arranges his material. He does not build with it. The pleasure we get from a book like *At the Sign of the Reine Pedauque* springs from grotesque contrasts. The salacious is followed by the lyrical, the philosophical by the picaresque. The patchwork manuscripts of Anatole France, posted into ledger-like notebooks from diverse rewritings, show the care with which he placed each sentence and each episode. No one could have arranged *bibelots* on a table more maliciously. But the failure to rise to the fullness of a great theme is curious in a brain and taste so greatly gifted. One is temped to turn away from literary criticism and to explain the failure, as Mr. Edmund Wilson has done, as the result of the lack of some comprehensive and energizing philosophy of life. Bourgeois culture has become static and self-contained. Anatole France has written enough about himself—and very honestly, too—to show that he was essentially a timid and egoistical writer; and one can understand how the first World War must have scattered his learned dreams by showing him History out on the hunt and with a purpose in its eye. But a writer cannot have a comprehensive philosophy of life just for the asking. And if there is no comprehensive view about mankind in Anatole France beyond the notion that we are going round in circles, there is a pretty constant view about one subject in his books—that is, the Church. There his skepticism could bite because it had something for his teeth to bite on. The fame and influence of Anatole France with the large public were due, one suspects, to his response to the religious crisis of the late nineteenth century. After all the sneers, the comedies and the satire at the expense of the Church there remains a nostalgia, like his own nostalgia for his childhood, which was typical of the minds of those caught in this religious conflict. And, especially in England, his sophisticated and Rabelaisian manner, alternating with the pretty manner of the folktale, soothed the struggles of our over-strenuous consciences. For at least a generation no English writer offered the same irreverent consolations.

My own taste is divided between the autobiographical books about childhood and the one or two realistic novels. *Le Petit Pierre* and *Pierre Nozière* are studied, but they are graceful and convey the dogged smallness and anxiety of childhood. They evoke, as *The Crime of Sylvestre Bonnard* does also, the life of the narrow streets of the Quartier Latin and of the Quais, so that one seems to be treading again the shadows of the plane trees and seeing the severe ripples of the Seine. The quality of meditation is filled with Latin sentiment; the fairy-tale charm is of the period. (That it may be a little fake is part of the charm.) The Bohemianism is harsh and native. It belongs to an entirely French society, unpolluted by the raucous Bohemia of Montparnasse. The tragedy of Anatole France was that he drifted from this fanciful world into the more violent world of religion, political and historical fable. The realism of books like *The Elm Tree on the Mall* or *The Red Lily* has a smaller scope, but its note is truer. One cannot call a book like *The Red Lily* a great novel about jealousy, but in its severe frame it reflects a few things perfectly and with supreme economy.

Formal and quite unspeculative, it makes its comment on "mœurs" with a clarity that is worth all the juicy Abbés, the tavern sluts and tedious scholars of the epicurean novels. These are good for a page, or good for a chapter, but they have the tedium of marginalia. They are a connoisseur's collection, a professor's conundrum, a bookseller's whisper. The great foot of Rabelais comes down upon the pretty pickle and leaves it looking flat.

THE RUSSIAN DAY

W HAT is it that attracts us to the Russian novelists of
the nineteenth century? The aristocratic culture made
more vivid by its twilight? The feeling, so readily understood
by English readers, for *ennui*? No. The real attraction of that
censored literature is its freedom—the freedom from our kind
of didacticism and our plots. The characters of our novels, from
Fielding to Forster, get up in the morning, wash, dress and are
then drilled for their roles. They are propelled to some practical issue in morality, psychology or Fortune before the book is
done. In nineteenth-century Russia, under the simpler feudal
division of society, there is more room to breathe, to let the will
drift, and the disparate impulses have their ancient solitary
reign. In all those Russian novels we seem to hear a voice saying:
"The meaning of life? One day that will be revealed to us—
probably on a Thursday." And the day, not the insistence of the
plot or purpose, is the melodic bar. We see life again, as we
indeed know it, as something written in days; its dramas not
directed by the superior foreknowledge of the writer, but seem-
ing to ebb and flow among the climaxes, the anti-climaxes, the
yawnings of the hours. Turgenev, who knew English literature
well, used to say that he envied the English novelists their
power to make plots; but, of course, he really disdained it. The
surprises of life, the sudden shudders of its skin, are fresher and
more astonishing than the imposed surprises of literary convention or the teacher's lesson. And in seeing people in terms of
their anonymous days, the Russians achieved, by a paradox, a
sense of timelessness in their books. Gogol, for example, seems

to date far less than Dickens. In the Russians there is a humility before the important fact of human inertia, the half-heartedness of its wish to move and grow, its habit of returning into itself. This is true of Turgenev; obviously true of Chehov, and I think also of Dostoevsky. His dynamism and complex narratives are the threshings and confusions of a writer who—if we consult his notebooks and letters—could never bind his mind to a settled subject or a fixed plot.

Yet the use of the eventless day could not alone give the Russian novel its curious power; indeed, it can be its weakness. No novelists are easier to parody than the Russians. These people picking their noses at the windows or trying on their boots while they go through passion and remorse! The day is a convention like any other. What gives those novels their power, and these persons their gift of moving us, is something which comes from a profound sense of a presence haunting the day. There lies on those persons, even on the most trivial, the shadow of a fate more richly definitive than the fate of any individual human being. Their feet stand in time and in history. Their fate is corporate. It is the fate of Russia itself, a fate so often adjured with eloquence and nostalgia, oftener still with that medieval humility which has been unknown to us since the Renaissance, and which the Russians sometimes mystically identify with the fate of humanity itself.

I have been reading Turgenev again and dipping occasionally into Avraham Yarmolinsky's thorough and discerning evaluation of him. It was a great advantage to the Russian novelists that they were obliged to react to the Russian question; a great advantage, too, that the Russian question was to become a universal one: the question of the rise of the masses. The consequence is that Turgenev's political novels—especially *Rudin* and even *Fathers and Children*—are less dated outside of Russia than they are inside it, for we can afford to ignore the detail of their historical context. I first read *Rudin* during the Spanish Civil War and, when he died on his foreign barricade, Rudin seemed to me (and still does seem) one of "the heroes of our own time." At the end of all Turgenev's political stories one may detect the invisible words "And yet . . ." left there by his hesitant and tentative genius. He is so close to the ripple of life's process of becoming, that at the very moments of decision, departure, farewell, he seems to revise and rejuvenate. The leaf falls, but the new bud is disclosed beneath the broken stalk.

Turgenev solved the Russian problem for himself, as he solved his personal question by an ingenious psychological trick. It is rather irritating, it is a little comic when we see it in the light of his personal character, but it was serious and successful. It was the trick of assuming a premature old age. Now this device was a legacy of Byronism. One can see how it must have infuriated his younger contemporaries to hear him declare that at thirty-five his life was finished; and then to have him live another thirty years in full possession of his gracious and pertinent faculties. The trick was a kind of alibi. For behind the mist of regret, that autumnal resignation, the tenderness and the wave of the scented handkerchief in a good-by that was never quite good-by, there was a marksman's eye. Yarmolinsky speaks of him stalking his characters as he stalked his grouse on the steppe of Orel or Kaluga. Every time he picks off his man and notes, as he does so, his place in the Russian fauna. Look at this from *A Nest of Gentlefolk*:

> I want above all to know what you are like, what are your views and convictions, what you have become, what life has taught. (Mihalevitch still preserved the phraseology of 1830.)

The comic side of this adroit sense of time—so precise, so poetic and moving in his writing—comes out in Turgenev's private life. His autumnal disguise enabled him to give his large number of love affairs a protective fragility. The autumn is the hunting season.

A Sportsman's Sketches, A Nest of Gentlefolk, Fathers and Children—those are the perfect books. Turgenev is the poet of spring who eludes the exhausting decisions and fulfillments of summer and finds in the autumn a second and safer spring. He is the novelist of the moments after meetings and of the moments before partings. He watches the young heart rise the first time. He watches it fall, winged, to the common distorted lot. The young and the old are his fullest characters: the homecoming and death of Bazarov and the mourning of his parents are among the truest and most moving things in literature. To this tenderness, this capacity to observe the growth of characters and the changes of the heart, as the slow days of the steppe change into the years that rattle by in Petersburg or Baden, there is, as I have said, a shrewd, hard-headed counterpart, the experienced shot:

> In the general the good-nature innate in all Russians was intensified by that special kind of geniality which is peculiar to all people who have done something disgraceful.

Or:

> Of his wife there is scarcely anything to be said. Her name was Kalliopa Karlovna. There was always a tear in her left eye, on the strength of which Kalliopa Karlovna (she was, one must add, of German extraction) considered herself a woman of great sensibility.

Or:

> Panshin's father, a retired cavalry officer and a notorious gambler, was a man of insinuating eyes, a battered countenance, and a nervous twitch about the mouth.

Looking back over the novels, one cannot remember any falsified character. One is taken from the dusty carriage to the great house, one meets the landowners and the servants, and then one watches life produce its surprises as the day goes by. Turgenev has the perfect discretion. He refrains from knowing in advance. In *Rudin* we are impressed by the bellows of the local Dr. Johnson; enter Rudin, and the brilliant young man demolishes the doctor, like a young Shelley; only himself to suffer exposure as the next day shows us more of his character. His people expose themselves, as in life people expose themselves, fitfully and with contradiction. The art is directed by a sense which the English novel has never had—unless Jane Austen had something of it—the sense of a man's character and life being divisible into subjects. Career, love, religion, money, politics, illness and the phases of the years are in turn isolated in a spirit which is both poetic and scientific. There is no muddle in Turgenev. Romantic as he may be, there is always clarity, order and economy. He writes novels as if he were not a storyteller, but a biographer.

It was Edward Garnett who, in defending the disputed portrait of Bazarov, pointed out that Bazarov ought to have been judged as the portrait not of a political type, but of the scientific temperament. (There is nothing wrong with Bazarov really, except that Turgenev showed him in the country, where he was a fish out of water, instead of in the city.) This temperament was Turgenev's, and because of it one easily discounts the inevitable sad diminuendo of his tales, the languid dying away which is the shadow of his own wish in his work. The rest stands clearly and without date. But the method has one serious weakness. It almost certainly involved drawing directly from life, and especially it meant that Turgenev was (or thought he was) stimulated to write by an interest in living persons for their own sakes. Turgenev knew his own lack of invention, his reliance on personal experience, and he studied character with the zeal of a botanist watching a flower; but, in fact, the study of character, for a novelist, means the selection or abstraction of character. What is selected is inevitably less than what is there, and since Turgenev was (as he said) governed by the actual life story which he saw, he does not add to or transform his people. They have the clarity of something a little less than life. What is missing from them is that from which he personally recoiled —fulfillment. There are spring and autumn—there is no summer. If success is described, it is by hearsay. Marriage, for Turgenev, is either scandal or rather embarrassing domesticity, something for a fond, indulgent smile, but a quick get-away. Strangely enough, it is his objectivity which leads to his limpness.

There are two qualifications to add to this criticism. One is suggested by *A Sportsman's Sketches*. His people derive a certain fullness from their part in the scene of the steppe, which none described better than he. In this book, his scrupulous habit or necessity of stopping short at what he saw and heard gave his portraits a laconic power and a terrible beauty. There the Russian day brings people to life in their random moments. The shapelessness of these pieces is the powerful shapelessness of time itself. The other qualification is the one I have indicated at the beginning of this essay. If his people lack the power to realize themselves because Turgenev himself lacked it in his own life, they have their roots in the fate of Russia. You localize them in a destiny which is beyond their own—tragic, comic, whatever they are—in the destiny of their society. They may fail, Russia goes on. One remembers that startling chapter at the end of *A Nest of Gentlefolk*, where, after the bitter end of Liza's love, the novelist returns to the house. One expects the last obligatory chords of romantic sorrow, but instead, there is the cruel perennial shock of spring:

> Marfa Dmitrievna's house seemed to have grown younger; its freshly painted walls gave a bright welcome; and the panes of its open windows were crimson, shining in the setting sun; from these windows the light merry sound of ringing young voices and continual laughter floated into the street.

The new generation had grown up. It is the most tragic moment of his writing, the one most burdened with the mystery of time as it flows through the empty light of our daily life.

THE HYPOCRITE

WE WALK down a street in the dead hours of the afternoon, looking at the windows of the villas as we pass by. They are glass cases; they are the domestic aquarium, and what our idle eye is seeking, is a sight of the human fish within. And presently we are taken by surprise. We see a face in one of those rooms. Agape, bemused, suspended like some torpid trout, a man or woman is standing alone there, doing nothing, and sunk in the formidable pathos of human inertia, isolation and *ennui*. It is always a surprising sight and, to a novelist, always a disturbing one. We are used to the actions of human beings, not to their stillness. We are taken aback suddenly to our childhood, when time went by so slowly, and when we, too, were shut in a room with some grown-up who was occupied entirely by the mysterious, enormous process of sitting. How they could sit! And sit alone! And how their figures grew larger and larger in our eyes, until their solitude and silence seemed to burst the room. It was, I think, one of the first intimations of mortality in early childhood.

The Russian novelists of the nineteenth century owe everything to their response to the man or woman sitting alone in his room, to the isolation, inertia, the off-beat in human character. They are naturally aware of what André Malraux has called, in a recent book, "the crevasse that separates us from universal life." The chief subject of the Russian novelists—the monotonous life of the country house which is scores of miles from its neighbors—draws this response from them. And as they stand alone in the room, drumming their fingers on the window and looking out at the slow, cumbrous changes of cloud in the Russian sky over the steppe, the characters of the Russian novel fill out with the unoccupied hours of life. Loneliness intensifies character. The great personages of literature have so often been the solitary natures who overflow into the void that surrounds them, who transcend their personal lives and expand until they become prototypes. The Russian novel abounds in such figures. Oblomov is an example. Stefan Trofimovitch in *The Possessed* is another. Iudushka of *The Golovlyov Family* belongs to this category. One is tempted to say novels are important only when they create these abnormal, comprehensive people. But in saying this it is important to note one difference between the Russian figures and those of the West. Those strong-minded, bossy, tyrannical Varvara Petrovnas and Arina Petrovnas who honk their way through Russian life like so many vehement geese; those quietly mad, stagnant, frittering men who spend their time dodging these masterful women, are different from the English eccentrics. Our eccentricity or excess is a protest against the pressure of society; the Russian excessives of the nineteenth century were the normal product of a world which was so lax that it exercised no pressure at all. "We Russians," Shchedrin wrote, "are not drilled, we are not trained to be champions and propagandists of this or that set of moral principles, but are simply allowed to grow as nettles grow by a fence." Iudushka and Oblomov are natural weeds of a neglected soil. They grow by running rife and they derive their force not from private fantasy alone, as Pecksniff or Micawber do, but from the Russian situation. They are puffed out by the sluggish, forgotten hours and days of the steppe. For in the empty hours and the blank distance which separate them from their neighbors, all the fate, the history, the significance of Russia itself, is gazing back at their gaping eyes.

After reading Shchedrin's *The Golovlyov Family* one sees why a character like Iudushka, the liar and humbug, is greater that Pecksniff who is, I suppose, the nearest English parallel.

Iudushka is greater, firstly, because he has Russia inside him, and, secondly, because he is encumbered with the dead weight of human dullness and vulgarity. He is greater because he is a bore. I do not mean that Iudushka is boring to read about. I mean that Dickens had no notion that Pecksniff was a boring and vulgar man; Dickens's mind was interested only in the dramatic and absurd exterior of the whited sepulcher. Shchedrin did not stop at the farce of human hypocrisy, for the tricks of hypocrisy are really too crude and blatant. Shchedrin went on collecting the evidence with the patience of one of those static realists like Richardson; and he presently came upon the really terrible thing in Iudushka's character. We can laugh (Shchedrin seems to say) at the obvious hypocrisies of Iudushka and, like his neighbors, we can grin at his eye-rolling, his genuflexions and his slimy whimsicalities; but there is something more serious. The real evil is the moral stagnation in Iudushka's character. The real evil is the muddle, the tangle of evasions, words, intrigues by which he instinctively seeks to dodge reality. We forgive his sins; what eludes forgiveness is the fact that his nature has gone bad; so that he himself does not know the difference between good and evil. He is a ghastly example of self-preservation at any price. In middle age he is befuddled by day-dreams. He will pass a morning working out fantastic conundrums such as, how much money he would make out of milk if all the cows in the neighborhood died except his own. He works out the most detailed but essentially ridiculous systems of bookkeeping, and imagines that he is working. Less and less is he able to face any decision, however small. He is a hive buzzing with activity—but it is the buzz of procrastination. I do not ever remember seeing such a picture of our character in any English novel; yet the humbug's art of evading an issue by confusing it is a universal one. There is one remarkable picture of Iudushka's evasion in the account of his behavior to the servant girl whom he has got with child. Iudushka manages never to admit that the child is his, but allows everyone around to say it is. His own reaction is to groan and to say "This is unbearable"—subtly conveying that his sufferings, not his act, are the unbearable thing. Iudushka reaches the sublimity of self-deception here. He has achieved detachment and isolation from his own actions. And the strange thing is that we begin to pity him at this point. He feels an agony and we wince with him. We share with him the agony of being driven back step by step against the wall and being brought face to face with an intolerable fact.

There is nothing notably remote from our experience in *The Golovlyov Family*. Neither the emancipation of the serfs which stupefies Arina Petrovna, nor the fact that one is reading about a remote, semi-feudal estate, makes the book seem exotic or alien to us. Our own Arina Petrovnas do not starve their sons to death, but they have driven some to alcoholism; our own Iudushkas do not publicly drive their sons to suicide. But, in the main, we must be struck by the essential closeness of Shchedrin's novel to the life of the successful middle class in England. Iudushka's prayers for guidance have a sinister echo. Walter Bagehot, I believe, said that the mind of the business-man lived in a kind of twilight, and the character of Iudushka is a remarkable example of a man whose cunning requires an atmosphere of vagueness and meaningless moral maxims. He has the stupidity of the slippery. In the end, it is not so much his wickedness that shocks his nieces, as the fact that he has become such a talker, such a vulgar babbler and bore. Cucumbers, pickles and the mercy of God indiscriminately mix in his mind. He bores one of the girls out of the house; and one of the most terrible chapters in the book is that one toward the end when the girl comes back to his house to die and wonders whether she can bear to spend her last weeks in the house of a man who never stops driveling on and on about trivialities. She can tolerate him only by persecuting him. This picture of the triviality of Iudushka's mind is Shchedrin's master-stroke.

The Golovlyov Family has been described as the gloomiest

of the Russian novels. Certainly the characters are all wretched or unpleasant, and the reader of novels who professes that strange but common English attitude to literature: "Would I like to meet these people?" must leave the book alone. Yet Shchedrin's book is not gloomy; it is powerful. It communicates power. It places an enormous experience in our hands. How many of the realists simply indulge in an orgy of determinism and seek only the evidence that indicates damnation. Shchedrin does this up to a point, but he is not looking for quick moral returns. His method is exhaustive and not summary. Old Arina Petrovna is a tyrant; but her lonely old age has its peculiar rewards. She enjoys guzzling with Iudushka, she adores his boring conversation; she is delighted to queer his pitch when he seduces the servant girl. The compensations of life are not moral; they are simply more life of a different kind. Here are the last years of her life:

She spent the greater part of the day dozing. She would sit down in her armchair in front of a table on which smelly cards were spread out, and doze. Then she would wake up with a start, glance at the window, and without any conscious thought in her mind gaze for hours at the wide expanse of fields, stretching into the distance as far as the eye could see. Pogorelka was a sad-looking place. . . . But as Arina Petrovna had lived all her life in the country, hardly ever leaving it, this poor scenery did not seem dismal to her, it touched her heart, stirring the remains of feeling that still smouldered in it. The best part of her being lived in those bare, boundless fields, and her eyes instinctively turned to them at every moment. She looked intently into the distance, gazing at the villages soaked with rain that showed like black specks on the horizon, at the white churches of the countryside, at the patches of shadow cast by the wandering clouds on the sunlit plain, at the peasant walking between the furrows, and it seemed to her that he never moved at all. But she did not think of anything or, rather, her thoughts were so disconnected that they could dwell on nothing for any length of time. She merely gazed and gazed until the drowsiness of old age began to ring in her ears, covering with a mist the fields, the churches, the villages, and the peasant walking far away.

No, Shchedrin is not gloomy because he does not soften. He undertakes to scald us with the evidence; he does not pretend that it will make vulgarity romantic or ignorance pretty. He is powerful because he remains severe. And so, at the end, when Iudushka and his niece, after their awful drunken quarrels, suddenly admit their despair to each other, and Iudushka makes the one truly heartrending cry of his life, we are moved beyond description. "Where are they all?" he cries, thinking of the mother, the brothers, the sons he has tricked and bedeviled into the very grave. He has felt the clammy coldness of a hand touching him—and the hand is his own. His cry is like Lear's. And it is all the more appalling that he utters this cry when his broken niece is still with him; if he had cried out when he was alone we would not believe. One had indeed not grasped it until then—the total disappearance of a family, the total disappearance of all that suffering and hatred. And the force of the book is all the greater because we do not look back upon a number of dramatic intrigues capped by their scenes, but we see Russia in our mind's eye, the steppe, the little-changing sky, the distance of people from each other, and the empty hours of all those lives. The English novel of family life inevitably turns from such a pessimism, but not, I think, because the English family is or was any nicer than the Golovlyovs were. The middle class, up to now, have lived in an expanding economy, which has enabled people to be independent where they could not be indulgent. If that economy becomes static or if it is put on the defensive, then a different tale will appear. The story of our money and of our religion has yet to be written.

THE GREAT ABSENTEE

IF LITERATURE were to follow the excellent custom of the Catholic Church which adds a new saint to the calendar in every generation, and with more than half an eye on the needs of the time, it is easy to see which character in fiction is now ripe for canonization. Not the propaganding figure of Don Quixote; not the innocent Pickwick; certainly not Robinson Crusoe, that too industrious town-planner knocking up a new society. The function of the saints is to assuage the wishes of the unconscious, to appeal to that part of a man which is least apparent to himself, and today we must turn away from the heroic, the energetic, expansive and productive characters. Falstaff the coward, Oblomov the sublime sluggard and absentee, seem to me our natural candidates. Oblomov above all. In a world of planners he plans himself to sleep. In a world of action he discovers the poetry of procrastination. In a world of passion he discovers the delicacies of reluctance. And when we reject his passivity he bears our secret desire for it like a martyr. For us he sleeps, for us he lies in bed day-dreaming, for us his mind goes back to the Arcadia of childhood, drinking the opiate of memory. For our sakes who live in clean rooms and who jump out of bed when the alarm clock goes, Oblomov lies among his cobwebs and his fleas, his books unread, his ink dry in the bottle, his letters unanswered. While we prosper, he is cheated. And at the end of our racketing day we see his face—the moon-like face of the obese and the slack, and with that wry kink of fret and faint madness which the moon sometimes has on it—we see his face looking upon us with the penetrating, disturbing criticism of the incurable, the mysterious reproach of the man who is in the wrong. Slowly, guiltily, his foot comes out of the bed-clothes and dangles furtively above the slipper on the floor and then, with a tremor of modesty before the implication of an act so obscenely decisive, the foot is withdrawn. Who knows what valuable grains of sensibility are lost to the soul when man is persuaded to stand upright?

In all the great mad literature of nineteenth-century Russia, Goncharov's novel is, to my mind, the gentlest and most sympathetic in its feeling. Like so many great books, *Oblomov* grew beyond its author's intention. Goncharov was one of the new realists and reformers. He wrote to satirize the sluggishness of the old-fashioned landowner. The industrialization of Russia was beginning, and he wrote to praise the virtues of the new businessman. *Oblomov* is an excellent example of the ambiguous value of propagandist purpose to a novelist: in a great novelist this will stimulate the talent until it swallows the purpose. Without genius Goncharov might have written a tract. Having genius, he has created one of the sublime comedies of all literature. After we have read this book we do not hate idleness, escapism, day-dreaming: we love Oblomov. We have discovered a man, a new man whose existence we had never suspected; a ludicrous Russian nobleman who, we realize, has dwelt for a long time not in Russia but in ourselves. And, so deceptive is the relation of moral purpose and literature, we are not in the least impressed by Stolz, the busy, cheerful man of affairs, who is held up for our admiration. It is easy and natural to admire *him;* we take *him* in our stride; our sense of justice, our humanity and our sense of adventure, demand more delicate and difficult tasks. Oblomov loses Olga, Stolz marries her; but, like Olga, after her years of happy and successful marriage, we have an intuition that something was lost when Oblomov was cast away. As Goncharov wrote—and he spent many years on this book—he began to see beyond the comedy of Oblomov's condition and discern the value of it. Propaganda does not become art until it has the grace and the courage to welcome the apparent defeat of its purpose.

There is reason to regret—though such regrets are really irrelevant to criticism—that Goncharov did have a purpose, and that he took it seriously enough to create the character of the virtuous Stolz. I do not mean that Stolz is a failure as a character. Goncharov had the gift of original observation, and he was incapable of palming off on us a wooden or sentimental idealization in the manner of our Victorian novelists. He has the kind of closeness to fact which Trollope had. One's criticism of Stolz is simply that he exists at all. The book could get on quite as well, indeed it might have taken a more startling and imaginative turn, without him. And this is not pure conjecture. We now know enough about Goncharov to see that he was not merely a pedestrian realist; Russian critics have pointed out that *Oblomov* is a much more subjective book than it appears to be at first sight. There is more than one hint in the drawing of Oblomov's character. That he should pay for his torpor by being filthy and getting swindled we easily see. What other price is there? Ill-health, of course. But there is something more. A faint furrow comes sometimes between those bland and mooning brows; a perceptible dryness gives, once in a while, an unguarded edge to his voice. Oblomov has the horrors. Under that passivity lies a possible madness, a frantic, abysmal, screaming despair. Now, that element is neglected by the book. Goncharov's preoccupation with Stolz took his mind from it. And so, once Oblomov has retreated from his affair with Olga with all the faultless strategic skill of the neurotic, he slumps to a comfortable, though pilfered, life in the arms of his landlady. He is ill. She mothers him. She recognizes in him an innocent. This is a shock to a moral man like Stolz, who believes in self-mastery, self-knowledge, the muscular development of human character; to Stolz, Oblomov is like a man who has gone native. But benign to the end, ineffectual, happy and blessed by Fate, Oblomov dies in his sleep, protected from his enemies and wept by the few who loved him.

Nothing could be more assuring. There is a transcendent gentleness, an ineffable prosaic delicacy, in the book. But we can't get away from it; the second part, although benign and moral, is dull. Suppose, for one moment, that Goncharov had not kept up his guard. Suppose that, undirected by Stolz and moral purpose, he had told much more of the truth. For Goncharov was, of course, a potential Oblomov—the fat man with the phlegmatic and malicious tongue, they called him. And Goncharov did have the horrors; he knew what they were. His life is one of those tales of mania that shadow literature, as we are said to be shadowed all our lives by our agonies at birth. Goncharov's minutely observant disposition concealed a nature eaten up by malice and jealousy. A slow, vegetating writer who wrote little, he could never forgive Turgenev for his adroitness, his skill and his success. He conceived the notion that Turgenev had stolen one of his plots and some of his characters, and even a humiliating public arbitration on the matter did not cure him. As the years went by and Turgenev's fame grew, Goncharov built up a fantastic dossier of Turgenev's supposed plagiarisms. Jealousy grew, as it will, into persecution mania. That is the drama which is missing: Oblomov's hatred of Stolz. Alternatively Oblomov's hatred of himself. Dostoevsky would have seen that; but, thank heaven, Dostoevsky did not seize the character of Oblomov. He would have made him one more Russian Christ.

Looking back on that paragraph, I begin to wonder if I have not strayed into a too strenuous conception of Oblomov's character and have forgotten his humility and its complement, his immense and passive conceit. No one can say that Oblomov is a divided man, he is as perfectly integrated as a blancmange. Oblomov's relation with the swindling Zahar, his servant, is like that of wife and husband; and the master rises to feminine heights in the wonderful quarrel which takes place in the early pages. Like some inured husband Zahar watches with resignation the familiar sight of Ilya Ilyitch Oblomov building up an emotional scene:

"Then why did you talk of moving?" said Oblomov. "Why, no man can stand it!"

"I merely thought other people are no worse than us, and if they move we can," Zahar said.

"What? What?" Ilya Ilyitch asked in surprise. "What did you say?"

Zahar was confused, not knowing what he could have said to cause his master's dramatic gesture and question. He was silent.

"Other people are no worse!" Ilya Ilyitch repeated with horror.

"That is what you have come to! I shall know now that I am the same as 'other people' to you!"

Oblomov bowed to Zahar ironically, looking deeply insulted.

"But Ilya Ilyitch, I've never said you were the same as anyone else . . ."

"Out of my sight!" Oblomov commanded, pointing to the door. "I can't bear to look at you. Ah, 'other people'! Very well!"

The scene goes on. Oblomov calls for kvass, and begins again on an ominously quiet note:

"Well, how do you feel?" Ilya Ilyitch asked gently. "You aren't happy, are you? Do you repent your transgression?"

"Whatever is this?" Zahar wondered bitterly. "Something heartrending, I expect; one is bound to cry if he goes for one like this. How have I grieved you, Ilya Ilyitch?"

"How?" Oblomov repeated. "Why have you considered what *other people* are? Comparing me to 'other people,'" Oblomov said. "Why, do I rush about or work? Don't I eat enough? Do I look thin and wretched? Do I go short of things? I should hope I have someone to wait on me and do things for me. Thank heaven I've never in my life put on my stockings myself. As though I would trouble! Why should I?"

And so he goes, pulling out all the stops, to the final words of this sublime quarrel, until Zahar is sobbing with contrition which—experience has taught him—is a necessary part of the play:

"And you," Oblomov went on, not listening to him, "you should be ashamed to say such things! That's the snake I've warmed in my bosom."

"Snake!" Zahar cried, clasping his hands and setting up such a howl that it sounded exactly as though two dozen bumble-bees had flown into the room and started buzzing. "When have I mentioned a snake?" he said amidst his sobs. "I never even dream of the cursed thing."

Both had ceased to understand each other and now no longer understood themselves.

Goncharov had all the comic gifts. He had the art of capping one absurdity with another yet more absurd. He is fantastic in this scene; but in the beautiful chapter which describes Oblomov's childhood and youth, he is also the master of the quieter humor of real record. The talk about the evenings drawing in, in the Oblomov drawing-room is a perfect fragment of satirical observation. Again his purely descriptive drollery is superb. There is the hour of the siesta when, the family and servants having guzzled in their plump and sunny Arcadia, all are asleep. It is a folk picture, a scene from the *Sleeping Beauty,* a fairy tale —to those scenes Russian humor owes a profound debt:

The gardener stretched himself out under a bush in the garden beside his mattock, and the coachman was asleep in the stables. Ilya Ilyitch peeped into the servants' hall; everyone was lying down on the benches, on the floor, and in the entry; the children, left to their devices, were crawling about the yard and rummaging in the sand. The dogs retreated into the depths of their kennels, since there was no one to bark at. One could walk straight through the house and not meet anyone; one could steal everything that was about and cart it away unhindered—but there were no thieves in these parts. It was an overwhelming irresistible sleep, a true semblance of death. There was no life anywhere: only sounds

HE LIVING NOVEL

of snoring of various pitch and quality came from every
corner. Occasionally some sleeper would raise his head, look
in senseless surprise about him and turn over or spit without
opening his eyes, and munching with his lips or muttering
under his breath, drop asleep once more. Another would suddenly, without any preliminaries, jump off his couch as
though afraid of losing precious moments, seize the jug of
kvass, blow the flies that floated in it, causing them to move
violently in the hope of improving their position, take a
drink, and again fall on the bed as though shot dead.

The undertone of dream and fairy tale runs through the book
like the murmur of a stream, so that to call Goncharov a realist
is misleading. Oblomov himself becomes one of those transfig-
ured characters which have grown over a long period of writing,
which exist on several planes, and which go on growing in the
mind after the book is put down. Now he seems to symbolize
the soul, now he is the folly of idleness, now he is the accuser
of success. He is an enormous character.

One other character ought to be mentioned: Olga. She is a
direct descendant of Pushkin's Tatiana. In drawing her Goncharov achieved something unusual. Ever observant, he set
about describing the birth and growth of a girl's personality;
and especially he set out to describe what most novelists—always
too much in love with their heroines—omit: the growth of their
will. Goncharov showed that the apparently incalculable Olga
was really quite calculable. You could show how much she would
change from week to week. It is an oddly cool psychological
analysis of "the young person" and something I do not remember seeing as clearly done anywhere outside of Henry James.
Much might be written about her, and much more still about
a comic masterpiece which does not agitate the mind as some
comedies do, but which seems to become grafted into it.

THE MINOR DOSTOEVSKY

I HAVE been reading the shorter novels of Dostoevsky. It is natural to pause before doing so for one last glance at the exalted glaciers of the major works. We stand in the sun on the modest contours of the foothills, looking up at the haggard and fog-hung precipices of Mounts Karamazov, Myshkin, Stavrogin and Raskolnikov, rather awed to think we have been up there, shuddering at the memory of it, impelled to go again, but glad of an excuse not to try it this time. We have been so lost on those heights; laughter at the wrong moments was so apt to cap the ecstasy of our expeditions. We would have periods of asking, with Tolstoy and Turgenev, whether our leader need be so shameless; and our Western natures rebelled at the notion of returning with the hangdog air of petty criminals. We conceived society to be our neighbors and their works; not a spawn of souls, half-born and without even an hour's civilization. And then, in the 'twenties, too heady a tradition of salvation was hung around those peaks, and it was the wrong kind of salvation. The world is not saved by novelists; and the unreason of the psychological mystics of the 'twenties seems to us now, I think, a rather shady attempt to get to God by the stage door. One thing scientific culture has done for us is to give us a desire for order and for intellectual propriety, and I hope we are beginning to see again that egging readers on to personal conversion is not one of the functions of the novel. In any case, the kind of salvation which Dostoevsky appeared to urge was not as private as it seemed to his adorers of twenty years ago; he did not offer a personal salvation in the form of a semi-re-

235

ligious psychoanalysis. The people of Dostoevsky's novels are notable not for their isolation but for their gregariousness. The infection is common. They run in crowds. If they plan to suicide or murder they tell everyone. They are missionaries in mass-morbidity, mass-guilt, and mass-confusion. Even when alone they are not absolutely alone; they have at least two selves. One hears not the private groan but the public lamentation. I can well imagine that the next time I read the great works of Dostoevsky—and we are growing nearer and nearer to his temper—I shall find he has everything to say to a Europe which is becoming a morass of broken pride, vengeance, humiliation and remorse. As a political journalist he will have a great deal to say about Christianity and Socialism, about Germany and Russia, about the criminality of Europe; as a novelist he will seem to show a profound instinct for the character of groups of people, their ideas and the common hungers that bind them.

The irrational is no longer the novelty it was, and we are consequently less struck by the madness of Dostoevsky than we used to be. A sensationalist he was; but now, whenever I open a novel of his, my first impression is one of realism and sanity. He knows the world from behind the scenes. The accent is decisive. The voice bristles with satire and expands with a capacious humor. Dostoevsky at his best writes like a hunted man who, for the moment, has fooled the bloodhounds and has time to confess and to laugh before the baying drives him on again. He is laughing hotly from the midst of experience. He is not laughing in order to forget it. The shorter novels of Dostoevsky —and in shorter works like *The Eternal Husband, An Unpleasant Predicament* and *Uncle's Dream,* we see the ground plan of all his greater works—are festive with experience of human society. Dostoevsky could see the terrors of our double natures, the fever in which our inner ghosts encounter each other, but he saw the raw comedy of this conjunction. It is frightful that we have so many selves and that the unconscious may wreck us; on the other hand there is something bizarre, something comic, something pitiable, in this squabbling assembly that has somehow got into one unpleasant pair of trousers. Look at *Uncle's Dream* for a moment. It is a farce; a masterful provincial lady in a scandal-mongering clique, attempts to marry off her beautiful daughter to a decrepit prince. One can picture the whole story as a very funny and quite unreal piece of theater. But even this mechanical piece of fooling lives on several planes. One moment the Prince, with his wig, his false beard and his derelict body, is a horror; the next moment he is ridiculous. Then, suddenly, he appears delightful. We long for him to appear again as we long for Stefan Trofimovitch in *The Possessed*. The Prince even attains a rickety dignity, and from dignity, he dwindles to a thing of pity. After all, we say, he did not really lie when he said his proposal of marriage was a dream. The conventional comic writer draws his characters to a single pattern of wit or makes the world a convenience for his joke. Dostoevsky does not do this. He is one of the great comic writers because, however satirically he may begin, he always grows into humor, and the humor is not imposed on life but arises out of it. He is aware of the collisions that take place in our natures. Somewhere—I forget where—Dostoevsky said he merely pushed things to extremes where other people went only halfway. And yet when we compare Dickens's *A Christmas Carol* with Dostoevsky's *An Unpleasant Predicament*, it is Dickens who seems to be the unreal and exaggerating artist. For Dickens exaggerated in seeing only one side of his characters. (Tony Weller's life is reduced to a reaction to widders, Barkis is merely "willin'," and so on.) Dostoevsky explored the whole, and the thing that is comic on one page may become tragic on the next. The profoundly humorous writers are humorous because they are responsive to the hopeless, uncouth concatenations of life.

In *An Unpleasant Predicament* we have the simple story of a pompous official who, in an access of philanthropical conceit, goes uninvited to his clerk's wedding celebrations, just to show that all men are brothers and that he is above social prejudice. Far from having a good effect, the visit ends in his total disgrace and almost succeeds in wrecking the marriage. The stages of Ivan Ilyitch's downfall, until he is carried dead drunk to the bridal bed and breaks up the wedding, are brilliantly described, and Dostoevsky, who, like all the nineteenth-century romantics, excelled in describing the moods of crowds, keeps us in uncertainty until the end. Exploring all the possibilities, that is to say raising all the mystifying issues which can be raised, as if he were writing a long novel and not a short story, he ends with justice to all. Ivan Ilyitch is not alone to blame. The poor clerk, with his pride and his private quarrels with his wife, is in a muddle as well. We cannot be made responsible for the unnerving manners of our friends. No one is malignant, but everyone is to blame. It is all very well to talk about humanity and brotherhood, but be careful that in doing so you are not forgetting your own pride when you contemplate the pride of other people. Each man and woman, I warn you (says Dostoevsky, the incurable novelist), is capable of becoming a novel in himself, a novel by Dostoevsky, morever. I warn you it is impossible to do anything whatever with any human being, unless you are fully willing to take the tumultuous consequences of his being human.

As I said before, it is odd that Dostoevsky should ever have been regarded as the novelist of the isolated soul. I can only suppose that very few readers read these comedies and do not know *The House of the Dead,* that wonderful documentary mine in which Dostoevsky describes his Siberian experiences, without hysteria or ideological puffing. In the great novels he is so blatantly the writer of spiritual headlines; in *The House of the Dead* he was content with the laconic news. No one who has read it can say that he ignored the problems of society. Like Balzac, on the contrary, he plunders society. He is acutely aware of class differences. So gregarious and populated is the unconscious, that in the typical dreams of his characters crowds of

people will appear. There are, for example, the dramatic
dreams in *The Eternal Husband,* Dostoevsky's most purely
intellectual and accomplished comic novel. The sinister gangs
of dream figures stamp up Veltchaninov's stairs and point at
him with horror as he lies asleep in his guilt. In this novel it
has been said that Dostoevsky parodied himself—it was written
after *The Idiot* and *Crime and Punishment*—and certainly all
his ideas are here: the double, the unconscious, the fantasies,
dreams, persecutions, suspicions, shames and exchanges of personality. Even a child is tortured. But surely this comic masterpiece, a comedy which (as always in Dostoevsky) carries its own
underworld along with it, stands completely on its own feet.
In the first place the growth of Veltchaninov's sense of guilt
from a vague irritation to mind and health into definite con-
sciousness is described with wonderful objectivity and suspense.
The value of psychological analysis to the novel lay, for Dostoevsky, in its latent dramatic quality. Psychology was dramatic;
for us it becomes more and more a metaphor or explanation.
The farcical duel between Veltchaninov and "the eternal husband" whom he has cuckolded, has an undertone of imaginative gravity which makes the farce more dangerous. Dostoevsky,
once more, is pushing things to extremes because at the end of
the extreme is the pity of human nature. Halfway—where
other writers leave this kind of story—lie the conventions of
melodrama and intellectual comedy; and, mad though the
story is, it is full of the madness we all know about in the lives
of people. The madness is the madness of life, not the madness
of the mind. No one will ever accuse Dostoevsky of failing to
complicate a situation, and this book is a succession of superb
complications. The very last one, in which "the eternal husband" is being bullied by his new wife, and has silently to beg
Veltchaninov not to cuckold him again, is one of the funniest
and most moving in comic literature. The unconscious, Dostoevsky discovered, gave probability to the most bizarre situations and turned coincidence into fate. And, it is interesting to

note, in the middle of this comic novel there occurs one of the very few pictures of normal, happy, family life to be found in his work.

The Eternal Husband is no doubt so refreshingly precise in its psychology, so well composed and economically written, so brilliant in its commentary because—for the time being—Dostoevsky had exhausted his anxiety for salvation. This is his one Western novel. It came from that part of him that liked to cut a social figure and was written during a rare period of equipoise and untroubled self-satisfaction. It has the genial air of a successful presumption, and it might easily have been written in our century, not his. And yet it could not have been. For the effect of psychological intuitions and discoveries upon our novel is to make it reminiscent, autobiographical, plotless; whereas in Dostoevsky's hands the novel became inventive, dramatic and far richer in plot than the rest of Russian fiction. How rich *The Eternal Husband* is in episodes; the absurd house-watching scene, the dramatic interviews, the discovery that the husband is torturing his child, the scandal at the brothel, the visit to the country, the nights which husband and lover spend together, where the husband first poses as his wife's ghost and later attempts murder! When one compares the realism of Chekhov with the romantic realism of Dostoevsky one sees how much was thrown away when novelists threw out plot. When plot went, the isolation of characters began; and though, by Dostoevsky's time, plots were stale, he showed that even the most hackneyed and novelette-like plot became rich and new when it was replenished by a new view of human nature.

A RUSSIAN CINDERELLA

AND what happened after the glass slipper fitted and Cinderella married the beautiful Prince? Marriage changes the character of women; what kind of woman did Cinderella become? Going back through the story and looking for those experiences which must have marked Cinderella's life, we cannot but be alarmed by the probabilities. How humiliation must have intensified her emotional and imaginative life! What a crowd of impulses will fly up, fierce and disparate in their flight, like birds suddenly set free, when the years and years of repression come to an end! What an appetite for life, for pre-eminence, for power, for perpetuating the glittering success, will come to the downtrodden and humiliated one. Heaven protect us (we say aloud, as we glance at the history of society) from the tongue, the will, the parading ego, the unstable moods of the slave set free! And how did Cinderella escape—if she did escape it—the worst evil that can puddle the eyes and slur the lips of a beautiful woman: the vice of touchiness?

I know of no book that presents this case with more imagination and percipience than Aksakov's *A Russian Gentleman*. Sofya Nicolayevna, in that most limpid of the Russian autobiographies, is a portrait of Aksakov's mother. For years she had been outrageously treated by a stepmother. Then had followed a time of extravagant social success. At the time of her marriage, when she came as a guarded and resolute stranger into the patriarchal family of pioneers who had settled in the swollen and luscious region of Ufa, the old Abrahamic grandfather of the family judged her character:

241

"Well, now, friend Ivan, what can say you of the daughter-in-law? As a man you are a better judge of the point than women are." Karatayeff, disregarding a signal from his wife, burst out with enthusiasm: "I do assure you, batyushka, that such another dazzler"—he always used this phrase of a beautiful woman—"as brother Alexyei has bagged is not to be found in the whole world. A look from her is as good as a shilling. And her cleverness! It's past all telling. But there's one thing, batyushka: she's proud: she can't stand a joke. When you try to have a little fun with her, she gives you a look that makes you bite off the end of your tongue."

And Aksakov himself says of the mother he adored and who adored him with all the violence of her heart, "Reluctantly," he says, "I must confess that love of power was one of her ruling passions; and the germs of this passion, now that she had been released from the cruel oppression of her stepmother, were sprouting actively at this time." Much, evidently, would depend upon the Prince. But power-loving women who are the belles of local society have a surprising tendency to fall for nonentities. They do not marry Princes. They look for slaves.

In Aksakov's father, Sofya Nicolayevna found a man whose deference, obedience and humility made him the perfect, the passionate slave. She would rule him, raise him up, mold him to the shape of her brilliant, town-bred ideas. She would scare him into wakefulness, blow him up in scene after scene till she had made him into another being. It was a bad beginning. But strong characters are often convinced that there is virtue not for themselves alone but for everyone else in violent purges of self-expression; and Sofya Nicolayevna was too young and too blindly herself to discern that violent outbursts appalled her husband, paralyzed him and drove him into the consuming daydreams of disillusion and resentment. She won her victory—but what a victory! It was empty. For she had begun by destroying his power of candor. Like many weak people, Alexyei had learned under the despotism of his father to develop a capacity for strategic retreat and adjustment. The weak—and how it

maddens the strong!—have their own resources. The strong—
and how it surprises the weak!—are so subject to sudden collapse, hysterical dependence, remorse and despair. Aksakov's
father had his moments of pre-eminence. And in any case there
are always compensations in life. He would leave the tumultuous bedroom to sit by the deep river which tumbled past the
house, watching the sight which—Aksakov says—no Russian can
resist: the sight of moving water. There was superb, Homeric
fishing at Ufa; and the end of a scene (Sofya Nicolayevna would
observe in despair) was often a fishing expedition, when the
perch came out of the river by the dozen and—engrossed now by
an unhuman antagonist—her husband would be seen in his
boat, playing an heroic bream. Flustered by human nature, he
could slip away from the incomprehensible campaigns of love
into a passion no less solacing or primitive, the passion of the
chase. In the crystalline air of the steppe and among the evening fogs of the water meadows and birch woods he would wait
for the rising quail which had been decoyed by the peasant's
flute, and shout, undeterred, at the hare bolting for cover.

The real Prince was Sofya Nicolayevna's father-in-law, the
stupendous grandfather whose portrait dominates the book and
whose wise, patriarchal mind and arbitrary nature seem to reign
over every page. In this old despot, with his terrifying rages, his
implacable regard for truth, god-like in the solemnity of his
habits, so that every eccentricity—chopping his shirts up on
the doorstep, dragging his wife about by the hair, or standing
more or less naked in the farmyard every morning to watch the
sun rise—had the weight of something like the whole Mosaic
Law behind it—in this tribal hero Sofya Nicolayevna recognized
a force more powerful than her own and an indispensable
ally among the jealousies of the family. Here she came upon
her match in love and found her quality justly estimated and
admired. The love of this old man for his daughter-in-law, in a
family rat-ridden with that fear and that jealousy which natures
too strong always create around them, is incomparably moving.

In this first volume of his recollections, when Aksakov was describing the early life of his grandfather and his parents, he was an imaginative artist of the highest order.

In the second volume of his recollections called *A Russian Schoolboy,* Aksakov reveals the second great passion of Sofya Nicolayevna. It was for himself. Intense in all her passions, she directed her whole life upon the ailing boy and he depended utterly on her. Their separations brought them both to fevers, fits and the brink of suicide. One must suppose that the fixity and joy of this overpowering and constant emotion must have been the cause of Aksakov's minute and exalted memory of his childhood, a memory that is hardly surpassed by Proust's. To Aksakov, childhood was the Golden Age. Not a bird song, not the flight of a butterfly or flash of a fish was forgotten. They were embalmed in the stillness of an unhesitating recollection. Like Goncharov's recollections of his childhood in *Oblomov,* Aksakov's have the warmth of some tale of the folk, where the sun always shines and where even the wickedness of man or the savagery of nature charms us as legends do, illuminating our lives without overpowering them. Aksakov's recollections are a retrospect without remorse. We are endeared by the permanence of human types and the profit and loss of living. The turbulent emotion of Aksakov's adoration of his mother has calmed into one of those deep and now untroubled feelings so beneficent to works of art. No other Russian writer, not even Tolstoy, has achieved the extraordinary stillness and ecstasy of Aksakov's picture of family life. No other Russian writer has held the mirror up to life so steadily, so that we see how the hours pass at Ufa in all their enchanting detail, without a tremor of the glass. In Proust, the act of remembering, the search for the past, the sensibility of the seeker, are important, perhaps the most important elements, in the task of memory; in Aksakov's mirror the agitation and flaws of such a brilliant egoism are not there to distract. Aksakov is not speculative. He is simple, tender, comic, delicate and factual.

The dinner passed off in the usual fashion. The young pair sat side by side between the old couple; there were a great many courses, one richer and more indigestible than another; the cook, Stepan, had been lavish with his spice, cloves and pepper, and especially with his butter. The bride ate the dainties pressed upon her by Stepan Mihailovitch, and prayed that she might not die in the night. There was little talking, partly because every mouth was occupied and also because the party were not good at conversation. Indeed, they were all uncomfortable in their own ways. Yerlykin in his sober intervals drank nothing but water, and hardly spoke at all at such times, which gained him a reputation for exceptional intelligence; and Karatayeff dared not open his mouth in the presence of Stepan Mihailovitch except to answer a question, and went no farther than repeating the last words of other people's remarks. If they said "The hay crop will be good if we get no rain" or "The rye made a good start till the sudden frost came"—Karatayeff came in like an echo "if we get no rain," "till the frost came"; and his repetitions were sometimes ill-timed. . . . Mazan with long boots smelling of tar on his feet, and wearing a long coat which made him look like a bear dressed up in sacking, handed round the loving cup. . . .

How is it that so still, so conservative a memory nevertheless conveys to us an impression of animation, excitement and suspense? For nothing like the airless gleam of a Dutch interior halts the descriptions of the scene. The answer must be that Aksakov's memory conceals the act of remembering, that his imagination works in hiding; he holds the mirror so still that we see not the writer but the movement of life itself, as the hunter or watcher of birds does when he sits in the fields unmoving for hours until life has the courage to resume its business. We watch with Aksakov and observe the huge suspense that hangs upon every detail of life from minute to minute.

Aksakov was a slavophile and a conservative. No hint of the political problems that were to disturb Turgenev and his successors comes into his work. To him the life of the country house in Russia—at least as he knew it—was as sound as an apple. It is true there may be sadistic and drunken landowners, who beat and even murder their serfs. It is true that his grandfather was a violent man who expected to be obeyed on the spot and gave summary punishment. But such things are in the order of nature. His grandfather prospered. His people or tribe prospered. To be relieved of evil we must all pray to God. One cannot say that Aksakov was indifferent or complacent. He was simply under a spell.

It was the spell of private life; that life which goes on whether there is justice or injustice, war or peace, struggle or inertia, the web we spin. One reads Aksakov now with a natural nostalgia—not indeed for the past, not for the delectable life of landed prosperity; not even for the abundance of food and drink—for what is the story of family life but the story of the hours spent between one meal and the next?—but for the fixed state of living, some settled condition of judgment. Aksakov's grandfather sat watching the happy young couple, Sofya Nicolayevna and her husband:

> His happiness had a shade of fear and of disbelief in the solidity and permanence of a state of things in itself so charming. He would have liked to speak his mind on the subject, to give them some hints or some useful advice; but whenever he began, he could not find the right words for thoughts and feelings which he could not make clear even to himself; and he went no farther than those trivial commonplaces, which, for all their triviality, have been bequeathed to us by the practical wisdom of past generations and are verified by our own experience.

What is it we admire about these words? We admire their closeness to a simple mind. But above all we admire the spaciousness of the experience from which they come. To that sense of space, in the Russian novels of the nineteenth century, we return eagerly again and again.

A RUSSIAN OUTSIDER

THE great Russian novels of the nineteenth century so dominate their scene that we forget they stand on the shoulders of minor figures who would impress the reader in any less fertile literature. One of these minor figures is Nicolai Leskov. I am not sure whether, considered as a writer of short stories, Leskov can justly be called minor. In England, translation of Aksakov came very late in the day, when his contemporaries like Turgenev and Dostoevsky were already established with us. There has been a greater delay in translating Leskov. A small collection of his tales called *The Sentry* was translated by A. E. Charnot and given to us by Edward Garnett in 1922; then in 1926 Gorki introduced us to *The Enchanted Wanderer*: and since then there has been one more volume: *The Musk Ox*, translated by Mr. L. Norman. Those who read *The Sentry* will remember Leskov's quality in that powerful story of squalid murder called *The Lady Macbeth of the Mzinsk District* and in the bishop's dramatic tale of his mission to Siberia, called *On the Edge of the World*.

Nicolai Leskov was born in 1831 and died in 1895. He was born of mixed class—clergy, merchants and the gentry were his forbears—and this puts his range of observation closer to Dostoevsky's than to the landowner writers. His origins are not very different from Dostoevsky's. For a long period of his life Leskov worked for an Englishman who was managing one of the great estates—the Englishman is amusingly drawn in the tale called *The Stinger* in Mr. Norman's translation—and he traveled all over Russia. When Leskov came to write he had a wide, travel-

ing experience of Russian life and custom to draw on, an experience which had been formed without literary intent. He
"went to the people" not as a self-conscious intellectual, but as
a practical man of affairs. One can see how this worked both
advantageously and disadvantageously on Leskov's talent. He
is, we are told, one of the "unplaced" writers of the nineteenth
century, very popular with the public but regarded with caution by the critics; and this caution comes from the suspicion
that many of Leskov's stories are ready-made. They come too
unevenly, too amateurishly and only partly digested out of life.
They smack sometimes of the reminiscences of a District Com-
missioner. It seems to be a fact that a writer of the highest class
must be driven by the instinct of the artist to strike a balance
between life and literature very early; then only will he have
time and place in his mind for the hourly discipline of imagination and sensibility which is essential to the well-being of a
talent. The sight of the self-conscious artist "going to the
people" or doing the opposite and shrinking from external
experience, is a subject for satire and, nowadays, for sociological
attack; but the artist is in the right of it. The greatest artists
have always rationed themselves. In the life of Leskov one can
see that he paid for the rich experience which enabled him,
among other things, to form an astonishing ear for the real
speaking habits of people by beginning to write too late in life.
One has only to compare his manner of narration with Turgenev's. Both Leskov and Turgenev used what is now considered
the old-fashioned device of setting a story within a story. The
Baron puts down his glass after dinner and is reminded of an
extraordinary man or woman he met years before. Or he retells
something he heard when he was a student, or when he was out
shooting. Now in Turgenev the convention is graceful, because
we feel that he has invented the setting. There never was such
a Baron with his glass of wine, nor such a student. The device
convinces because it is an artifice. In Leskov one has no similar
illusion. We feel that his beginnings, his containing stories are

muddled up with real life and, by the great paradox of art, they are distracting and unconvincing just because they are probably true.

Another reason for the uncertainty about Leskov's talent and the neglect of it in Russia is said to be political. A practical and experienced man, Leskov attacked the Left, especially the Nihilists, and was boycotted by the Liberal papers and critics for the rest of his life. He was also especially interested in the religious subject, and was accused of being a debased clerical writer fond of mixing lewdness and religion. He deserted the impressive ranks of Russian pessimism for a gentler, more tolerant and warmer view of life. I can only say that I do not believe Leskov's position was seriously affected by these sins. Dostoevsky did far worse in *The Possessed,* and Turgenev went almost as far in *Fathers and Sons* and *Virgin Soil,* and both survived the anger of the political fanatics. Aksakov was a Conservative of the Conservatives. If Leskov's position was unsatisfactory to the critics the reason is plain. He brought the independence, the originality of the man who has put his own life and experience before his political and religious views. Revolutionaries, Liberals and Conservatives all disliked him; and perhaps they had some right on their side, perhaps there is no special merit in refusing to be labeled. That kind of independence is frequently egotistical and unstable.

There are eight stories in *The Musk Ox,* and many of them stop at the point where Dostoevsky would have begun to inflate them. Leskov is in many respects a Dostoevsky without the epileptic fits. The tale called *The Musk Ox* is about an uncouth and vagabondish fellow who is deeply religious and is in training to be a priest. But he cannot get on with people. He is dirty, he is difficult, he has no pliancy. He becomes a tutor and finds the family he is with are corrupt, and goes scowling away at a moment's notice to tramp the roads. Everyone, according to him, is tainted. There are fewer and fewer people worth seeing or talking to, and so, tramplike and morose, refusing to work, demanding his bread at any door, he loses himself in the depths of society, looking for signs of the resurrection of the human spirit among the outcasts and disinherited. In the end, he finds a reformed estate run by a hard and thriving businessman who recognizes his originality and lets him hang around. The businessman knows that "the musk ox" will try and upset his workers by preaching his peculiar Gospel Hall revolution to them; but the businessman also knows that the workers will regard the tramp not as a messiah but as a comedian. And so it turns out. They love "the musk ox" and humor him. Everyone loves and humors him, and this is too much. "The Musk Ox" has depended on getting on badly with people; humored, he goes and hangs himself.

Like many of Leskov's stories, this one is slow in starting. He is best in describing the unexpected reactions of peasant people and in recording their devious or stone-walling conversation. And he is especially attractive because of his sympathy. Leskov had a particular gift for leading one, step by step, into the quiet obstinacies of sainthood, and for creating the awkward, the almost humdrum saint, the very ordinary man who has become isolated from the beliefs of his fellows by the force of experience. Where other writers interest us in ordinary people by giving them some bizarre habit of life or mind, or by turning them into eccentrics, Leskov sticks closer to his observation. The King Charles's head is not an amusing decoration in these people's lives; it is very often the main, clumsy, immovable piece of furniture. In one of his tales, the mournful chair-mender who is made to change his name by an erratic nobleman, lives with the new name all his life, as if it were a sofa or a sideboard he was keeping for someone. He lives with it religiously, without comprehension; there is nothing eccentric in this. For the new name is his luck. Too perturbing to be thought ludicrous, too useful to be inquired into. Again and again in Leskov's stories, something comes into the lives of the people and settles there immovably like an animal. There is the sensation of a thing or a presence mysteriously "in occupation," a sensation one has also in stories of Kafka's. When the Lady Macbeth of the Mzinsk district commits adultery, we detect at once a change in the character of her husband's house. She herself walks about like an empress giving orders, quieting the whispers about her adultery, with gifts, until the servants say, "That's all. It's her affair—she will have to answer for it." When she goes from adultery to murder, we see guilt living in the house. In a remarkable passage Leskov actually gives a form to this presence—there is a symbol in all his stories—without deviating into fantasy, but indeed by adding to psychological truth. After her first murder when she is lying down on her husband's bed dreaming of her lover, Katerina Lvovna sees a cat come on to the bed and she strokes it. She is puzzled because there is no cat belonging to the house. She does not realize that she is dreaming the cat.

In this dreadful story, in all of Leskov's best work, every sentence adds and tells, and Katerina moves toward her doom trammeled by her crimes, and only death can set her free of them. Circumstance, we feel, has moved into her life like the hostile figures of a dream, and has ousted her will. Her drama is impelled. And because of the laconic simplicity of the writing and the awkward garnishment of plain but real dialogue, her lot seems to us unanswerable and cuts speculation short.

Leskov's powers as a writer were brought out most strongly in his religious stories; but unlike most religious writers he was capable of many moods. He comes closest, I suppose, to the one or two Irish writers who are sometimes pious, sometimes skeptical, sometimes even ribald; and while he satirized the clergy or described religious failure, he also described the search for pure religion. And he did this, as a novelist should, without being didactic. His mind was saturated with the religious folklore of the peasants. Leskov seems to have a more genuinely religious nature than "the great sinner," as we can see in the story called *On the Edge of the World*. Here the mystery of faith and the question of the nature of Christ are described as a search, and indeed, paradoxically, as a gradual shedding of what is formally thought to be Christian. A young bishop is obliged to put his life in the hands of a pagan tribesman during a Siberian blizzard; they exist together on an animal level, and at every turn the dull, ignorant peasant who refuses to be baptized and whose simple mind argues in a maddening and small circle, obliges the bishop to shed one certainty of dogma after another. The setting is unforgettable. In some way the religious mystery has moved into the bishop's life in the shape of the stinking, stoical, immovable tribesman. And the bishop is not presented as an obtuse or conventional figure of satire; he is sensitive, educated, courageous and altogether a delightful human being. There is a wonderful scene at the height of the blizzard when the peasant covers the bishop with a reeking reindeer skin and then crawls underneath with him, puts his nose against him and snorts his bad warm breath into the bishop's nose in order to keep him alive.

The Musk Ox is not as good a selection of Leskov's stories as *The Sentry* is, nor is it as well translated. The translator of Leskov has a cardinal difficulty. Leskov excelled as a writer of common speech and wrote many of his stories as they would be spoken in a kind of vernacular, which he sometimes stylized. This must have given his work a quality which escapes translation.